Eternal Family
in the
Alphabet

God's Purpose for Mankind
Seen in the Ancient Hebrew Alphabet

By
Paul Devereux

Eternal Family in the Alphabet

Copyright © 2024 Paul Devereux

First edition published 2024.

The moral right of the author to full ownership of the copyright of *Eternal Family in the Alphabet* has been asserted. All rights are reserved. The book may not be reproduced in part or whole without prior written permission from the author. However, extracts for the purpose of Bible study, sermons, and reviews in magazines, newspapers, radio and television, and quotations in other books are allowed.

Cover photo by:	Paul Devereux
Cover Design by:	Wordwyze Publishing Ltd
Edited and Prepared for publication by:	WordWyze Publishing Ltd http://wordwyze.nz
Published by:	Devereux Books

Most Scripture quotations are taken from the King James Version (KJV) Perpetual Copyright by the King of England, Public Domain in the USA and other countries, by various publishers.

Scripture quotations marked (NIV) taken from The Holy Bible, New International Version® (NIV®) Copyright© 1973, 1978, 1984, 2011 by Biblica, Inc.® Used by permission.www.biblica.com.

Copies of *Eternal Family in the Alphabet* are available in New Zealand and can be purchased direct from Paul Devereux (email: paulrdevereux@outlook.com).

Discussions regarding the content of this book can be found on Facebook on a page called, The Eternal Family in the Alphabet.
URL: https://www.facebook.com/profile.php?id=61553474849709

Printed in New Zealand by YourBooks.com

A catalogue record for this book is available from the National Library of New Zealand.

Paperback ISBN: 978-0-473-72570-9

Contents

Dedication x
Endorsement xi
Digging Up Layers of Meaning Hidden for Thousands of Years 13
Ancient Timeless Wisdom 24
The Original Language 30
The Miraculous Hebrew Language 33
How the Semitic Word Works 36
Tools for the Explorer 40
    Guide to the Pronunciation of Sounds 43
    The Danger of Doctrines 47
An Alphabetical exploration 52
A – Aleph – Ox 53
    The Alphabet and Aleph Taw 55
    Three in Two in One 57
    The One nature of God 63
    The Dual Nature of God 65
    The Tri-nature of God 66
    The Universal Fractal of Life 67
    Living the Universal Fractal 69
        The Divine Level 69
        The Human Level 70
        The Physical Level 71
AL (God) and LA (The Idol of Humanism) 72
ALHYM – Almighty God 78
ADM – Humanity 80
ANSh – man and woman 82
    How is the Woman a Help to Humanity? 84

- AWT – Miraculous Sign ... 86
- The Symmetry of the AlephTaw ... 89
- AB – Father ... 92
- AM – Mother ... 94
- B – Bayt – House ... 95
  - On This Foundation I Will Build My Family ... 99
  - BN – Son ... 105
  - BRA – Create ... 108
    - Science and Creation ... 110
  - BThX – Trust ... 112
  - BT – Daughter ... 116
- G – Gimel – Foot ... 119
  - ARGMN – Purple ... 121
  - GB – Pride ... 122
  - GAL – Kinsman-Redeemer ... 124
  - GN – Garden ... 125
- D – Dalet – Door ... 128
  - DM – Blood ... 128
    - ADM – Red, Man ... 130
    - DMWT – Compare, Likeness ... 131
    - DMM – Quiet ... 134
  - DBR – Word ... 134
  - ADNY – My Lord, Adonai ... 138
  - D? – Knowledge ... 139
- H – Hey – Behold ... 141
  - HYH – I Am ... 142
  - HL – Hallelujah ... 145
  - HB – Give, Love ... 146

- HSH – Silent 148
- W – Waw – Tent Peg 150
- Z – Zayin – Plough 152
  - ZD – Proud 153
  - ZKH – Pure 153
  - ZHB – Gold 154
  - ZAB – Wolf 157
  - ZBX – Sacrifice 160
- X – Heth – wall 162
  - AXD – One 162
  - XZWN – To See What Was Hidden 164
    - XZH – Perceive 165
    - AXZ – To Realise Something 166
  - XZQ – Courage 166
  - XTh – Sin 167
  - XY – Life, Stomach 171
    - XYW – Beast 173
    - XLL – Pierced 178
    - XNN – Beauty 179
    - XSH – Refuge 180
    - XPShY – Free 181
    - TWXRT – Beyond the Immediate 183
- Th – Teth – Basket 185
  - ThWB – Good 186
  - ThHR – Cleanse 187
  - ThWT – Fasting 188
- Y – Yud – Throwing Hand 191
  - YDA – Praise, Thanks 192

- YHWH - Yahweh 193
- YWNH – Jonah 195
- YM – Day 198
  - TWRH – Teach, Torah 199
  - YRWShLM – Jerusalem 200
- K – Kaph – Palm of Hand 202
  - KL – Completion 203
    - TKLT – Blue, Violet 205
  - AKN – Sure 207
    - KHN – Priest 211
  - KBR – Multiply 212
  - KPR – Atone, Cover 213
  - KTB – Write 215
- L – Lamed – Shepherd's staff 216
  - LB – Heart 216
  - LBN – White 218
  - MLQWSh – Latter Rain 219
- M – Mem – Ocean 221
  - The M in AL-HYM – Elohiim 223
  - MLH – Word, Speak 224
  - MLK – Kingdom 225
  - AMN – Amen 226
    - AMNT – Truth 229
    - MYN - Man 232
    - YMN – Right Hand 232
  - MRYM – Bitter 233
  - MShH – Moses 235
  - MShYX – Messiah 236

MWT – Mortality, Death	238
N – Nun – Sprouting Seed	241
NAH – Pasture	242
NDB – Offer Willingly	243
NXSh – Serpent	244
NSA – Forgive	245
NR – Light	248
NHR – River	249
NShA – Debt	250
S – Samech – Thorn	253
SBB – Surround	254
SR - YShRAL – Israel	255
SLTh – Pardon	257
SMX – Rejoice	258
ʕLZ – Triumph	262
ʕLTs – Be lifted	263
GYL – Rejoice	263
RNN – Sing for Joy	264
SWS - Joyful	265
SPR – Sapphire	266
ʕ – Ayin – Eye	269
ʕBRY – Hebrew	270
ʕD – Witness	271
ʕZR – Help	273
ʕDN – Eden	273
ʕSR – Tenth	275
ʕT – Time	277
P – Pe – Open Mouth	278

- PDH – Redeem 278
- PLL – Pray 282

Ts – Tsad – Man on Side 284
- TsDYQ – Righteous 285
- TsWM – Fasting 287

Q – Qoph – Sun on Horizon 289
- QDSh – Holy 291
- QShR – Conspiracy 293

R – Resh – Head 297
- ARGMN – Purple 299
- RWX – Spirit 300
- RʕH – Friend, Shepherd 303
- RXB – Liberty 305
- RXM – Compassion 307
- RShʕ – Wicked 308

Sh – Shin – Teeth 310
- ShBYʕY – Oath, Seven 312
- ShBT – Sabbath 313
- ShXT – Pit of Destruction 314
  - ShXH – Worship 316
- ShWH – Equalise, Stilled 318
- ShLM – Completion 318
- ShMYM – Sky, Heaven 321
- ShNA – Hate 322
- ShQTh - Quiet 324
- ShQWTs – Abomination 325
- YHWShʕ – Joshua, Jesus 327
- YShʕ-NAH – Hosanna 329

T – Taw – Marker	330
TW – Completion	332
TMM – Perfect, finish	334
TʕH – To Wander Away	335
The Completion	337
About Paul Devereux	339

Dedication

This book is dedicated firstly to my own children Krystal, Ellie (step daughters) and Leanne, Ataahua and Angel (foster children), in the hope that I can pass on something to aid the next generation in their eternal journey.

I also thank my wife Maria for putting up with me tapping at my computer in the oddest of places – in hospital waiting rooms, holidays and in the evenings.

I have a strong place in my heart for the people of the Middle East, not only because they share the language which was descended from Adam, but because I have made so many good friends there to the point where I feel like they took me in as family. The relationships I had in Arabia were of a much higher quality and depth than any I've been able to have in New Zealand.

So, I dedicate this book also to the people of the Middle East and Israel in the hope that it will help to unlock the door of eternal life and family for them.

This book may be like an ancient treasure chest full of lost gold treasure and precious stones. It's full of ancient wisdom set in place by God, in the words He designed and gave to Adam. A seeking heart will find something of great and eternal value. I hope you can find what I've found.

Endorsement

This book comes across as well-researched, authoritative, and challenges some present-day theological views. Paul Devereux has a mixture of personal views and current understanding of God, the Bible and people – and he balances this well with his understanding of the Hebrew language revealed by its letters, and sound constructive arguments to add meaning to the key points he wants to deliver. The Strong's Concordance references help the reader to relate to Biblical words, but I found that while Strong's brings more meaning to a word, it can be limiting in its actual meaning in a specific verse. The author does bring a more multi-dimensional application to the word here.

The way Paul introduces Bible verses relating to the word he is focussing on, brings that word to life. May the Bible, as a whole, come to life more as people read this book.

This book will appeal to the person seeking truth in their relationship with God. It will appeal to those wanting deeper meaning of the Bible, particularly in the Hebrew-based writings. Paul deals with the 'meat' more than the 'milk', so could be heavy-going for some readers. Overall, his approach is to logically, and as simplistically as possible, present his wonderful revelation of God's desire for His family relationship – and it is all unfolded in the Hebrew alphabet and language!

~ Gary Woodward

Electrical Inspector and Apprentice co-ordinator, New Zealand
Former pastor and elder of the Saturday Fellowship in Hamilton, and a scholar of Hebrew and the Bible.

Digging Up Layers of Meaning Hidden for Thousands of Years

My journey of discovery into the ancient writing began while working in the deserts of the Arabian Peninsula. While doing a survey of water resources in the desert regions, visiting all the Bedouin camps we could find, I was shown in many different places, ancient writing on rocks which all shared a similar simple style. No one knew what they meant. These are not highly detailed and carefully crafted images such as seen in Egyptian hieroglyphs. They were not drawn in highly respected places like tombs or temples, but drawn in common places such as camping sites and watering places. One local had collated thousands of images into a book and had traced their origin back to the original settlers of the region – a people called Ad. I met him while visiting Salalah in Oman. The name Ad is interesting because when the Israelites crossed the Jordan to enter into the Promised Land after escaping Egypt, some of them stayed on the East side of the Jordan river. They set up a memorial pile of stones which they named Ad – which means, 'a witness between us'. The descendants of the people of Ad in southern Arabia, can still understand the Aramaic language – which Jesus and Abraham spoke. Could there be a connection between the people who stayed on the East bank of the Jordan river and those who reside today in Southern Arabia?

Because of the ultra-arid climate in Southern Arabia, this area had very little human activity for thousands of years, so these ancient relics have been well preserved. On the high plateaus above the wadis where many writings were found, you can easily find shells and fossilized sea life strewn around on the ground. This was the same land which was thrust up from the bottom of the sea thousands of years ago, likely during the time of Noah's flood about 5000 years ago. It's been largely untouched since then! It hasn't been covered by sand because the wind has blown all the sand into the centre of the Peninsula – the Empty Quarter sand desert. The salt laden wind and no moisture has made it impossible for anything to grow on the tops.

I did some research and found publications about the various ancient Proto-Semitic writings of the Middle East.

Perhaps the most useful publication was entitled, *'The Ancient Hebrew Lexicon of the Bible – Hebrew letters, words and roots defined within their ancient cultural context'*, by Jeff A. Benner (ISBN 1-58939-776-2). I might not agree with most of his interpretations of how each letter brings meaning to a root, but it's a good start. I've used the symbols he published as fonts, though there would have been considerable variation of those symbols in ancient times. There was no mechanised printing, so there would be much less consistency in the way people wrote letters of the alphabet. The exact form of the letters is not as important as the meaning which they carry.

Other dictionaries I use via a computer program, *'Bible Works'* (which is no longer available) are entitled, *'Whittaker's Revised BDB'* and *'Theological Wordbook of the Old Testament'*.

With that information, and having studied four Semitic languages including Arabic, Amharic (Ethiopia), Hebrew and Mahri (Eastern Yemen) – and having a lifetime of reading the Bible; having lived in the Middle East in 8 different regions for a total of 10 years, I was well placed to put together many pieces like a jigsaw puzzle to see patterns which make a lot of sense.

I bring this to you not because I'm an accomplished writer, but because this is a treasure which I believe is important and should be shared. If you receive it, I believe you will be benefitted eternally in God's family. If you reject it, keep on searching.

Before we go further, I should clarify what I refer to as Ancient Hebrew. I'm ultimately talking about the language God used with Adam. Now the first person to be called, 'Hebrew' was Abraham – who lived around about 2000 years after Adam. So, in a way, we shouldn't call the language which Adam used, 'Hebrew'.

Some call this original language, 'Proto-Semitic', meaning that it's the ancestor of all the Semitic languages. But that takes the language only back as far as Shem, the son of Noah. I believe Adam was speaking the language about 1000 years before Noah.

So perhaps we should call it Adamic – the language of humanity.

But because the language has been carried through to Abraham, and Hebrew has been the main language of the Bible, we'll call it Ancient Hebrew.

Spoiler alert – I'm going to tell you what the end purpose of the Bible story is – because God himself did it by putting the end purpose of the whole story right at the first letter of the Bible. That letter is the letter B which was named 'bayt' and written as ב. This letter talks about God's family dwelling in his house. Notice how the symbol represents a plan view of a house. Everything in the Bible and the Hebrew concepts explored in this book all point to that end goal. In this journey of life, God wants us to know what the destination is, as early as possible – that way we don't waste time in heading off in wrong directions. Unfortunately, most of us haven't spent much time looking at the beginning of the Bible, nor have we had the tools to understand the Hebrew letters. But without that, God still manages to make Himself known to us in many other ways.

We may think that each person sets their own destiny – which is partly true. But God is the Designer of the universe which, of course, is far larger than any of us, so we do well to follow the end purpose He has told us about – to be His Eternal Family.

The story which the Hebrew alphabet brings, is not one which most people will readily accept, and much of my interpretation is outside the box of accepted, standard theology of Christianity and Judaism. But I'm not writing this to please anyone or make a lot of money! The only reason I'm writing this, is to share my discoveries which I see are too good to remain hidden. I think this is amazing revolutionary stuff and I just hope that people will be able to understand it and see how important the themes are! There are many other interpretations and traditions around the Hebrew alphabet which are worlds apart from my observations and I make no apologies for that! I need to be true to what I've seen. I don't expect you to click, 'Buy Now' on what I'm writing, but you may like to put it on your watch list because I believe that what you read here will start to make more sense to you as you walk with God in these very weird end times.

Allow me to describe in one page some of my life experiences which have worked together to form the concepts written in this book. This book is not a purist observation of Biblical Hebrew but does include some of my own views derived from my own journey.

I was born in 1966 to parents who were Salvation Army officers. From as early as I can remember I was hearing Bible stories every day. Soon after I could read for myself, I was reading the Bible every day – a chapter from the Old Testament and a chapter from the New. God's word was the lamp for my life. As a teenager, the walls and ceilings of my room were almost totally covered in homemade scripture posters. At age 13, I discovered a real personal connection with God as the leader of my life. God's word has remained my lamp the whole of my life, which gave me a good understanding of the whole picture as found in God's Word – in the context of real-life application.

After a year in Bible college, I went on to study Bible Translation and Field Linguistics for two years. I then studied Arabic full time in the Middle East for two years. While studying Arabic, I was told by my Arabic tutor about the root system of Semitic words, which became a strong part of my language learning.

For the following 8 years, I worked with agricultural development in Bedouin desert communities. In the evenings, I worked on language analysis and writing a dictionary. While travelling in the Southern Arabian desert regions, I saw many examples of simple ancient writings on rocks. This led me to explore the origins of these – which led me to the original ancient Hebrew alphabet. After discovering that each letter has a meaning, I've spent many thousands of hours discovering patterns of meaning and observing how those letters tell a story within their words.

In order to see patterns while putting together a jigsaw puzzle, it helps to see a picture of the completed puzzle. My time reading the entire Bible hundreds of times, and then being immersed physically in the original language and culture, has certainly given me a view of something much closer to a picture of the completed puzzle. But to have found the research of others on the original letters, was the game changer.

It's important to understand that modern archaeology only tells a small fragment of the history of humanity. We can make a hypothesis about what we understand to be historical and then test it against what we actually find. Or if we claim to be completely impartial, we could start with what we find and then form a hypothesis around that. Either way, there's a lot of connecting dots which are very far apart in many cases.

My hypothesis is that the ancient Hebrew writing system and language spoken about in this book is the original writing system and language which God gave to the first humans – Adam and Eve.

My main reason for putting this thesis forward is that I see miraculous design though-out the language at multiple levels. This design reveals God's purpose for humanity.

We can see how this original design would have influenced all subsequent alphabets including Sumerian, Egyptian hieroglyphs and Chinese writing. All these subsequent writing systems are far more complex and stylized in their use of symbols. But their complexity doesn't make it a better system. Complexity was only added because the original system didn't suit the new languages, many of which are tonal to the East, towards China.

The original Hebrew language is profound in its simplicity. But though it has an outward simplicity with just 22 characters, it has a design which goes deeper with at least three types of meaning for each character and three levels of meaning in each word – as I'll explain.

Though complexity has been added to the original alphabet throughout history to form many descending alphabets, complexity doesn't equate to advancement of design. The simple structure of original Hebrew shows a highly advanced design with a minimal number of characters. In modern alphabets, we can easily see how they may have originated from this Proto-Semitic alphabet.

As I see from looking at a range of writers on the meaning of Hebrew letters in words, that there are a wide range of interpretations. We should be wary of those claiming to have a definitive understanding of the meaning of letters. I myself can't claim to have an infallible understanding. I often find myself revising my understanding of words. So where does that leave us? Do the meanings of Hebrew letters have any value to us?

I see it in a similar way in which we hear the voice of God speaking to us. Everyone hears God in a different way and will interpret scripture in a different way and will find their understanding of scripture growing with time. Does that invalidate the notion of God speaking to us? I don't believe so. Apart from the aspect of faith in the unseen, I do see that there are some consistent patterns across all levels of meaning in the Hebrew language, especially in the context of the Bible. Patterns, frequency and consistency are what gives strength to meaning. And the strength of those meanings becomes greater as a person sees a wider range of text and contexts. Noone can claim to have a full and comprehensive understanding of the depth of meaning in scripture. Therefore, those who continue to seek will continue to find more treasure. It's important to be open to continually revising our understanding and not be set in concrete. This is one reason I believe why God commands us in the Ten Commandments not to make a carved image of God in material such as stone – because that image of God will be very inadequate and our understanding of who God is cannot be static. We may carve for ourselves an image of God in stone, but we can also be tempted to carve an image of God in static words on paper. Both limit our understanding of who God is and can hinder the understanding of others if we force our notions on others via managing membership to a particular group or sect.

We should not force our understanding of scripture on others, but everyone does well to be honest to what they read and not try to twist a limited scripture to fit with their own desires.

For me to find what I consider to be the path closest to the truth, I've been careful not to let mysticism (such as Kabbala and Numerology) influence my understanding. I've also put aside extra-Biblical traditions found in Judaism and Christianity. The original documents of these religions are true, but a lot of extra-Biblical traditions have been added which cloud the clarity of the original. I've taken meanings of letters and words entirely from their textual context in the Biblical story. Christians keen on following Jewish traditions, should be aware that Judaism departed from the original Hebrew script and language during their exile to Assyria, so the alphabet which Judaism uses today is very different and many of the meanings which they attribute to those characters are very different to the original Hebrew which Abraham and Moses knew.

The most important rule for understanding any unit of meaning in any language is context. Context provides the meaning. The more varied and extensive the contexts, the wider and more reliable the understanding you get. For example, let's examine the English word, 'run' in the context of, 'I will run in the marathon', it suggests moving along rapidly so that both feet leave the ground simultaneously. In the context of, 'run the tap', it talks about opening the tap to let water come out. In both examples, we can see something in common, that there is something moving. This is the root or core meaning of the word 'run'.

The central theme of this book is what I believe to be God's central purpose for humanity – to be His eternal family. We will see this theme introduced at the very start of the Bible, and its thread will be seen through-out the Hebrew language and alphabet.

Although my knowledge of the Hebrew language may be limited, what I've sought to do is to find patterns which serve to weave together concepts into a larger tapestry. These aren't patterns which I've invented but patterns which appear to be very deliberate in God's design. It's the larger picture which we need to understand. Seeing the details and patterns help us to understand the bigger picture.

The Hebrew word spelt ARG [arag] means 'to weave'. This is a child of the root RG which includes the meaning of, 'thought'. Thoughts grow and develop as we weave concepts together. It's all about the energy of relationships.

I'm not claiming to be bringing divine revelation, but I hope as the reader discovers hidden truths, that those truths will be a divine communication at the right time.

For myself, the process of discovering what the Hebrew letters tell us, has brought clarity to the message God is bringing to us about His ultimate destination for us and how we can get there. I hope it will do the same for you, the reader.

Some will ask, "If the message is so important, then why is it hidden from us? Why not make it more up front in plain English?"

The answer to that is that I believe the original reader in the original language would have been well aware of the meanings of the letters. We must remember that English is a relatively "young" language, made up of words borrowed from many others, so that it is far removed from the original language of mankind.

We may also consider that there are many speakers of other languages that have developed over time – who will also have missed out on that message – to whom God wants to communicate, as well. God communicates in specific ways to specific people in specific times. The concepts in this book have their appointed time for appointed people. It could especially be brought to light to bring the Hebrew and Semitic peoples to Himself in the time of the final harvest. A translated version of the Bible does tell us what God's purpose for us is, and the translations are relevant to the people and to the time in which they are communicated.

I believe that the patterns and truths found in the hidden layers of the Bible and Hebrew language are among the most important truths we can get our head and heart around. These layers don't bring new information to what you might read in a translation of the Bible, but they bring clarity and focus. Many truths of God's Word have become hidden behind a veil of language, time and human tradition. This book is about exploring *without* the bounds of accepted tradition; but exploring *within* the bounds of the ancient Hebrew language, the Biblical record, and how that relates to the real world around us.

Some may say that we should be able to find and come to God without needing to delve into the hidden depths of the Bible. A simple translation of the Bible should be sufficient. That's certainly true, in fact, it's possible to find a relationship with God without even reading the Bible – just by trusting Him. But it's a bit like seeing a flower which we can admire from a distance; the closer we get and the more detail we see, the more we become awe-inspired and the more clarity we see in the patterns and purpose God has designed in it. The more we discover about God's plan and design, the better we can keep our lives on track with His plan for us.

The very best way we can understand the Bible is by reading it in its original language (Hebrew)[1], with an understanding of that language, culture and alphabet which the original audience will have had. The further away we get from that original, through time and translations, the further away we get from a clear understanding of what the author intended us to understand.

Much of what you will read here will be unfamiliar and strange to most. Why is that? It's because it takes three keys working together to unlock what was hidden.

Key One: belief that God has a design for everything in His creation – which includes the creation of the Hebrew language and alphabet.

Key Two: some understanding and acceptance of the ancient Hebrew language and alphabet. For centuries, the Western Christian church has been divorced from its Hebrew heritage which means this important key to unlocking the completion of God's Word has not been available.

Key Three: a belief in the validity of the Old and New Testaments of the Bible which includes the acceptance of Jesus as the Son of God. By accepting the whole, we see the complete picture and everything falls into place.

---

[1] The source text of the New Testament is Greek, but that also is a translation of the language of the central New Testament characters, (namely Jesus and his disciples) which was Aramaic and Hebrew.

The combination of these three keys working together is a rare thing in today's world.

A fourth key which is useful but not essential has been **my ten years living in the village culture and language of the Middle East**. It's Semitic languages and cultures are all descended from the same source.

As the reader, you can decide for yourself whether this book is fiction or non-fiction. I don't need nor expect anyone to believe everything written here. In fact, I wouldn't want the reader to blindly accept everything written here because even I hold my observations lightly. This is a journey towards a better understanding. To move forwards in that journey, we must be willing to sometimes modify or move on from an existing camp.

We should always be willing to add to what we understand and at times even backtrack on something we've already thought was set in concrete. This has happened multiple times in my writing of this book, and I wouldn't rule it out happening again. Does that uncertainty give us a weak foundation to build our lives on? I don't believe so, because our faith in God is not based on our full understanding of everything. Our faith is based on a trust relationship in God. It's like a child trusting their parents. The child may not understand everything their parents say but the child does trust that their parents have everything in hand. This is why we don't need to fully understand such questions as why an innocent child should experience suffering beyond their age. Many have said that there can't be a God if suffering of the innocent is allowed. Be assured that God anguishes over the suffering of humanity, but he doesn't want to force his love on us. He gives us a choice to follow his plan, but many reject that plan, which has resulted in suffering for wider humanity.

The stubbornness and pride to resist moving from our set understanding is exactly why the educated people of Jesus' time refused to accept the newness of what Jesus was saying and doing, despite clear visible proof of His supernatural abilities.

There may be some middle ground between fiction and non-fiction. This is where an idea may be beyond the immediate understanding of the reader but can be accepted by heart, instead of brain. This is the realm of trust and instinct. Trust in God often requires us to let go of reliance on our own strength and intellect. When we can do that, we can move further to trust the integrity of God and His Word. Our heart is what leads us in relationship. It is true that our brain plays a part in good decisions but it's not everything. When we have everything sewn up in our own intellect and learning, we have no need to trust God or others. The real world exists beyond our ability to perceive and understand it.

My interpretations of the Hebrew letters used in Hebrew words are based on my belief and observations that God designed each letter in a word to bring meaning to that word. Therefore, I try to find an explanation for how each letter brings meaning to the word it is used in.

I may not always be correct in my interpretations, but I do try to follow regular rules and patterns which I see repeated in the language. The explanations shouldn't be set in concrete as an absolute fact, but they represent what seems to make the best sense to me, based on observing how the letter operates in a wide range of words and contexts.

I hope this book will help you to grasp the clarity of the nature of God and His purpose for humanity. If you can grasp what's in this book, you may be making one of the most important discoveries of your life. I present this book to you with the urgency and responsibility akin to alerting people to a fire in the house. And much of what you read here will be uncomfortable because much of what you learnt from human traditions may get singed or burnt!

My role in digging up the ancient treasure is not much different to the shepherds in Israel who, last century, found the ancient Dead Sea scrolls in a cave while searching for their lost sheep. I didn't write any of this treasure, instead I bring to you a discovery.

Ancient Timeless Wisdom

This book is very much about ancient yet timeless wisdom. The truest most reliable things don't change with time. Despite what many will tell you, truth is not relative to where you are now and what you want.

God designed humanity and put us in this universe for a specific purpose right from the start. That truth didn't change when Adam decided to reject God's purpose and make his own truth and rules. Adam left God's purpose but the consequences of departing from the master plan are not usually pretty. It's like trying to use a coffee machine to bake a roast dinner.

Adam chose knowledge and personal gain over wisdom. Today, even the word, 'wisdom' is disappearing from our modern language and society.

Many are obsessed with the idea that scientific knowledge is the rock on which to build our brave New World. It's said that no one can argue with science, and Science is enlightenment. It's the pinnacle of human achievement. Our schools tell us that scientific knowledge will lead us into a sure future which will save humanity and the world. It's claimed that science is absolute and above unreliable human minds and emotion.

It's said that humanity has grown up and we're leaving behind our dark superstitious past. Humanists claim that we are entering the age of Enlightenment. But in fact, the further we go away from God's truth, the further we go into darkness. And, of course, the Serpent[1] will have us think that it's enlightenment!

We're being moved away from the original plan where humanity comprises spiritual beings created for a spiritual purpose – to be God's family. We're being falsely taught that humans are essentially no different to animals. We're even hearing how humans are responsible for all the destruction of the world and so we need to be brought under control. It's being said that the best way to do this is to remove spirituality, human

---

[1] Throughout this book, whenever "Serpent" is mentioned with a capital S, I am referring to our soul's enemy, who Revelation 12:9 explains of the dragon: "the 'serpent of old', who is called the devil and Satan, who deceives the whole world."

emotion and politics from the equation. Some even want to reduce the human population. Their proposal is to be more pragmatic and be led by 'the science'.

We would be naive to think that science is impartial, without human bias and is the most reliable indicator of truth we have. It's all too apparent when you observe on the internet how scientific reports are on both sides of the fence on any issue. Who do you believe? Most will choose a politically sanctioned narrative on mainstream media and school text books. The science of today is strongly driven and influenced by funding from political ideologies, corporations and lobby groups.

Science and archaeology may well give us some supposedly clear points on a page, but it's usually up to the human mind to connect the dots in a meaningful way – meaningful to whoever is observing those dots. Having said that – even the dots are moveable as we progress in scientific discovery. Science and knowledge are all about the visible, tangible, measurable and physical world. But reality and God's purpose are not limited to the physically measurable. Nor is it limited to the scope of the human mind.

There's another whole way of looking at life which we are being divorced from – wisdom and relationship. Wisdom is all about how we relate to God and one another. It has everything to do with heart and spirit. The Dark Ages of our history certainly contained many absurd beliefs and practices, but let's be careful not to 'throw out the baby with the bathwater'.

I'm proposing that there is a measure of truth and direction which is not based on human knowledge, discovery and creativity – though there are places for these - as you'll see. Personal knowledge, pride and attainment should not lead us. Instead, relationship and trust in God should lead us.

The difference between wisdom and knowledge has everything to do with relationship and spirit.

What ultimately is truth? In the ancient Biblical language of Hebrew, we see that truth is all about what leads us to our ultimate purpose and design. Truth is what points us in the right direction. What is that direction? Is it merely here and now according to current scientific knowledge? Is it all about immediate gratification? Or is it in the future?

God has revealed a direction to us which is all about a future and eternal outcome. The Hebrew word translated as 'God' is pronounced 'el' and spelt 'AL' and its actual meaning is 'to guide'. Each letter of a Hebrew word brings its own meaning to the word. And each letter has both a physical and a spiritual (abstract) meaning.

In our personal lives, the prevailing culture around us tells us that our direction and what we do should be determined by our own needs and wants and even fantasies. There's two ways of living life we need to choose from. One is led by self, and the other is led by God, which is very much to do with relationship – what's between us and others.

Should a person do something if they don't feel comfortable doing it? The answer may seem to be a straightforward, 'no'. After all, everyone should have the freedom to do what they want with their own lives. That is certainly true.

However, if we believe in a God who has a design for humanity, then there is a direction and purpose greater than ourselves. We can take it right back to Adam and Eve. God asked them not to eat from the tree in the centre of the garden. That was a directive beyond themselves. Adam and Eve decided that they would not listen to God's directive but instead do what pleased themselves and what they were comfortable with. They chose what was 'good' for themselves but not good for relationship with others and the greater plan beyond themselves. Because they broke with the greater plan for which they were designed, the consequences would not turn out as good as it could have been. A fork doesn't work so well if it's used to drink soup!

This is a huge issue of our times, which is why many are breaking with the parameters of objective reality (the parameters of what we were designed for) and seeking freedom beyond it and into fantasy.

Sometimes we may need to do things which we are not comfortable doing because it's for the greater good or because we need to develop ourselves in areas which we would rather not face.

This is because we are part of a greater plan for humanity. We were not designed to be an island. We were designed to be part of God's family with Himself as the Father providing the direction. Sometimes, following that direction will stretch us beyond our comfort zone.

Here's an example from my own experience. One of my personal policies for my life is to avoid stress because stress will reduce the quality of my life and be a detriment to my health – which I have experienced at times. However, I also believe in the importance of family. I have decided that family is more important than my own needs. I have realised that being in a family is better for my long-term well-being. The result is that there are many more stresses in my life than if I was living as an island. I have to work harder to care for the more dependent members of the family and there is very little time and money to do many of the things I would like to do. Being around others in the confines of a house can take its toll.

Living beyond ourselves and into the realm of relationship with others is essentially stepping beyond living merely in the physical and stepping through into the spiritual realm. This is where we discover true meaning and identity for our lives. The real power of meaning lies in relationship. Many may think that they can find meaning in personal satisfaction, but I believe that to be a shallow mirage.

In Ancient Hebrew, there were no spaces between letters and no punctuation, but the fluent speaker would know how to read it. There was of course frequent ambiguation.

The Proto-Semitic symbol on the above image, to the right has the sound 'A'. The symbol on the left has the sound 'L'. Together they spell AL, meaning 'to guide'. Most English Bibles translate this word as 'God'. *(Note that the Proto-Semitic – or Ancient Hebrew – is written right to left. Later in the book, I will write the English letters left to right, with the Ancient Hebrew right to left. More information on this is found in the section titled, Tools for the Explorer.)*

The **noun** meaning of the letter A is 'Ox'. The verb meaning is 'to be led or guided'. If you turn the English letter A upside down, you'll see an ox head with horns. The English alphabet is descended from ancient Hebrew.

The **spiritual** meaning of the Ox being led, is, 'humanity being led'. I'll discuss how that works later.

The **noun** meaning of the letter 'L' is 'shepherd's staff', and it's **spiritual** meaning talks about 'giving direction'. The hooked top of the staff was for catching sheep. You can see the hook in the modern letter 'L' – which has been straightened out. The hook was likely formed by a fork in the branch.

So, if we put 'A' and 'L' together, in that order, we see humanity being led – by God. This is why God is spelt AL.

If we turn the letters around in the opposite order, you get an opposite meaning. 'LA' means, 'empty idol'. 'L' before 'A' tells us about leading to humanity. The biggest idol in human history is the idol of humanism, yet it's empty. It doesn't lead us anywhere meaningful. Meaning is found in relationship – not personal attainment!

The Arabic word spelt 'LA' means 'no'. This is not the way to go! (Arabic is descended from ancient Hebrew, as well!).

Humanism goes right back to where Adam and Eve decided that eating from the tree of knowledge, for instant self-gratification, was more important than relationship, and in particular, relationship with God. The results were fatal and long-lasting.

Later, at the Tower of Babel, humanity banded together to try to make a name for themselves, and to try to be bigger than God. They said, 'Let us do things our way!' So, they built a large tower.

When Moses led the Israelites through the desert, he went up on Mount Sinai. The people tired of waiting for him, so – led by Moses' brother Aaron, the people said, "Let's not wait for God, let's build ourselves an idol."

Today, people are still saying, "Let's not wait for God. Let's go our own way."

The Original Language

In the beginning, God created the heavens and the earth. And it's also very apparent to me, that He created, or already had in existence, a language with an alphabet. Since He created the unfathomable universe, it would seem a small thing in comparison to create a means of communication for the human He also created!

The original language of both the Old and New Testaments of the Bible is Hebrew with some exceptions. Many will say that the original language of the New Testament is Greek. That may be true in that the oldest surviving manuscript of the New Testament is in Greek, but the original language the New Testament people spoke was Aramaic and Hebrew (which are basically sister languages and closely related). It was subsequently retold or translated into Greek. Some of the Apostles may well have written down their accounts of Jesus' life in Greek at first, but the language they used to speak to Jesus was Aramaic and Hebrew. Aramaic was their everyday language and Hebrew was used for scripture.

The Hebrew language is, to me, clearly Divinely designed.

Biblical Greek has traces of the original language of Hebrew which God gave directly to Adam and Eve. The Greek language is the result of thousands of years of change from a myriad of influences.

Linguists estimate that today's languages originate from about seven language families. It's my belief that these seven languages originated at the Tower of Babel. Therefore, it seems to me that there is Divine design in those languages, too. But only Hebrew has the connection to the Divine design of the Hebrew Bible.

When we say that Scripture is Divinely inspired, I would say this applies only to the original words in the original language. If it's been changed at all through translation or the adding of traditions and culture, then we start diverging from the original intent and depth of the words and language. As I've seen first-hand while working for a Bible translation organisation, many translations are translated by people who don't even believe in God, or have political and denominational motivations, so it's quite possible that their translations are not Divinely inspired. When we try to understand what God is saying to us in a translation of the Bible, we can only go so far. In fact, some English words can lead us astray somewhat from the original meaning. This is because we have loaded English words with the meaning our culture and tradition bring to such. As an example, two important words which have lost much of their original meaning and dynamic are the words 'church' and 'worship'. The original word Jesus used for 'church' was most likely the Hebrew word spelt 'BYT' ✡︎ [bayt] – which means, family and house. 'House' is a physical picture of the spiritual concept of family. God's ultimate plan is not for a building but for a spiritual family. The word 'church' has become so loaded that now it has strong connotations of a building, or institution, and a place to meet once a week. This is far from the meaning of 'BYT'.

The Hebrew word for, 'worship' was spelt 'ShXH' ✡︎ [shakhah] which has the central meaning of 'a low place'. It's talking about bowing down to God – not only in a physical sense, but in a sense of putting ourselves lower than God, in humility – to fully trust Him with our lives. The English sense of the word has become loaded with many other ideas, so that now when we hear the word, we think firstly of a gathering where we sing songs and have a spiritual buzz. It can easily become all about seeking spiritual kudos and a sense of personal comfort. 'Worship' should not be equated only with singing songs to God in a group in a church building.

Below is a time chart showing Adam's language running down the centre. Sometimes the language is carried by descendants of Adam and Abraham. At other times, those descendants find themselves in foreign lands and so lose the original language. But the language remains in written form. Pronunciation can be found in other Semitic languages such as the South Semitic languages including Mehri, Shehri and Amharic which haven't had as much foreign influence. The pronunciation of modern Hebrew is greatly influenced by European languages, notably Spanish and German.

The history of Adam's language (aka Hebrew)

God gives Adam a language
↓
Tower of Babel falls. Diverse languages created and dispersed. Descendants of Shem remain in Iraq.

↙ ↓ ↘

Descendants of Ham to Africa?

Abraham leaves Ur (Iraq) to live in Canaan (now Israel) where he is called, 'Hebrew'.

Descendants of Japheth to the East?

Semitic language influences Indo European languages e.g., Greek, Russian, English

Abraham's grandson Jacob becomes Israel – the Hebrew speakers.

Some Semitic families disperse to Southern Arabia and Ethiopia

Abraham has a son Ishmael by Hagar the Egyptian. Ishmael becomes the ancestor of Arabic speaking people of central Arabia.

The Hebrew Bible remains in Israel and is taken by Jews with them around the world.

Israel is exiled to Assyria and adopt Aramaic language and script. Israel later again leaves the homeland to be dispersed among the nations.

The Hebrew written language is retained in the Bible. We can get a good idea of the original pronunciation from the South Semitic languages (not influenced by foreign languages)

The Miraculous Hebrew Language

There is a Hebrew word spelt AWT ✝Y𝒴 [awt][1], which carries the meaning of a miraculous sign. It also talks about the connection between divinity and humanity. The root AT points us to the name of the Hebrew alphabet – AlephTaw – which is comprised of the names of the first and last letters of the Hebrew alphabet A and T. The Hebrew letter W seen in the word AWT means, 'and'. It talks about connecting. In this instance humanity is connecting with divinity. A miraculous sign is essentially talking about God communicating with humanity. These communications don't always need to be seemingly supernatural. The sign of the rainbow is one example. God can communicate in any way He sees suitable.

The ancient Hebrew language can still be read today. Its amazing feature is that it has meaning at many levels starting with the letter itself. Each letter had a sound and a name which was written with a symbol which connected with the name. That name carried a meaning. A letter can have many different meanings depending on its context, much like a flower can have different meanings and functions in different contexts. It can bring pleasure to one person and sneezing to another! It's unwise to nail a letter down to one meaning.

It is apparent that, unlike other languages which developed an alphabet invented long after having spoken it, the Hebrew alphabet was formed at the same time as the language. That is indicated by the fact that the position of a letter in the alphabet gives it a numerical value. And often we see that the numerical value has meaning beyond the number, and that meaning is brought with the letter to words. Of course, that doesn't make sense to many modern academics. This is because it was divinely designed from the start rather than the product of language and cultural evolution.

Most languages today have developed a writing system and alphabet. There are two main categories of alphabet in use today – the sound system and the meaning system.

---

[1] Strong's 226

The **sound system** spells words with symbols which represent a sound. This is the case with most Western languages. The letters within a word tell us how to pronounce the word but the letters by themselves in a word don't bring any information to the meaning. You have to know the meaning which is associated with the entire word.

The **meaning system** writes words with a symbol which has a meaning. Examples are the Egyptian hieroglyphics and Chinese characters. You can get a good idea of the meaning from looking at the symbol, but you will have no idea how to pronounce the word. You have to know the sound which is associated with that symbol.

You could make a sweeping generalisation (with some exceptions) that the languages to the West of Babel (central Iraq) started out with a sound-based alphabet, and the languages East of Babylon adopted the meaning-based alphabet. Another curious tendency is that the languages West of Israel which are predominantly Indo European, write from left to right, while many languages East of Israel write from right to left. You could observe that they are both heading in the direction of Israel!

Man's first alphabet started in the garden of Eden and remained around the Iraq area until the Tower of Babel where God dispersed the peoples by giving them different languages. As mentioned, the first alphabet had both a sound and meaning for each character. It seems that those who found themselves speaking a tonal language (mostly the Eastern languages) could no longer use the sound alphabet because there was too much sound complexity in their language. Therefore, they used the symbol-equals-a-meaning system. Those who spoke a language with a simpler sound system eventually retained just the sound-based alphabet.

Indo-European languages are the closest relation to the Semitic languages. The Indo-European area is said to be just north of Iraq though I would put it in Iraq. Iraq is the homeland of the Semitic languages. The Indo-European languages are most of the Western languages including Russian, Spanish,

Italian, Greek, German, Sanskrit of India, Iranian and English. I see many Semitic influences in the English language. We can see many Adamic influences in the modern English alphabet.

In this book, we'll look at each of the 22 letters of the Hebrew alphabet in order. We'll look at key words which start with each of the letters.

There are many different interpretations of the letters and you'd be forgiven for wondering which version to believe. I'm not following the Judaism tradition which is based largely on a later Aramaic alphabet. Judaism has added many human traditions and mystical ideas to the meanings of the letters. The Kabbala tradition has added yet further mysticism and New Age ideas.

My approach has been to use only the names of the letters and to confirm their meaning by looking at how they are used in the context of the Hebrew words in the Torah. I haven't drawn on any famous Rabbis, commentaries, traditions, or doctrines of Judaism or Christianity, though I have read many of these. I have used dictionaries as a reference. But I use the context of the text as the final verdict on what a letter and word mean.

I've put the words in the context of God's entire plan from start to finish – which includes the Old and New Testament in the Christian Bible.

How the Semitic Word Works

In Hebrew, most who study and learn the language concentrate on the surface words – the words which are written on a page or spoken. But there are two layers of meaning below the surface word – the root and the letter.

In addition to the three layers of meaning in a word, my view is that there are three prominent **types** of meaning for each of those three layers: Verb (directional), noun (tangible manifestation) and abstract (relational). These three reflect the tri-nature of God. A linguist could identify many more types of meaning, but I see that these three umbrella categories are significant.

The three layers of meaning also reflect the tri-nature of God as I'll explain soon.

I believe it's important to understand the meaning of the roots of Hebrew words. Roots in the Hebrew language consist of one, two, three or four consonants. Mostly two because two provides a relationship between two consonants. That relationship provides meaning which is greater than the sum of its parts.

The joining of two or more letters is like the joining of two people together to form a mother and father (parents) A two-letter root can have many children. A three-letter root has less and a four-letter root less again. It's as if the three- and four-letter roots are also children of the two letter roots.

The order of letters in a root are also significant because they tell a story of what happens in a concept, for example the story may tell about a change in state. A reversal of letter order can bring an opposite meaning. The root can be understood better by looking down a layer at the meaning of the individual letters, and up a layer to the words which it gives birth to (it's children).

Some Semitic language dictionaries will have the main entries as roots and then list the children beneath them.

To understand the meaning of the letters, there are multiple methods which all need to be used – as follows:

The first and essential factor is the **name** of the letter. For example, the letter B has the name bayt[1], which has the dictionary meaning of, house, 'to be in', family and tribe. Note the three **types** of meaning: 'house' is the literal meaning. 'Family and Tribe' are the abstract meanings. 'To be in' is the verb meaning.

The second way to understand the meaning of the letter is from the **form** of the written letter. However, this is where things can and have gone horribly wrong, because some traditions have, in my opinion, put too much weight on the written form.

Hebrew has changed its writing form over 6000 years. It started with a more picture type writing, similar to basic hieroglyphics. In my opinion, this was the form God gave the writing to Adam in. It slowly became more stylized – which is what Moses would have used. At one point, Israel was exiled to Assyria where they lost the picture style script and began using the Aramaic script of Assyria – which they use to this day. Judaism has attached a huge amount of meaning to the form of this script to the point where many claim it was the original script given to them by God. Archaeology provides many variations on the history of Hebrew writing, so we can't say that any one form is correct. In those days there was no standardised printing of script. But from looking at a wide range of examples, we can get an idea of what the basic shape would have been and with the aid of the name of that letter, form a fair representation of that letter.

Thirdly, we need to look at the ***context*** of a letter's use. This is perhaps the most important method. We should be able to see some clear indications from words as to how the letters bring meaning to those words. For example, in the word AB[2], meaning, 'father', the letter A (Ox) brings the idea of leading and strength. The letter B means, 'family'. The father is the leader of the family. That's the abstract meanings. The physical, literal meaning of AB is, 'tent pole'. The letter A (Ox) likely brings the idea of strength. The letter

---

[1] Strong's 1004
[2] Strong's 1

B brings the idea of house. So, we see that the tent pole is the strength or centre support of the house. After looking at many words, we get an idea of the range of meaning which letters bring to words. The meaning of a letter is not always the same because it will also depend on the context. But we should ideally be able to trace the meaning of a letter back to its core identity.

The three levels of meaning in Hebrew words

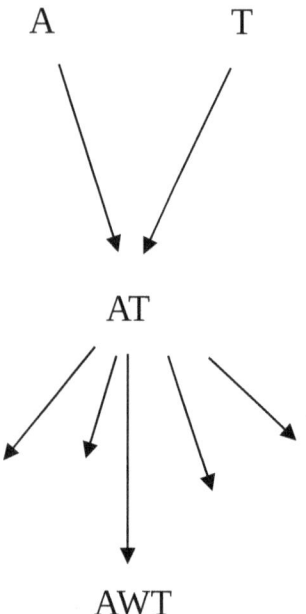

The first layer of a word is the letters. Each letter has a range of meanings. They are like single people – each with their own unique identity.

The second layer of a word is the root. The root introduces a relationship dynamic between the letters (mainly consonants). It's like the parents of a family. At their marriage they become as one.

The third layer of a word is the spoken word. It has vowels added which enable it to be spoken. It's like the children of the root. There can be numerous children from one root. Grammatical and derivational affixes consisting of consonants and vowels can be added to modify the basic root meaning.

Each of the three **layers** (letter, root and word) and **types** (noun, verb and abstract) of meaning reflect the tri-nature of God and the tri-nature of life which we'll look at later - loosely described as follows:

The three layers of meaning are the letter, root and word.
1. The letter is the foundational identity of meaning. This relates to God the Father.
2. The root forms a relationship. This relates to the Holy Spirit.
3. The word is the pronounceable and tangible expression. This relates to Jesus – the manifestation of God.

The three types of meaning are the verb, abstract and noun.
1. The verb is all about an action – it's directional. This relates to the Father.
2. The abstract is all about relationship. This relates to the Spirit.
3. The noun is about what's tangible and visible. This relates to Jesus.

Tools for the Explorer

Before we start into the excavation of ancient wisdom, there are some tools the reader can use for themselves in addition to the interpretations I bring in this book.

Much like an archaeological dig, there's usually a lot of earth to move before you find the treasures. Then we need to put everything on the table to try and make sense of it. Some of what we find may not immediately make sense in the wider picture – but those pieces may make sense at a later date, so we need to keep them in mind. Hopefully, we will find patterns which can help us learn something useful for our lives.

I could be wrong about anything I've written in this book, but hopefully, you will see patterns which are self-evident and therefore speak for themselves as to their accuracy and truth.

The Bible

An important tool for finding the meanings of ancient Hebrew words is looking at their context in the Bible. I don't believe any one English translation of the Bible is any better than the other and you certainly shouldn't compare one translation to another – that would be like comparing a copy to another copy. No translation is as good as the original. In this book, I quote mostly from the New International version and sometimes from the King James, where the wording better reflects the original Hebrew.

The Strongs Concordance

In the text of this book, wherever you see a Hebrew word, I have inserted a footnote which gives a reference to a number in the Strong's Concordance (hereafter known as 'Strong's'). When you look this number up in Strong's, that number will give you all the references where the Hebrew (or Greek for the New Testament) word occurs in the Bible. You should be aware, though, that a Hebrew word may have multiple English words which it has been translated into.

Also, some Hebrew words are not translatable into English, so you will not see any indication of their meaning in an English translation.

You can find a Strong's Concordance in an App store, online or as a hard copy.

The Ancient Hebrew Lexicon of the Bible

This book is a dictionary of the Biblical Hebrew words. It's written by Jeff A. Benner. He sells a hardcopy, but it can also be found online as a PDF. The key entries are arranged according to the order of the Hebrew alphabet using ancient Hebrew characters. He provides references to the Strongs numbers, shows modern Hebrew pronunciation (which is different to the original Proto-Semitic) and script and gives his interpretation of how each letter brings meaning to the root.

In this book which you are about to read, I have instead used what I understand to be Proto-Semitic pronunciations [shown in square brackets], based on what I have heard from other Semitic languages in the Middle East and in particular Southern Arabia, which linguists consider to be the closest existing representation of the original. This is likely because these ethnic groups have had the least amount of influence from foreign languages. The Hebrew-speaking peoples have been away from their homeland for thousands of years, living among speakers of other languages, so their pronunciation has a higher chance of being influenced by those languages. In contrast, speakers of the languages of Southern Arabia such as Mehri and Shehri have remained in one place for thousands of years. Their environment is ultra-arid so their land hasn't been desirable to foreign invaders.

Also, linguists have observed after comparing all Semitic languages that the languages of Southern Arabia (not to be confused with Southern Arabic), show structure more consistent with what they call a Universal Semitic language.

For example, the word spelt AB, meaning 'father' would be pronounced in modern Hebrew as 'avva'. But the modern Hebrew pattern of B becoming V between vowels doesn't exist in any other Semitic language. Another prominent difference between modern Hebrew and Proto-Semitic is the pronunciation of the letter T. Modern Hebrew will often pronounce it as 'th', for example BYT will be pronounced as 'beth'. In contrast, other Semitic languages will pronounce it as 'bayt'.

So, a reminder to modern Hebrew readers – my pronunciations in square brackets [...] represent a more Proto-Semitic pronunciation – not modern Hebrew. It will be more consistent with an English reading of the letters.

Benner writes the Hebrew characters both in the Aramaic script (Modern Hebrew script) and in English capitals. I have used those same English capitals in this book. However, from my analysis and study of the sound system of the Southern Semitic languages which are considered by modern linguists to be the best example of Proto-Semitic languages (closest to the original), I could change that considerably. One example: the letter written by Benner as Ts (based on a modern Hebrew pronunciation) would be written instead as Dh – a backed alveolar stop.

In my two years analysing the sound system of Mehri while living in Southern Arabia, I found a very symmetrical system of sounds which comprised of 7 main points of articulation (e.g., denti-alveolar, velar, pharyngeal) which each had three modes of modification: voiced, voiceless and backed. So, the letter Dh for example belongs to the set of denti-alveolar sounds including t (voiceless denti-alveolar stop), d voiced denti-alveolar stop, and dh (backed[1] voiced denti-alveolar stop).

---

[1] A backed modification of an articulation is often known as a retracted tongue root, though I think speakers normally think of it as being simply backed – which I think is a more accurate label because the backing doesn't always involve the tongue root- it's just backed in relation to the others.

Guide to the Pronunciation of Sounds

As mentioned, in this book I'm not following the pronunciation system of modern Hebrew but am trying to get back to what I understand may have been the original pronunciations based on my study of modern Semitic languages which haven't been so influenced by other languages.

Here's a description of those sounds in the Hebrew alphabetical order:

Short vowels weren't written but were understood. The general rule for pronunciation of those vowels is that there are three main vowels. This is based on a phonology study I did of the Southern Semitic language of Mehri – a language which is considered to be the closest to the original Semitic languages.

Here's a guide to the pronunciation of the three vowels:

[i] as in ski, not hit.
[a] as in car, not hat
[u] as in full, not pot

There was a rare occurrence of [e] as in tent. This is half way between [i] and [a] so may have been an allophone of one of these. [i], [a] and [u] are very symmetrical, and [e] goes against that symmetry.

To tell the truth, it's hard to know exactly which short vowels were used in each word though there are some rules around which vowels are used to bring certain meanings. I want to move away from the modern pronunciation of Hebrew which has picked up phonological rules from European languages.

Here's a guide for the pronunciation of what's termed by many Semitic linguists as the 'radicals' – the letters which were written in ancient Semitic languages.

A א: Has a long 'ah' sound. The 'a' sound is that found in the word 'car'. 'A' is a long central open unrounded vowel.

B ⌂: b as in 'bat'

G ⌐: g as in 'go'

D ⍱: d as in 'door'

H ⍭: h as in 'happy'

W ⌇: w as in 'went'. It can also double as a long 'u' vowel. A close back-rounded vowel. Unlike modern Hebrew, it's never pronounced as 'v'.

Z ⌿: z as in 'zoo'

X ⍬: This is not found in English. It's pronounced much like clearing saliva from your throat. Position your mouth to form a k and produce friction at that point. It's a voiceless velar fricative. In this book, I've written it as X in the roots, and as [kh] in the pronunciation brackets. Some dictionaries write it as [ch] but I've wanted to avoid confusion with the sound 'ch' as in 'chair'.

Th ⊕: as in 'theory'. It's voiceless so not the voiced th as in 'the'.

Y ⌐⌐: at the start of a word, it will be y as in 'yellow'. But in between consonants it will act more as a lengthened 'i' such as in 'skiis'. In that situation we may write it more as [ii].

K ⍲: as in 'keep'.

L ∠: as in 'lamb'

M ⌇⌇: as in 'mum'.

N ⌐: as in 'noon'.

S ⌇: as in 'sun'

ʕ ⟨eye⟩: This sound is called an Ein. It's not found in English. It's a characteristic Semitic sound like a camel moo. It's a voiced pharyngeal fricative. The closest English sound would be the [h] which is also a fricative (having friction). But [h] is further back in the glottal region. Bring the [h] forward into the pharyngeal region and add voicing. The friction sound is not so distinct as the X sound. Try to pronounce Ein but pull the E back into the throat with the back of the tongue.

P ⟨mouth⟩: Not as in 'paper'. There is no p sound in Semitic languages. Modern Hebrew I understand pronounces [p] when at the beginning of a word and [f] inside the word or at the end. This is most likely a habit derived from European influences.

Other Semitic languages use the sound [f] in all positions, so for example the Arabic word for 'mouth' is [fam]. The Hebrew word for 'mouth' is [pey]. In Proto-Semitic, the P was written with the symbol of a mouth. It's possible that in ancient times the P was pronounced like an [f] but with friction formed between the lips (voiceless bilabial fricative) rather than from the connecting of the top teeth and bottom lip as in [f]. This Semitic sound between the lips may have been the origin of the English wh. Today we pronounce 'when' as [wen] but there must have been a reason to write the wh. I understand old English pronounced wh with some friction between the lips but not with the lips so close together.

Ts ⟨glyph⟩: Most Semitic languages don't use the pronunciation of the [ts] sound. Instead, they will use a soft 'd' sound, often written as 'dh'. Modern Hebrew will say the word meaning 'earth' as [erets]. Arabic will say [ardh]. The dh sound is a retracted d with the root of the tongue pulled back. It sounds much like a muffled thudding d. Dh is part of a set of sounds [t] voiceless, [d] voiced and [dh] backed.

Q ⟨glyph⟩: This sounds like the English letter q. But in English we pronounce q much like k. In the Semitic languages q is part of a set of three sounds: [k] voiceless, [g] voiced and [q] backed. So [q] is much like [k] except that [q] has the tongue root pulled a little further back like you're swallowing a k.

R: This is not the English pronunciation of r where the tongue doesn't touch any part of the mouth. The Semitic languages pronounce it as an alveolar flap with the tip of the tongue briefly touching the gum at the back of the upper teeth. It's called an alveolar flap.

Sh: as in 'shine'.

T: as in 'tea'

Here's a chart showing the ancient symbols and a rough guide to the meanings and numbers connected to each letter.

			Name	Noun	Verb	Abstract
	1	A	Aleph	Ox	Guide	Humanity
	2	B	Bayt	House	Dwell	Family
	3	G	Gimel	Foot	Walk	Humility
	4	D	Dalet	Door	Go in/out	Reciprocal
	5	H	He	Person	Behold	Existence
	6	W	Waw	Peg	Connect	Relationship
	7	Z	Zayin	Plough	Work	Physical
	8	X	Heth	Wall	Hide	Beyond the physical
	9	Th	Teth	Basket	Protect	Safe keeping
	10	Y	Yud	Arm	Throw	Destiny
	20	K	Kaph	Hand	Tame	
	30	L	Lamed	Staff	Direct	Direction
	40	M	Mem	Sea	Query	The Unknown
	50	N	Nun	Seed	Continue	Design
	60	S	Semech	Thorn	Grasp	
	70	ʕ	Ayin	Eye	See	Knowledge
	80	P	Pe	Mouth	Open	
	90	Ts	Tsadhe	Lying down	Lie down	
	100	Q	Qoph	Sun set	Condense	Intensity
	200	R	Resh	Head	Be on top	Headship
	300	Sh	Shin	Teeth	Cut	Separation
	400	T	Taw	Marker	Agree	Completion

The Danger of Doctrines

Much of what's in this book will be strange to many Christian academics. So strange that it may be bordering on heresy in their minds. So, at this point, let's think about what heresy is and the nature of doctrines.

The best way to avoid making false doctrines, is to not make doctrines at all. That, no doubt, might sound crazy to many.

Didn't the church fathers write doctrines to keep people on the straight and narrow? Doctrine is like one person's snapshot of who they think God is. People can then use that image to determine who is 'in' or 'out' of their group. Subsequently, the church has split into thousands of different groups based on their own diverse doctrine. Sadly, submission to a set of doctrines is often the basis for who gets privilege and money in a church.

We need to ask who the people were who formed these doctrines, and how did the doctrines come to be part of our church tradition?

The Nicene creeds are perhaps the most prominent creeds in Christian tradition today. The people who were brought together to formulate the Nicene creeds were bishops who had graduated from Greek universities where they were immersed in Greek philosophy. But before that, the early church of Acts was instructed to choose leaders based on whether they were known to be full of the Spirit, not based on academic qualification from a state-sanctioned institution.

In addition to the change in method of choosing leaders, the state church in the time of the Nicene creeds had rejected the Hebrew language and the heritage of the Bible. We can assume that they used none of these critical resources when making important decisions on Christian belief. They were chosen by the Roman Emperor Constantine, who claimed to be a Christian. It appears to me that he was not a true follower of Jesus, evidenced by the fact that while claiming to be a Christian, he had some of his relatives murdered, as was the custom in those times when someone threatened his rule. That was certainly not in the spirit of Jesus. When the bishops couldn't agree on the final set of doctrines, the emperor made the final call and chose one set of doctrines which one Bishop had formulated. The emperor, of course, was in no way qualified to make any decision on Biblical truth and practice.

Previous Emperors had persecuted and killed Christians, but that only served to spread and multiply Christianity. As was the habit of Emperors, Constantine felt the need to bring control and order to his empire. To do this, he set about to enforce a common set of beliefs for the church. The Serpent couldn't squash Christianity, so he set about to control it.

Constantine forbade people from meeting in their own homes for worship. Instead, they were required to meet in temples and be led by his own authorised priests. The church became an institutionalised stage show which has largely remained so to this day. He banned the love feasts and the family model of gathering which Jesus had put into place.

Of course, many churches do have a sense of family, but God's family are severely debilitated by the model of control and the idea that to be a Christian, all you need to do is say yes to a set of doctrines and meet in a particular building once a week. There is just enough Christianity to keep people hooked. It's all good for our spirit to be stirred by a good singsong, but does our practice of Christianity extend beyond that to being a family for the whole of life? Or is the one hour of inspiration and spiritual personal satisfaction, once a week, inoculating us to a fuller practice of our faith?

What I call the Constantine model of church, became cemented into church practice by military force and fear where it remains to this day. It has become the norm in Christianity today for both Catholic and Protestant churches. People have forgotten the origin of the Constantine practice.

It can be compared to the conversion of many Islamic communities in the Middle East. In the time of early Islam, the prophet Muhammad sent envoys out to many communities inviting them to join Islam. Many communities rejected the offer. Muhammad subsequently sent an army to take control of those communities to force them to accept Islam. Now today, the practice of Islam is entirely normal in those communities. Most are oblivious to how and why their communities came to Islam.

The Constantine church model has deflected people from God's central purpose of being a family, supporting one another in every aspect of life, 7 days a week, in homes, and in the community.

A family has everyone participating, but the church model has everyone sitting in rows watching what is often a stage show. Most people only participate by playing a game of Simon Says - do this and do that. And for most people, this is the entire extent of their Christian experience. Only a handful of chosen people are permitted to participate if they are known to be safe, and qualified to uphold the tradition of that church, or have passed an audition! Those who pay their money, get to have 'Premium Membership' and privileges. Of course, genuine Christian family does exist within many Constantine churches, but their vitality can be greatly muffled.

Some of these words may be saddening and shocking to many. It will not be palatable to many in the church, but the time has come for us to be a family where we can all pull together as a body, and not rely on a paid professional to run the show. Leaders should be chosen according to whether they are known by the community to be full of the Holy Spirit – not according to whether they have completed a state-approved qualification. In many cases, these people are chosen from outside the community according to their qualifications on paper and approved by church and state authorities. Usually, there is little to no effort to train up local people. Is there still a place in today's Christian leadership for smelly fishermen and dusty carpenters – as was the case in Jesus' time?

Constantine had the state power and authority to cement the doctrines of his choice into church tradition where they remain to this day.

To me, all those factors are certainly not a good foundation for Christian doctrine and practice. In fact, I believe that doctrines are only formulated to bring control. They are effectively an engraved image of who someone thinks God is – often, according to one person and tradition.

The Ten Commandments forbid us from making graven images of God which people are then required to worship. Doctrines are essentially a written image (like a graven image) of who someone thinks God and theology should look like – and people are required to worship this image if they want to be in a particular religious institution.

Churches have subsequently formulated a whole range of doctrines which have only served to separate God's family into thousands of different factions.

People will always express in spoken word and writing who they understand God to be. Everyone will have a slightly different understanding. The important thing, though, is whether they set up that version to be worshipped by others. Will they separate themselves from others based on their own version?

Jesus gave us only one rock on which to build his family, which was the statement of Peter to Jesus,

"You are the Messiah, the Son of the Living God.

Jesus replied, "Blessed are you, Simon son of Jonah, for this was not revealed to you by man, but by my Father in heaven. And I tell you that you are Peter, and on this rock I will build my church, and the gates of Hades will not overcome it." Matthew 16:16-18.

The confession and belief that Jesus is the Messiah, the Son of the Living God is the only doctrine (rock) which should determine who is in God's family.

≈

While living in rural Middle East communities, I observed how families and tribes have a close connection. People would turn up unannounced and a large plate of food would be placed on the floor for all to share. Everyone participated in the conversation and helped each other in everyday life. To me, this was closer to the model of family that Jesus had in mind. If we are to be family, this tribal model is way better than the model of people just meeting once a week to sit in pews and not having much to do with one another for the rest of the week. In the tribal model, if anyone walked into the house, they would be greeted by every person in the room. In the Constantine model, I have walked into large churches where not one person greeted me. Even in smaller churches which I have been part of, I have wanted to offer my abilities and gifts, but have not been permitted to do so because I'm not stage show material or good enough to draw a crowd. God's family is not about having a larger crowd or giving a polished performance, it's about being a family.

Let's get back to the model which Jesus put in place: sharing food as a family on a regular basis and being a family in every aspect of life. Instead of investing many thousands of dollars into a large building, we can invest in helping the poor. Instead of employing professionals to serve the church, by each person in the family having a one-on-one relationship of helping the needy, we will attract others into the family. It's about the family engaging with the wider community, not a professional representing an institution.

An Alphabetical exploration

What follows is an exploration of key words for our journey towards our destination - arranged in alphabetical order according to the Ancient Hebrew 'AlephTaw'. With each word we study, we gain a better understanding of how the letters bring meaning and how the language works. Hopefully, we'll also gain a better understanding of how we were designed to function as God's masterpiece.

The script written with large Proto-Semitic picture-like characters is read from right to left. This type of ancient writing didn't include vowels.

All other text written in Roman script is read from left to right.

A – Aleph – Ox

Aleph is the first letter of the alphabet and has the sound Ah. It's often pronounced in Hebrew as Eh but most other Semitic languages pronounce it as Ah.

Being the first letter, it also has the numerical value of one. The English letter A takes its first position from the Hebrew alphabet. The letter A was originally written with the symbol of an Ox head with horns. It was later turned upside down to form the Latin, then English letter A. Who knows why it was turned upside down? A crazy theory I have relates to the Satanic habit of turning sacred things upside down. Could this have been a practice back in ancient times? The Serpent certainly was around and his mission is to turn humanity upside down, so why not turn the letter which represents humanity and is also the first letter of the word meaning God, upside down? It may have inadvertently been done to distinguish or distance it from the Hebrew alphabet and culture.

The letter A introduces the two main players in the Biblical story – God (AL)[1] and humanity (ADM)[2] [adam]- appropriately at the beginning of the alphabet.

The letter A was given the name, 'aleph' which means, 'Ox', 'to learn', and 'thousand'.

As we've seen, Semitic letters and words have three types of meaning: a noun (e.g., Ox), a verb (e.g., to learn) and an abstract (e.g., thousand). An abstract is something you can't see, and it frequently talks about a relationship or the spiritual.

---

[1] AL Strong's 410
[2] ADM Strong's 120

We can expect all the three meanings ('to learn', 'Ox' and 'thousand'[1]) to form one scene. So, this would say, 'the Ox is guided for a thousand'. The thousand doesn't seem to make much sense in that context because a plough line could be any length.

Let's introduce another Semitic feature where visible physical things serve to illustrate a spiritual or abstract concept. In this case, the Ox is figurative of humanity being guided by God over units of a thousand years. Humanity (represented by Adam) has been led by God (AL) in units of a thousand in three different eras: Firstly, four thousand years from Adam to Jesus being led by the Law. Secondly (the current era) we are led for two thousand years by the Spirit. Lastly, we will be led for one thousand years being led by Jesus in person. Note how with each era, the period is halving each time – 4000, 2000 and 1000. I'm presuming the current era to be 2000 years based on the pattern of halving.

So, we could expect Jesus to return 2000 years after His death. The biggest problem is that we don't know exactly when He was born but many put it at between 4 to 6 BC. We do know from the Bible that He began His ministry at age 30, and we understand He was crucified after 3 years of ministry. So, this puts his death at age 33. Add 2000 to that and we arrive at His possible return. We could make predictions about when He returns, but I simply want to bring to your attention God's pattern, and that Jesus' return is imminent. This is by no means meant to be "prophetic". I am simply proposing a possibility, based on my observations and understanding. Only 'time will tell' if I'm anywhere near accurate on this!

Now the Bible does say that we won't know the day or the hour at which Jesus will return, but I think we're starting to get a clearer picture. We may not know the day nor the hour, but we may get a good idea of the month or year. We know from ancient wedding custom that the groom would return from building the house to take his bride at a time when the bride would not know.

---

[1] Strong's 505

Be ready for when the Groom returns – don't be caught sleeping, because many Christians will fall into the trap by following the status quo.

The Alphabet and Aleph Taw

A key word we need to look at which begins with the letter A is the word Aleph Taw.

In English, the name we give to the entire collection of letters is, 'alphabet' which is comprised of two words, alpha and bet. These are the first two letters of the Greek alphabet. They were derived from the first two letters of the ancient Hebrew alphabet where they were called aleph (Ox and humanity) and bayt (house and family).

The Semitic name for the ordered collection of letters is, 'aleph-taw' – a word which is formed from the first and last letters of the Hebrew alphabet, A and T.

When we put these two letters together to form AT, we get the root which talks about the ox (A) moving towards the marker (T). AT brings us the idea of the plough marker. In ancient times, and still today in many farming communities, the plough driver would steer his ox towards a marker at the end of the field in order to keep a straight furrow. When I was at horticulture school, I was taught this same principle while ploughing with a tractor.

As with most meanings in Hebrew, there is a physical picture which helps us to understand a spiritual or abstract concept. The physical picture of the ox being guided towards the marker, is a spiritual picture of humanity being led towards our destination or ultimate goal. The word Aleph not only means ox but also means, 'to guide', and 'thousand'. We are being led towards our destination in units of a thousand years: 4000 from Adam to Jesus first coming, 2000 till the second coming of Jesus, then 1000 years of the rule of Jesus on earth before the folding up of the physical earth.

The word spelt AL is translated as, 'God' but actually means, 'to guide'. This word is related to the word ALPh (Aleph).

Children of the root AT include:

AT 𐤕𐤀 'plough point' (the leading tip of the plough). '**Sign**'[1] (a reference marker). '**At**' (a word used to point to a location – so AT is very likely the origin of the English word 'at').

ATH[2] 𐤄𐤕𐤀 [ata] '**arrive**' (to arrive at the destination).

AWT[3] 𐤕𐤅𐤀 ['owt] '**Agree**' (a common destination or end outcome shared between two or more people). The most common form of agreement in ancient times was the marriage agreement, so AWT has a strong connection to the betrothal.

'**Mark**' (a mark used as a reference point). This word is also used in the context of a miraculous sign such as the mark of the rainbow which God gave to Noah. The rainbow served as the sign of an agreement between God and Noah, that God would not destroy the earth with a flood again. Another use is with the signs God gave to Pharoah to harden his heart such as the plagues of locusts and the death of all first born. The letter W in AWT is the tent peg, which brings the idea of connecting two together. So, A (humanity) is being connected to T (divinity – I'll explain that meaning soon) by a marriage agreement.

AYT[4] 𐤕𐤉𐤀 ['ayt] '**entrance**' (the place where you enter in at your destination). The letter Y (arm) talks about throwing or destining something towards a target. The entrance is our destination. Ultimately that entrance will be the house of Father God where we will dwell in the room which the Son (groom) has prepared for us. It's common practice even today that when a son gets married, he builds a room onto his father's house for

---

[1] AT Strong's 852
[2] ATH Strong's 857
[3] AWT Strong's 226
[4] AYT Strong's 2978

his wife and family. That room is called a house – a house within a house. The word meaning, 'house' is spelt BYT and pronounced as bayt. It also means, 'family'.

In the word bayt, notice the use of the letters ayt, talking about an entrance. The letter B means, 'house' and 'family'. Put B and ayt together and you get something like, 'family entering in'.

Three in Two in One

The letter A has the numerical value of one. So, this is a good place to talk about how God is one.

My exploration of the tri-nature of God has led me on a very difficult and long journey spanning many years. The result is that I no longer support the Nicene view that God is three persons in a Trinity. Instead, I see God as having a tri-nature of Father, Son and Spirit, but with two persons – the Father and Son. It is however debatable whether or not the Nicene creeds did pronounce a three-person nature of God. The Greek word they used to describe what we translate as 'person' was 'persona' – which was used to talk about a mask or facet – so not necessarily three persons. Persona and person is not the same thing.

So, I can agree with the original Greek wording of the creed but not the translation into English.

To come to this current understanding has taken a lot of literal tears and anguish – mostly as the result of witch-hunter control-freak Christians sending out emails far and wide to discredit me and warn about what I was writing about. There was a time of at least a year where I dreaded opening my email.

It started with a very exciting journey of discovery. I was living in Jordan, studying Arabic and was learning from a Muslim tutor. I chose not to learn Christian Arabic at the Christian language school because I wanted to be able to communicate with Muslims and understand where they were at. I met a student named Shadee at the University where I started learning

Arabic, who was Jordanian Bedouin. He was a top student studying law. His father was the leader of his village Mosque. Shadee was able to recite the whole Quran by the age of 10. He also learnt a lot of English by studying the English dictionary from cover to cover.

I often visited and stayed at his family home in a rural village so was able to see how people lived and how it was very similar to Bible times, ploughing the ground with animals, growing grapes, wheat, olives and pomegranates through the seasons of cold winters and hot summers. On a couple of occasions, I even went to pray with him in the Mosque, saying that I was going to pray to God, not his prophet. He was fine with that. I was able to learn first-hand how people prayed and what their faith was all about, including all the language that went with it. Other missionaries would have had a panic attack if they'd found out I had prayed in a mosque. But I felt that relationship was important.

I spent hundreds of hours with him unpacking the Arabic language going deeper than most Arabic speakers do in normal life. At that stage, I wasn't aware that letters had meanings nor did he. For every new word I learnt, we looked at the root of the word, which is going one step below the meaning of the actual spoken word. We looked at families of words which shared the same root consonants (like parents) and how they were made different to bring a variation of meanings.

Sometimes we visited the ancient ruins of Roman occupation. I was able to see how people lived in the Biblical times. I was aware that Islam has a belief that God is one. I knew also that Judaism also believes that God is one. Now, while I'm on the topic of one, the Hebrew word meaning one is spelt AXD[1] אחד, which means to join two together as one. So, in one, there's actually two. I found that out much later.

It was clear that Muslims and Jews find the Christian belief that there are three persons in God to be a significant barrier for them to come to Jesus. I also discovered that Muslims have a misunderstanding of what Christians believe about a trinity. And Christians haven't helped the situation by

---

[1] AXD Strong's 259 'one'

insisting that God is three persons. Many Muslims have the misunderstanding that the Christian trinity includes Jesus, *Mary* and God. They understand that Christians believe that God had sex with Mary to produce Jesus – which is highly preposterous and blasphemous to them – and to Christians!

Therefore, I sought to find out whether or not the trinity idea was a necessary barrier and how it actually got there. The sticking point to me was the Holy Spirit, so I looked up every reference to the Holy Spirit in the Bible to see if the Spirit truly demanded being a person in its own right. Now before we get hung up on pronouns – whether the Spirit is an 'it' or a 'him', we need to remember that the Hebrew language doesn't have a non-gender pronoun, 'it'. There is only he or she – even for objects. So, when we see a gender pronoun (he) referring to the Spirit of God, that doesn't automatically mean that the spirit is a person. I believe that spirit is not an 'it' but is part of every person.

One of the first things which I noticed, was that people have a tri-nature which resembles the tri-nature of God. The Bible says that man was created in the image of God. It seems that we share the same tri-nature, image or pattern. God's tri-nature includes Father, Son and Holy Spirit.

The first thing to notice is that we both have a spirit. So, it seems that to be a person, we need to have a spirit. The Bible says that God has one spirit. If God was three persons, then there would need to be three spirits. But there is only one spirit. The vast number of references to the Spirit in the Bible use the phrase, 'Spirit of God' – which supports the idea that the Spirit belongs to the person of God – the Spirit is not necessarily a person in its own right.

But then we also have the phrase, 'Son of God', referring to Jesus. This is where I see the Son as being a subset of the whole person of God, in the same way that the Spirit is a subset or part of the person of God. Just as a person has a body which is a subset of that person, so Jesus is the physical manifestation of God – part of the person of God – a subset of God. If God has only one spirit, then it seems that Jesus shares that same spirit with God the Father. Jesus said:

John 10:30 "I and the Father are one."

So, there are three aspects within each of the two persons within one person – three in two in one.

The next step is noticing that the Son Jesus has a human body – just like we do. That accounts for the physical nature we share.

The Father is the aspect of God's tri-nature which has to do with giving direction. This relates to the aspect of a human which has to do with will – the part of us which directs us. This likely relates to the word translated as, 'heart' in the Bible. However, the Hebrew word spelt LB ⌂ℓ [1] which is translated as 'heart' has nothing to do with the heart organ. English translators used 'heart' perhaps because the word included the idea of internal feelings. The letter L means to lead, and the letter B means family or relationship. The heart leads us *in* relationship and *to* relationship.

Where does 'soul' fit in? The Hebrew word translated as soul is NPSh[2] ଏହି [nefesh]. Its dictionary meaning is 'refresh' and 'soul'. But the word 'soul' doesn't really tell us what it is. We'll need to look at the context.

> *Genesis 1:20 And God said, "Let the water teem with **living** (NPSh) creatures, and let birds fly above the earth across the expanse of the sky."*

This is the first use of the word, and we see it's used to talk about something all living things have – a kind of life force. I'd say it relates more to the physical life of something.

> *Genesis 1:30 And to all the beasts of the earth and all the birds of the air and all the creatures that move on the ground--everything that has the **breath of life** (NPSh) in it--I give every green plant for food. And it was so.*

We see it relates to the breath of life which all living things have.

> *Psalm 6:4 Turn, O LORD, and deliver **me** (NPSh); save me because of your unfailing love.*

---

[1] LB Strong's 3820 heart
[2] NPSh Strong's 5315 soul

Here's it's used to talk about the whole self. In Arabic the equivalent word NPSh [nafis] has the meaning of, 'self'.

If the word relates to animals as a whole living being, then it will also relate to the whole person – and most likely to the whole physical person. Not an aspect of that person who will live on after the breath of life has left such as the will or the spirit.

Then it occurred to me that physical objects also have a tri-nature in the same pattern. The will or direction aspect relates to the order or design of an object. We can see this right down to the smallest visible particle.

A physical object also has energy. Energy is all about a relationship between particles. Energy in itself is not visible. This must relate to the spirit in a person, which is also not visible but is all about the connection we have between persons. Perhaps the spirit also connects body with will.

An object has a physical presence or visible manifestation. Jesus is the physical manifestation of the person of God.

As we've seen, this tri-nature is also expressed in the three layers of meaning in a word and the three types of meaning in a word[1].

Life and the Bible are full of this pattern of three. It's the basic pattern for all of life.

The single, dual and tri-natures of God can be seen in the Star of David. Whether this was intentional or not in its original design, I don't know. But it is a very good visual illustration of the nature of God – three in two in one.

The whole star shows the one nature.

The two triangles show the dual nature. Each triangle represents one person.

Each triangle shows the tri-nature of a person.

---

[1] See the section: How the Semitic word works

It's a mystery as to where the Star of David came from and what it's meaning is. As with anything with ancient origins, perhaps we'll never know. It's not mentioned in the Bible. The only mention of the word Star and David in one sentence is in Revelation.

> *Revelation 22:16 "I, Jesus, have sent my angel to give you this testimony for the churches. I am the Root and the Offspring of **David**, and the bright Morning **Star**."*

Here we see that Jesus is the Offspring of David and the bright Morning Star. So perhaps the star refers to Jesus! Jesus is the physical manifestation of God and therefore does represent each of the three levels in the Star of David!

The Hebrew word for star is spelt KWKB[1] כוכב [kow-kab] which is from the root KB. K has the value of 20 and B the value of 2 which gives us 22. Notice how the only mention of Star and David within one sentence is in Revelation 22, the last chapter in the Bible. And 22 is the last letter in the alphabet. I believe that the 22nd letter represents the new era into eternity. The 21 previous letters talk about the three stages or eras of human history on earth, each with 7 letters.

The Israeli flag has the Star of David in blue. The Hebrew word translated as blue is TKLT[2] תכלת [tekelet] which I understand to mean violet – the final colour of the colour spectrum. T is also the last letter of the alphabet. So, the blue star also has a strong connection to the last chapter of the Bible. Jesus, while on the cross, pointed us to Psalm 22 by saying the first line of it, 'My God, my God, why have you forsaken me?' This Psalm was prophetic of his suffering and final victory.

The Morning Star would appear to refer to a star which is seen in the morning. It comes up over the horizon just before dawn. It effectively signals the start of a new day – the new era. The arrival of Jesus in His second coming to earth is the star which signals the arrival of the new dawn. The morning star is seen while it's still dark – just before the start of the new day.

---

[1] KWKB Strong's 3556
[2] TKLT Strong's 8504

This is known to be Venus, which is the brightest and first star visible in the morning sky.

Some say that according to archaeology, the Star of David existed before David in other Middle Eastern cultures. From what it shows about the nature of God being one, dual and tri, I would say it's divinely inspired. Perhaps it was even revealed to Adam by God. God may have made it as a kind of sign, in much the same way that the alphabet is a communication from God to humanity.

In the following sections, we'll take a closer look at what the first three and last three letters of the alphabet tell us about the single, dual and tri- natures of God.

The One nature of God

A T

*Deuteronomy 6:4 Hear, O Israel: The LORD our God, the LORD is **one**.*

The first and last letters of the alphabet - A and T tell us something about how God is One. We could expect them to tell us about oneness because they're the first from the beginning and first from the last – as in a reflection of one another.

The name for the letter A is, 'aleph' which means, 'to lead/guide'. God gives us one direction. When we **listen**, we will hear one voice from God. We won't hear three different directions.

The name for the letter T is, 'taw' which means, 'mark' – which is a physical mark with a meaning. It could be a cross on the ground, a writing, a cross stuck in the ground as a plough marker. The plough marker was a target and focal point for the plough driver to keep a straight line towards the completion point at the end of the field. The letter T is at the end of the alphabet and so has the meaning of completion and end purpose. God is about one direction towards one end target.

The Hebrew word for, 'one' is spelt AXD[1] ߺ߃ߊ [ached]. We see it used in Deuteronomy 6:4. Notice the use of the letter A. The word AXD talks about joining together. So, it would seem that oneness is actually talking about two or more entities.

Another important word starting with the letter A is spelt ALHYM[2] ߺ߃ߊ߃ [elohiim] and is used in Deuteronomy 6:4. This verse uses two names for God – translated as God and LORD. 'God' is translated from the Hebrew word 'Elohiim' – spelt ALHYM. The word 'LORD' is usually translated from the word spelt YHWH ߺ߃ߊ߃ [Yahweh].

The word ALHYM is made of two parts – AL and the affix HYM. AL means, 'God' and 'guide'. HYM has two meanings: It can mean, 'plural' which is two or more (Hebrew has a dual but is used only for natural pairs such as legs or eyes). The word elohiim is sometimes used to describe multiple gods such as idols.[3]

The second meaning talks about something great, awesome and majestic.

The word YHWH[4] [Yahweh] means something like, 'he exists' akin to God's other name, 'I am' which uses the same letters HWH. The H alone means 'to exist' and was drawn with the picture of a person. So, in HWH we could observe that here are two persons. The letter W (tent peg) which connects the two means, 'and'. It's connecting the two together. Therefore, in Deuteronomy 6:4, we clearly see a theme of there being a unity of entities to form one direction.

> *Deuteronomy 6:4 Hear, O Israel: The LORD [YAHWEH] our God [Elohiim], the LORD [YAHWEH] is* **one***.*

---

[1] Strong's 259
[2] Strong's 430
[3] For example, Genesis 31:30 "…why did you steal my gods?"
[4] Strong's 3068

The Dual Nature of God

    B   Sh

To learn something about the dual nature of God, we can reasonably expect to look at the second letter of the alphabet B, and the second to last Sh.

The letter B has the name spelt BYT[1] [bayt] which means house, family and tribe. Being the second letter, it has the numerical value of 2 which denotes relationship because relationship starts with two or more entities. There is relationship in the nature of God because there are two persons Father (divine) and Son (human).

The letter Sh (teeth) talks about separating – which is the opposite of relationship. However, God the Father is truth and purity, so He separates Himself from falsehood and uncleanness.

There is a reflective symmetry in the nature of God. In reflective symmetry there are two sides which appear to be opposites, yet they work in harmony. Relationship is directly opposite to separation. God's truth brings judgement and separation. Yet His Son Jesus brings relationship, mercy and forgiveness. Actually, you can't have one without the other. You can't have relationship if there weren't two separate persons. It could be argued that you can't have forgiveness if there wasn't separation. When we sin against one another or against God, it brings separation in the relationship, and forgiveness brings about the continuation of the relationship. It seems to be in God's plan that we should be separated so that we can come to Him again with our own free will and learn to trust Him.

These two aspects of relationship and separation tell us about the two persons of God – the Father (who gives us the directives and law and needs to be separated from sin) and the Son who brings relationship and connection. Many say that there is a third person, the Holy Spirit. But I

---

[1] BYT Strong's 1004

believe that to be a Greek invention put into place at the Council of Nicaea by bishops who were all graduates of Greek philosophy and who were divorced from the Hebrew heritage of Christianity. The Nicene creeds became cemented into Christian tradition through military force, by the emperor Constantine who commissioned the Creeds as a control tool. The Holy Spirit is, however, part of God's tri-nature, just as a person in God's image has a spirit as part of his tri-nature. God doesn't need three persons to begin relationship. Relationship is defined as being two or more.

The first phrase of the Bible is, "In the beginning God…" In the beginning of the Hebrew Bible is the letter B which has the value of two. This is certainly another clue pointing to God being two who created the heavens and earth.

The Tri-nature of God

      G   R

The letter G, being the third letter in the alphabet, and the third to last letter R, tells us something about the tri-nature of God. The letter G (foot) relates to the humility of Jesus and the letter R (head) to the headship of God. The tri-nature is not about the number of persons – which is two, but about the three aspects of his nature: direction (Father), relationship (spirit) and physical manifestation (Jesus).

Notice that direction relates to God's one nature, and relationship to his dual nature. It seems to follow then that the physical manifestation will relate to the tri-nature. The physical nature is that part of God's being which is expressed as a fractal symmetry – with the same pattern seen in God, the person of Jesus and the physical body of Jesus. At this point, it's a bit hard getting your head around that. For more explanation, see the section on the Universal Fractal of Life.

The letter G has the name Gimel – spelt GML. Each letter of this word talks about the tri-nature of God.

The name Gimel means, 'foot' – the lowest part of the person, which gets dirty and so talks about the humility of the physical person of Jesus – made from dust. The physical foot walks in the dust and is made from dust. Jesus is the physical manifestation of God.

Now to the third from last letter in the alphabet: The letter R has the name Rash - spelt RASh ܫܐܪ.

The letter R talks about the physical aspect. Rash means 'head'. God expresses himself in physical form through the person Jesus, who sits as head to rule the nations – beginning at the thousand years of rule. Notice that when we look at the tri-nature of Jesus, the physical aspect of that tri-nature is about humility, but when we look at Jesus as part of the tri-nature of God, the whole person of Jesus becomes the head – the physical manifestation of God's rule.

The Universal Fractal of Life

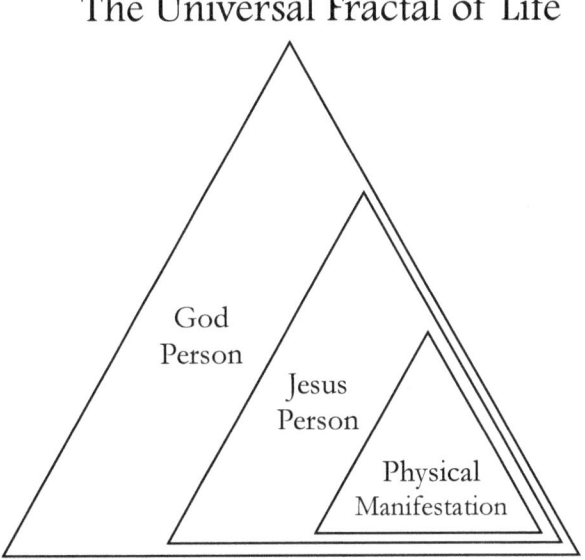

A fractal is a pattern repeated at successive levels.

There is a tri-nature fractal in all of life beginning with the tri-nature of God. We could also call it a universal fractal because it includes every type of existence at every level.

The tri-nature pattern is repeated at the levels of God, man, and physical objects.

The pattern which is repeated is order, relationship and visible manifestation.

At the level of God, the pattern is seen as Father (order), Spirit (relationship) and Son (visible manifestation).

At the level of Jesus, the human person, the pattern is seen as will (order), spirit (relationship) and body (visible manifestation).

At the level of a physical manifestation, the pattern is seen as design (order), energy (relationship) and visible manifestation. A visible manifestation is the result of design and energy working together. In the physical world (as described by quantum physics), there isn't anything visibly solid at the smallest level. There is no visible or measurable 'particle'. What we see and touch is the result of the interaction of design and energy.

Notice the beautiful symmetry of the tri-nature pattern seen in multiple dimensions – vertically (three levels) and horizontally (three elements of the pattern). In the vertical pattern, God represents order, Jesus is the agent of relationship between God and His creation, and physical manifestation is just that.

It's hard to define the basic pattern with just these three words, so I'll explain them in a little more detail:

Order. This talks about a basic identity and design. It's all about direction and purpose.

Relationship. How something or someone relates to other things and persons. For example, there is a gravity relationship between an object and the earth – seen when an object falls to the earth.

Physical manifestation. An interface with others, usually a visible physical manifestation.

Living the Universal Fractal

We can apply this pattern as we live our life so that we get the whole picture of living in this life and universe.

We can apply it at three levels in three ways:

The Divine Level

This talks about our relationship with God in all three aspects. This is the level many of us leave out because we live with our physical bodies in a physical world. But we have the design within us to operate at this level whether we're aware of it or not. Don't fall for the humanistic talk that we're mere chemical and physical beings descended from single celled organisms and monkeys.

The first aspect has to do with Father Elohiim. He is a person but at a higher level to us as humans. He is the one who gives us direction, purpose and design. We can connect to his purpose and design for us by seeking it out in the Bible – but not just with our head – we need to engage our love for him and listen with our heart. There are many stumbling stones in the Bible which I believe are placed there deliberately to filter out those who aren't true seekers of God's purpose for their lives.

His ultimate purpose is that we become his family and children now and into eternity.

The second aspect relates to the Son Yeshua (Jesus). He is a person who is part of the divine being, but is also at our level as a human. He's a physical manifestation of God so that God can relate to us at our level as humans. Jesus is called the Son of God and we too are regarded as children of God – sons and daughters.

Yeshua is supremely important to us because he is the physical representation of God to humanity. He was born as a human and walked among us to guide us towards God's family. He also died to pay the price for us to become his bride and so enter into his family. It's for us to accept or reject that offer of marriage. We enter into his family not by our own merit, understanding or work but because we have trust in Yeshua as our beloved husband and lover (not in a sexual sense but in the true sense of love).

The third aspect relates to the Holy Spirit of God. This is the means by which we connect to God. The Spirit is not visible but the reality of the Spirit is real just as the gravitation force is real between us and the earth. Without this force we would fly off into space! The gravitational analogy is at the physical level of the Universal Fractal. We are talking about what pulls us to the divine Father. His Spirit guides us in our hearts and gives us the power to follow his leading.

The Human Level

Humanity is created in the image of God, which I understand to relate to us having the same tri-nature of a will, a spirit and a body.

Regarding our will, we need to use it to choose our ultimate path. When we choose that path, that involves day to day decisions which keep us on that path. Ultimately God designed us to be his family, so if we choose to follow that plan, that will affect the way we live and everything we do in the present. Living as his family starts now, not when we reach the Pearly Gates. If we have the view that salvation is like having a ticket to the theatre and we don't need to do anything till then, we're mistaken. When we get to the great ticket office, the Father will say he doesn't know us. And he would be right because we haven't spent our time expressing our love for him by the way we live on earth.

Many people don't choose their course of life but instead are led by their physical cravings and the environment around them.

Regarding our physical body, we use it to express and outwork our love for Yeshua by loving those around us in practical physical ways. If we allow it, we will be led away from relationship with God if we are led by what our body wants. Our body is not evil as many religions have claimed, rather it's a gift from God. We are invited to love God with all our being and all our physical strength and resources.

Regarding our spirit, we use it to connect with one another and with God. Spirit is all about relationship. You could say it's the abstract part of our nature – you don't see it but you are certainly aware of the state of your relationships. In fact, I observe that relationships are the most important aspect of our being. It's very much to do with our ultimate purpose in life to be God's family. If our relationships are bad and toxic, that will certainly have a toxic effect on our physical bodies – for example cancer, stress and addictions.

Our heart (LB) is the non-organic part of us which leads us in relationship.

The Physical Level

Our physical body is a subset of our human person. The physical world extends far beyond our human body into the humanly unfathomable universe. Some would say that humanity pales into insignificance in comparison to the universe. But I believe the physical universe is merely a stage where humanity learns to trust in God – this is the ultimate purpose for all of the physical creation.

We are to honour God with our physical bodies:

> *1 Corinthians 6:19,20: Do you not know that your body is a temple of the Holy Spirit, who is in you, whom you have received from God? You are not your own; you were bought at a price. Therefore, honor God with your body*

Our appreciation of the physical world aids us in our appreciation of God:

> *Psalm 19:1 "The heavens declare the glory of God; the skies proclaim the work of his hands."*

I believe we should keep the physical universe in perspective as secondary to the spiritual world in importance. We may think the visible world is the real reality but let's consider that when we get down to the smallest known constituent of physics – the quark, there is actually nothing to see – there is no size or shape! According to quantum physics, there is literally nothing solid or tangible! It's all ordered energy. Order plus energy equals a physical manifestation. And that order and energy is from God.

AL (God) and LA (The Idol of Humanism)

*Genesis 14:18 Then Melchizedek, king of Salem, brought out bread and wine. He was priest of **God (AL)** Most High*

The word translated as 'God' is written in Semitic as AL[1]. The word AL means, 'ox', 'oath' and 'power'. An oath is about a binding agreement between two parties. It has power to guide direction.

Let's look at each letter. The A was drawn with the symbol of an ox head – and figuratively humanity. It also carries the idea of being guided.

The letter L was drawn with the symbol of a shepherd's staff and brings the idea of leading.

So, put them together and we have the idea of the ox being led which is a picture of humanity being led.

Now when the letters of a Hebrew root get reversed, we often get a reverse meaning. If we reverse AL, we get LA[2] – which means, 'not', 'nothing' and 'idol' - essentially, 'empty, worthless idol'. It's talking about the ox leading – the ox is worshipped as an idol.

The spelling of LA is a root which has the underlying meaning of something pointless and worthless.

---

[1] Strong's 410
[2] Strong's 408, 408, 3809

It's children (derived words) include LAYA[1] 𐤀𐤋𐤉𐤋 meaning, 'idol', 'worthless', YLA[2] 𐤉𐤀𐤋 'foolish'.

Since the letter A (ox) is figurative of humanity, the root LA is talking about being led to humanity – essentially humanism. Humanity is worshipped as an idol. The word humanism is not in the English Bible, largely because Hebrew doesn't use words with 'ism' (ideology) meanings. It talks more about specific actions. We can certainly see humanism in action in the Bible – known by its fruits. And the following Biblical examples are certainly reflective of the actions of Humanism today – perhaps even prophetic.

The first example is when Adam and Eve decided not to listen to God but to their own knowledge and desire[3]. About 2000 years later, humanity decided to join together to make a name for themselves by building the Tower of Babel reaching to heaven[4].

Then there's the account of Moses' brother Aaron building a golden calf for the people to worship[5]. I understand the calf to be figurative of humanism. The reason he built it, was based on human rationalism – in contrast to trust in God.

The people of Israel had left Egypt and were travelling to the promised land. This in itself is a figure or type of our journey to the spiritual promised land. On the way, Moses went up the mountain to receive the Ten Commandments from God. But...

> *Exodus 32:1-5 When the people saw that Moses was so long in coming down from the mountain, they gathered around Aaron and said, "Come, make us gods who will go before us. As for this fellow Moses who brought us up out of Egypt, we don't know what has happened to him."*

---

[1] Strong's 457
[2] Strong's 2973
[3] Genesis 2:19 to 3:6
[4] Genesis 11:4
[5] Exodus 32:1-5

> *Aaron answered them, "Take off the gold earrings that your wives, your sons and your daughters are wearing, and bring them to me." So all the people took off their earrings and brought them to Aaron. He took what they handed him and made it into an idol cast in the shape of a calf, fashioning it with a tool. Then they said, "These are your gods, O Israel, who brought you up out of Egypt."*
>
> *When Aaron saw this, he built an altar in front of the calf and announced, "Tomorrow there will be a festival to the LORD."*

The people did not want to wait for and trust God – so they took matters into their own hands – Humanism. They turned their attention from the unseen spiritual and instead to the visible and tangible. It was a blatant lie that the wealth of gold and the skill of men to make the gold into images had brought them out of Egypt.

Today we see the same behaviour as the human worship of science to the exclusion of the spiritual and God. I see it played out in the heartless actions of humanist institutions. An example is the Covid lockdown where people were forbidden to be with loved ones who were dying in hospital. The cold hard truths of science were being put before spiritual relationship. The cold hard physical facts took precedence over the unseen spiritual. I have a theory that more elderly would have died through isolation from their loved ones than died of covid.

The same is true of many human ideologies in history. A classic example is Hitler who put an ideology over the value of spiritual life. He heartlessly killed millions.

Today, Humanists are putting the ideology of Climate Change above the value of spiritual life and politics. Prominent humanists today claim that politics is standing in the way of saving the world from a climate disaster. It seems to me that the logical follow on from that comment or ideology is that they want us to do away with politics. They would say that decisions need to be made based on, 'scientific evidence'.

So, what do we do? It seems like they want to do away with human error and introduce a technological leader for humanity – one that does away with human sentiment and emotion. God help us! They're saying that the saviour of the world will not be human spirituality, but what humans have made – which will essentially be their god (leader and saviour) – an empty idol void of human relationship and meaning.

What the humanist New World Order is doing is bypassing politics and governments and putting on the sheepskins of pandemics and climate change to create the illusion of an emergency which is so critical that we must put aside normal political procedure and institute a state of emergency which will override politics.

Aaron, the brother of Moses, had the audacity to claim that the calf god was responsible for the salvation of the people – as today humanism claims that humans are the salvation of humanity and the world.

Then Aaron brought religion into it to somehow try to sanitize or justify it. He stated that they would be worshipping God by making a festival to the Lord. This religious act was a pure façade as is the case for many who claim to be worshipping God today. True worship of God is to submit yourself to God, to wait for Him and to trust Him. Aaron was doing none of these. He was putting his trust only in human power.

There are many churches today who put on a good stage show and can draw the crowds. They claim that their music is worship. But is it truly about submitting to God or is it just to have a good time and feel a warm spiritual buzz?

Could the ox equate to the Beast talked about in Revelation whom the nations will worship? We only have a Greek translation of Revelation, but Revelation is following on from the end-time prophesies of Daniel. The Hebrew or Aramaic word Daniel uses for, 'beast' is spelt XYWA[1] 𐤀𐤅𐤉𐤇 [khaywa]. It means simply, 'living creature'. It's from the underlying root XY𐤇 meaning, 'stomach' and 'life'.

---

[1] XYWA Strong's 2423

Another word translated as, 'beast' in the Old Testament is spelt BHMH[1] 𐤔𐤌𐤄𐤁. This word often refers to cattle. It's from the root BM which has the idea of something high or tall.

Note that the Beast of Revelation was given the power of life and the ability to talk[2] – implying that he didn't have it before. Could the Beast be a robot built in the image of a man, given the power of artificial intelligence and speech? The Dragon gave the Beast authority. The robot embodies all the scientific achievements of humanity, much like the Tower of Babel embodied the united achievements of humanity in its time. Humanism has aspired to 'reach the heavens' to be like God by creating life. The pinnacle of Humanism's achievement would be to create a 'living creature' – which would then be given the authority to rule all of humanity. Kind of like an impartial puppet who would embody all the ideals of humanity but without the flaws of a human with a spirit.

Here's a quote from

www.computer.howstuffworks.com/dna-computer:

> *You won't believe where scientists have found the new material they need to build the next generation of microprocessors. Millions of natural supercomputers exist inside living organisms, including your body. DNA (deoxyribonucleic acid) molecules, the material our genes are made of, have the potential to perform calculations many times faster than the world's most powerful human-built computers. DNA might one day be integrated into a computer chip to create a so-called biochip that will push computers even faster. DNA molecules have already been harnessed to perform complex mathematical problems.*
>
> *While still in their infancy, DNA computers will be capable of storing billions of times more data than your personal computer. In this article, you'll learn how scientists are using genetic*

---

[1] BHMH Strong's 929
[2] Revelation 13:15

material to create nano-computers that might take the place of silicon-based computers in the next decade.

That's how a lifeless robot could be given life! The core of life is DNA. The pinnacle of human achievement would be to harness that life for their own purpose! Remember the word BHMA translated as beast actually means something high or tall. This could essentially equate to a high aspiration – a pinnacle of achievement. Does this sound like the tall tower of Babel built by the combined efforts of Humanism?

We are warned in the book of Revelation not to take the mark of the beast or to worship his image[1]. The mark of the beast is mentioned 7 times in Revelation. It's hard to miss, so there are no excuses – except that the Beast will use deception. Like the deception the Serpent used with Adam and Eve, he will offer us something we find hard to resist – something which appeals to our human desires and leads us away from trust in God. Something which appears to be a good cause. Could it be a global pandemic or climate change – something which sways the masses through controlled mass media?

> *Revelation 13:17 And that no man might buy or sell, save he that had the mark, or the name of the beast, or the number of his name.*
>
> *Revelation 14:9 A third angel followed them and said in a loud voice: "If anyone worships the beast and his image and receives his mark on the forehead or on the hand, he, too, will drink of the wine of God's fury, which has been poured full strength into the cup of his wrath.*
>
> *Revelation 19:20 But the beast was captured, and with him the false prophet who had performed the miraculous signs on his behalf. With these signs he had deluded those who had received the mark of the beast and worshipped his image. The two of them were thrown alive into the fiery lake of burning sulphur.*

I believe the Beast equates to humanism. In a literal sense, the beast may likely be talking about an ox – which in a spiritual sense represents humanity.

---

[1] Revelation 14:9

If we worship humanity, that becomes humanism. We must be very careful in the present time not to follow the Beast down his path of Humanism.

Could it be that Freemasonry is at the helm of Humanism? It's symbol of a divider intersected with a square resemble the capital letter A which represents humanity. Freemasonry was founded on the building of grand edifices to the glory of man. At the time, they would say that the grand cathedrals were built for the glory of God, but personally, I think that was an excuse to build to the glory of man, in the same way that the golden calf of Aaron was given a religious cover.

Some levels of Freemasonry forbid the discussion of religion and politics. Under their ideal global rule, the freedom of religion and politics will certainly be banned. Humanism is already today steering us in the direction which says that religion and politics are divisive and harmful to society as a whole.

ALHYM – Almighty God

*Genesis 1:1 In the beginning **God**(ALHYM) created the heavens and the earth.*

ALHYM[1] [Elohiim] is the first name God is known by in the Bible.

It's translated as simply- 'God', but in my view should be translated as, 'Almighty God'. The word spelt ALHYM is made up of two parts. The central noun is the word AL – meaning, 'God' or more exactly, 'leader of humanity'.

HYM can function both as a derivational affix and as a grammatical affix at the same time. As a derivational affix, it means 'almighty'. As a grammatical affix it marks plurality – meaning more than one.

---
[1] ALHYM Strong's 430

Here's a breakdown of the letters in the affix HYM: The letter H was written with the symbol of a person with hands raised. It has the name Heh[1] which means, 'to exist'. As a lexical unit, it brings the idea of, 'behold'. It can also bring the idea of 'wow'.

The letter Y ⌐ (arm) often brings the idea of throwing something – and in an abstract sense destining something – projecting something. The unit of measure known as a cubit was the forearm.

The letter M ∿ (sea) brings the idea of something unfathomable, unknown and awesome.

So, put together HYM could be saying something like, 'behold, consider the dimension of the unfathomable.'

Those who believe that God is three persons (Trinitarians) have used this plural marker to support the theory of the existence of three persons. However, the HYM can be used for two or more. There is a dual marker in Hebrew, but this is used only for identical pairs such as eyes etc. Anything else which is not an identical pair and is two or more receives the HYM plural marker. I observe that God is two persons – Father and Son. The Spirit is part of God's Tri-nature. God's dual person and tri-nature is well illustrated in the Star of David – which is two triangles overlaid over one another. Each triangle represents a person. Each person has a tri-nature. Both persons are part of one person.

Also, if we follow that the plural marker is showing more than one, then it will imply that there is more than one God because the plural marker is on the word, God. The Bible is fairly clear that God is one. Even trinitarians state that there is only one God eternally existent in three persons.

Put together AL and HYM add up to mean something like, Almighty Leader of Humanity, or Unfathomable Guide.

---

[1] HEH Strong's 1933, 1934

ADM – Humanity

*Genesis 1:26 Then God said, "Let us make **man (ADM)** in our image, in our likeness, and let them rule over the fish of the sea and the birds of the air, over the livestock, over all the earth, and over all the creatures that move along the ground."*

The word spelt ADM[1] [adam] has a wide and awesome range of meaning.

Adam was the first person. But ADM is more than the name of a person. It also means, 'man' which includes wider humanity, males and females. In contrast, the word ANSh is also translated as 'man' and 'husband', but refers specifically to male man.

Notice how the distinction between ADM (humanity) and ANSh (male man) plays out in the account of the fall of humanity:

Genesis 3:6 When the woman saw that the fruit of the tree was good for food and pleasing to the eye, and also desirable for gaining wisdom, she took some and ate it. She also gave some to her husband (ANSh), who was with her, and he ate it.

Soon after, God seeks an account from humanity:

Genesis 3:9 But the LORD God called to the man (ADM), "Where are you?"

God then asks humanity how they realised that they were naked.

Genesis 3:12 The man (ADM) said, "The woman you put here with me-- she gave me some fruit from the tree, and I ate it."

We can see from the above verses that the author is squarely putting the responsibility on humanity, even in the account of the man (humanity) blaming the woman.

The root of ADM is DM which brings the meaning of both, 'blood' and 'likeness'.

---

[1] ADM Strong's 120. ADM is translated as 'man' and 'Adam'.

How do these meanings come from the letters?

The word, 'blood' is the name for an object. The word, 'likeness' is an abstract idea. So, we will explore the root from these two angles.

Let's look at, 'blood' first. The letter D (door) brings the idea of being reciprocal – a coming and going. This relates to blood being something which goes back and forth from the heart. The letter M (sea) brings the idea of liquid. Blood is a liquid which moves back and forth.

The word, 'likeness' requires us to look at the letters and their relationship from an abstract, spiritual angle. The letter D (door) may talk about a comparing back and forth between two items. The letter M (sea) brings the idea of an unknown. Because it talks about an unknown which seeks an answer, it's used in most question words in a similar way that the letter W is used in most English question words. So, we're looking backwards and forwards to compare and asking the question of what is alike.

What's significant about the meaning of, 'likeness'?

> Genesis 1:26 Then God said, "Let us make man ADM in our image, in our likeness DMWT."

Another Hebrew word spelt MN[1] [min] connects to the idea of man: It includes the meaning of, 'from' which answers the question, 'from where'. This word is likely the origin of the English word, 'man' and so talks about being from God. MN is also the root of the word, 'Manna', the food which fell from the sky to feed the Israelites. They asked, "where is it from?", hence the name, 'manna', meaning, 'from where'.

The addition of the letter A to the root DM, brings the idea of being guided, and connects the letter A to humanity.

The letter A is the first letter of the alphabet, so also refers to Adam being the start of the human story.

It's also no chance that DM means blood, which talks about the colour red. Red is the first colour of the colour spectrum. This is in symmetry with

---

[1] MN Strong's 4478, 4479, 4482. Arabic has the meaning of from and who.

the last letter of the alphabet T which is the first letter of the word TKLT meaning, 'violet' – the last colour of the spectrum.

ANSh – man and woman

In the creation of the first woman, there's some curious things (perhaps even mysteries) which need looking into more, which we don't see in an English version of the Bible. But to get an overview, let's read the English translation. In brackets, I've shown the original Hebrew word:

> *Genesis 2:21 So the LORD God caused the man (ADM) to fall into a deep sleep; and while he was sleeping, he took one of the man's ribs and closed up the place with flesh.*
>
> *22 Then the LORD God made a woman (ANShH) from the rib he had taken out of the man (ADM), and he brought her to the man (ADM).*
>
> *23 The man said, "This is now bone of my bones and flesh of my flesh; she shall be called 'woman' (ANShH), for she was taken out of man (ANYSH)."*
>
> *24 For this reason a man (ANYSh) will leave his father and mother and be united to his wife (ANShH), and they will become one flesh.*

Why did Adam name the woman with the Hebrew name ANShH? The man explains the reason as: "(Because) she was taken out of man". So, what does the name ANShH tell us about being taken out of man? The best explanation I can see is that the name ANShH is derived from the word ANYSh (man). Both names share the same parent root ANSh. The addition of the letter H to form the woman's name is a way of forming feminine nouns in Hebrew.

Another child meaning of the parent root ANSh is 'sick'.

ANSh appears to be talking about the mortality and sin (sickness) of humanity.

Notice how the writer uses two different Hebrew words (ADM and ANSh) for 'man'. In the English translation we see only the one word used – man. In verses 21 and 22 the writer uses the word ADM. Then in verses 23 to 24 the writer switches to using ANSh.

Note how in verse 22, God took the rib out of ADM (humanity), but then in verse 23 he describes the woman as being taken out of ANSh (male man). Why the change? Perhaps it's setting the scene for verse 24 where the ANSh (the male) leaves his parents to be united with his wife.

Both ADM and ANSh are used extensively throughout the Bible.

> *Genesis 6:5 The LORD saw how great man's (ADM) wickedness on the earth had become, and that every inclination of the thoughts of his heart was only evil all the time.*

In the contexts of use, ADM could easily be translated with the idea of, 'humanity'. Obviously in Genesis 6:5 it's not just male man that had become wicked, but the whole of humanity - male and female.

See the verse where both ADM and ANSh is used:

> *Genesis 2:23 The man (ADM) said, "This is now bone of my bones and flesh of my flesh; she shall be called 'woman,' for she was taken out of man (ANSh)."*

The context of "For she was taken out of man", requires man to be specifically male (ANSh). The use of ADM seems to be directing us to think of the first creation of man as essentially the creation of humanity. In a similar manner, God separated the waters into two different waters – the waters above and the waters below.

So, with that separation in mind, perhaps we could conclude that the Sh (teeth) in ANSh refers to the humanity which has been separated out into male and female.

The letter A (ox) in ANSh, likely refers to humanity being led. The letter N (sprouting seed) refers to the continuation of life. Perhaps this continuation refers to humanity being the continuation or multiplication of God's family. An important aspect of that continuation is forgiveness – which is about allowing life to continue. The letter N has the numerical value of 50 which links to the Year of Jubilee where all slaves were to be freed and debts forgiven. Receiving God's forgiveness is the only way back into God's family.

How is the Woman a Help to Humanity?

*Genesis 2:18 The LORD God said, "It is not good for the man (ADM) to be alone. I will make a **helper** (ʕZR[1]) suitable for him."*

Of the 21 occurrences of the noun ʕZR ('helper' or 'help') in the Old Testament, it's used almost exclusively for help given by God, for example:

*Psalm 70:5 Yet I am poor and needy; come quickly to me, O God. You are my **help** and my deliverer; O LORD, do not delay*

The only time it's used in relation to help from man is where the help is expected but not actually delivered, for example:

*Isaiah 30:5 "Everyone will be put to shame because of a people useless to them, who bring neither **help** nor advantage, but only shame and disgrace."*

It should be noted that when the word ʕZR is used as a verb 'to help', then it is used frequently in relation to humans giving help, e.g.:

1 Chronicles 22:17 "Then David ordered all the leaders of Israel to help[2] his son Solomon."

Other Hebrew words are translated as 'help' and relate also to help given by men. These include ʕZB[3], TShWʕH[4] (salvation), YShʕ[5].

---

[1] Strong's 5828
[2] Strong's 5826
[3] Strong's 5800
[4] Strong's 8668
[5] Strong's 3467

So why is the noun ʕZR used in relation to help from woman when it's only used elsewhere in relation to divine help? Could it be that divine help would come through a descendent which requires the creation of the first woman. I understand that descendent to be Yeshua (Jesus).

Also, the need for help was expressed in relation to ADM (humanity), not in relation to ANSh (male man). The meaning of the word ADM relates to humanity both male and female, so the help is in regard to help for humanity. I had always thought that (according to the English translation) woman was created so that man wouldn't be lonely. This would seem like a natural assumption. But surely Adam wasn't lonely with God. However, after ADM rejected God's command, there is now a greater issue in mind – the eternal separation of mankind from God.

Could Genesis 2:24 be a physical picture of our spiritual separation from God (our Father) and subsequent uniting with Jesus (our groom)?

For this reason, a man will leave his father and mother and be united to his wife, and they will become one flesh.

The picture is limited though to one concept, because we will eventually dwell with both the Father and Son, but only after we've accepted the Son.

What does the word ʕZR tell us about divine help?

The letter ʕ (eye) likely relates to seeing the need. The letter ʕ is used in the word YHWShʕ (Joshua – the Hebrew name translated as Jesus). YHWShʕ is comprised of two words YHW and Shʕ. Shʕ means to delight in – to be seen and admired. So, a help is more than being seen, it's being valued.

The letter Z (implement) usually relates to work – action which meets the need.

The letter R (head) likely relates to an important purpose or end goal and our return to our original intended state – which is to be in God's family as Adam was in the garden of Eden.

In a Hebrew reading of Genesis, the word translated as 'rib' is TsLʕ[1] [Tselaʕ]. In all other contexts of use in the Bible TsLʕ is used to mean 'side' – not specifically a rib bone. So, there's no contextual basis to translate as 'rib'. It appears that the position of the side is more significant than the anatomical part. A rib is not only the side of a person anatomically, it's wraps around the entire torso, so would be technically inconsistent with the specific meaning of 'side'.

Adam says that Eve was 'flesh of my flesh and bone of my bone' – which appears to talk about flesh and bone being taken. It's significant that woman is at man's side – not in front or behind, not only in a literal sense but in a relationship sense also.

AWT – Miraculous Sign

*Genesis 9:13 I have set my rainbow in the clouds, and it will be the **sign (AWT)** of the covenant between me and the earth.*

AWT[2] [awt] is certainly one of the most amazing words to exist. It means, 'miraculous sign'. So, we would do well to pay careful attention to this word.

As you'll see, the word is itself miraculous. It's meaning goes a lot further than the meaning of, 'miraculous sign'. It's used exclusively to talk about a communication between God and man, or a communication of God's purposes to man. Here's some examples:

*Genesis 17:11 You are to undergo circumcision, and it will be the **sign** AWT of the covenant between me and you.*

*Exodus 3:12 And God said, "I will be with you. And this will be the **sign** AWT to you that it is I who have sent you: When you*

---

[1] Strong's 6763
[2] AWT Strong's 226

have brought the people out of Egypt, you will worship God on this mountain."

*Exodus 4:8 Then the LORD said [to Moses], "If they (Egyptian rulers) do not believe you or pay attention to the first **miraculous sign** AWT, they may believe the second."*

*Numbers 14:11 The LORD said to Moses, "How long will these people (Israel) treat me with contempt? How long will they refuse to believe in me, in spite of all the **miraculous signs** AWT I have performed among them?"*

*Joshua 2:12 Now then, please swear to me (Rahab) by the LORD that you (Israeli spies) will show kindness to my family, because I have shown kindness to you. Give me a sure **sign** AWT*

This last example in Joshua 2 talks about a communication between the Israeli spies and Rahab so seems to break the rule of AWT relating solely to a communication between God and man. But she had affirmed that she considered that God was with Israel and was responsible for their success. I think this puts it at another level above a sign between humans.

Here's how the word works. As we've seen, the letter A represents humanity, and it's the first letter in the alphabet. The letter T is the last letter of the alphabet and represents God and his end purpose for humanity. The letter W is the peg which is for joining together. So, in AWT, humanity is being connected to divinity – by a communication and a covenant.

The letter T was drawn with the symbol of a plough marker which was a marker placed at the end of the field to act as a target to keep the plough line straight. Also being at the end of the alphabet it brings the meaning of a completion point. The name of the letter T is Taw, which brings the idea of a completion and especially the completion or final fulfilment of a covenant or agreement – such as the marriage contract.

The root of AWT is AT, which is said as 'Aleph-Taw' which is the Hebrew name for the alphabet – the letters which form the foundation for language and communication

Aleph and Taw are the first and last letters of the Hebrew alphabet.

Divinity　　　　Completion　　　　Humanity

There's a reflective symmetry happening in the alphabet – humanity (A) at one end of the alphabet and divinity (T) at the other. At the centre of the alphabet and at the centre of the reflective image of opposites are the letters K and L. These letters combine to form the word KL, which means 'completion'. The joining together of humanity and divinity is the completion of God's purpose. The word KLLH is from the root KL and means 'bride'. Those of humanity who accept the marriage proposal of the Son of God, will become His bride and dwell with the Son in the house of the Father for eternity. This is the joining together of humanity and divinity.

The word AKLT is from the root KL and means, 'to eat'.

> *Genesis 3:11 And he said, "Who told you that you were naked? Have you eaten from the tree that I commanded you not to **eat** (AKLT) from?"*

In Genesis, eating the forbidden fruit resulted in Adam losing eternal life. But when Jesus came, eating together was a key element in the betrothal ceremony – which was the Passover meal before his crucifixion.

> *Luke 22:15 And he said to them, "I have eagerly desired to **eat** this Passover with you before I suffer."*

Jesus also said that eating his bread would bring eternal life:

> *John 6:51 "I am the living bread that came down from heaven. If anyone **eats** of this bread, he will live forever. This bread is my flesh, which I will give for the life of the world."*

There's a connection between eating and completion which I don't completely understand, but the two meet at the point where we find completion as the bride of Jesus. Humanity and divinity join together and become a family. The root KL is the point where both sides of the alphabet meet in the middle. Eating is the point where the family come together in the middle of the house and the life of the family to share a common food.

In many Middle Eastern cultures, even today, sharing food together creates an important bond. I have found that a person won't accept even a casual offer of food unless they're willing to enter into a relationship. Sharing food together has always been an integral part of God's family right from before Jesus' time. It's one of the central characteristics of a physical family. It's an expression of generosity, care and unity – and meeting the physical needs of all, equally. It's a physical picture of the spiritual coming together.

The root of AWT is AT, which also functions as a Hebrew word, but has no English translation or equivalent, though it is likely the origin of the English word, 'at' and has a similar meaning. The English, 'at' points to a location. The Hebrew word AT also serves as a pointer. AT is used in the first sentence of the Bible:

> *Genesis 1:1 In the beginning God created the AT heavens and the AT earth.*

AT marks and points to the things which are created by God – the heavens and the earth. Likewise, the word AWT also points to the things which God has done – in the context of His relationship with humanity.

The Symmetry of the AlephTaw

Let's review:

The first three letters of the alphabet (A, B, G) talk about the tri-nature of the human Jesus. The last three letters of the alphabet (R, Sh, T) are in reflective symmetry with the first three and talk about the tri-nature of divine God.

The letter A (ox) and its opposite T talk about the visible manifestation. Both represent the visible ends of the colour spectrum. A refers to the physical blood (red) and body of Jesus. T refers to the completion (violet) of God – found in the combination of divinity with the human Jesus.

The letters B (relationship) and Sh (separation) both talk about relationship and spirit. B refers to the spirit of Jesus which is all about relationship. This contrasts to the Spirit of God which is all about holiness – being separate – set apart from evil. The word, 'holy' in Holy Spirit means to be set apart – separated from evil. The word, 'holy' is spelt QDSh[1].

Jesus has both these aspects in his spirit – relationship and holiness – seemingly opposite but working in harmony.

The letters G (foot) and R (head) both talk about the basic identity of the person. The foot refers to the humility of the will of the person Jesus. The head refers to the headship of the Father.

There is another symmetry happening. The colour red is spelt ADM and the colour violet is spelt TKLT. Notice how red starts with the letter A and the colour violet starts with the letter T. Red and violet are at opposite ends of the colour spectrum. The word TKLT is also from the root KL meaning complete – because violet is at the end of the colour spectrum.

The colours red and violet when combined, produce the colour purple. Jesus was dressed in purple by the soldiers on the night before His death. Jesus is the combination of humanity and divinity. Purple cloth was very expensive to produce so was reserved for rulers. It would have been the only time Jesus wore purple.

On the cross the three colours were dominant. The red blood of his humanity was all over his body. His body would have been violet and purple from the bruises received the night before. The cross itself was the shape of the letter T which is the symbol of the completion of God's purpose.

The colour purple is written as ARGMN[2] [argawmawn], which is from the root RG which means to weave together. The letter R means, 'head' and the letter G means 'foot'. The head represents headship and talks about the

---

[1] Strong's 6942
[2] Strong's 0713

divine nature of Jesus. The foot talks about humility and refers to the human nature of Jesus.

The letter G is the third letter of the alphabet, and the letter R is the third to last. They are in perfect symmetry both in their positions and in their meaning. But the root spelt RG has them crossed over – just like weaving crosses over the threads – which is another reference to the cross of Jesus.

In the English translation of the book of Revelation, God describes Himself as the Alpha and Omega. This is from the Greek translation and represents the first and last letters of the Greek alphabet. This is a translation of the original Hebrew first and last letters of the alphabet – Aleph and Taw. The original significance of these two letters has been lost in translation and in the early church's divorce from its Hebrew heritage.

Revelation 22:13 I am the Alpha and the Omega, the First and the Last, the Beginning and the End.

The Aleph and Taw describe God as the first and last and the beginning and end, but there's so much more to it.

As we've seen, the word AWT comes from the root AT which has the underlying meaning of a destination marker. Let's look at the letters to get a picture of how that works.

We have seen how AT denotes leading humanity (A - ox) towards a destination (marking the end of the ploughline – T).

So, what is that destination? Here's some important and obvious clues – we'll look at the beginning of the Bible and we'll look at the end.

The very start of the Bible – the very first letter, is the letter B. You can't get any closer to the start than that! The first phrase of the Bible is, 'In the beginning'. It's written as BRAShYT which means literally, 'at the head'. The head also refers to what is at the top – what is the most important. The most important is at the very start. The letter B brings the meaning of family dwelling in the house. We'll examine the letter B in more detail in the chapter about the letter B.

What's at the end of the Bible? The last letter of the Old Testament is the letter M and is part of the word XRM – which means curse. The last phrase talks about the curse of the earth. The letter M (ocean) talks about a great unknown.

If we stop at the Old Testament the outlook is not great! If we stop at the physical earth and its law, it's only a curse!

So now, lets' move beyond the physical law and go to the New Testament. The last letter of the New Testament is N and is from a Hebrew word, 'amen'. The letter N (sprouting seed) tells us about continuation – specifically referring to the continuation of God's family. This certainly is the opposite to a curse and a great unknown! This is repeated elsewhere, but it's worth the repetition!

The last chapter of the last book (Revelation) is the 22nd chapter. The letter T is the 22nd letter of the alphabet. No accident!

In the last chapter of the Bible, we can see the completion of all things. The bride has finally joined her husband the Messiah Jesus, to dwell in the house of his Father.

AB – Father

*Psalm 68:5 A **father** to the fatherless, a defender of widows, is God in his holy dwelling.*

The word AB[1] is the first word in the Hebrew dictionary. It has three meanings:
- Stand (verb/directional meaning)
- Pole and fruit (noun/physical meaning)
- Father (abstract/spiritual meaning)

---

[1] AB Strong's 1

When letters are put together, they tell a story which unfolds chronologically. There may be different angles on a story which are all relevant.

So, A with B would tell us that humanity is being guided to family. This is truly the whole purpose of humanity, spelt out right at the start.

It appears that the physical meaning is talking about the central tent pole – or perhaps a central supporting pole for the house roof. The tent pole is a physical picture for the spiritual Father – the central support for the family.

What do the letters A and B tell us about the tent pole? The letter A (ox) talks about strength. The letter B talks about the house. The tent pole is the strength of the house.

God is referred to as father though this is not His regular title.

> *Psalm 103:13 As a **father** has compassion on his children, so the LORD has compassion on those who fear him.*

> *Psalm 89:26 He shall cry unto me, Thou art my **father**, my God, and the rock of my salvation.*

This verse refers to Jesus the Messiah, who calls God his Father.

We also see the Messiah being called Father, because the Messiah is also God:

> *Isaiah 9:6 For to us a child is born, to us a son is given, and the government will be on his shoulders. And he will be called Wonderful Counsellor, Mighty God, Everlasting **Father**, Prince of Peace.*

Another way of looking at the word AB is to see the meaning of A as talking about leading humanity to B family.

AM – Mother

*Genesis 2:24 For this reason a man will leave his father and **mother** and be united to his wife, and they will become one flesh.*

You will notice that all three members of God's family are linked by the letter B – AB (Father), BN (Son) and BNT (daughter-in-law – those who accept the marriage proposal of the Son). The only member of the family which seems to be missing in this pattern is the mother – spelt AM[1]. It would appear that our spiritual mother isn't a person as part of the family. Some have the idea that God is both mother and father, but I can't see that in the Semitic language or Bible.

Let's look at the word AM a little closer and see what it tells us.

Its meanings include, arm, mother.

Children of the root AM include:
AYM[2] (glue),
AMH[3] (bondwoman).

There seems to be the underlying meaning of holding together.

How do the letters A and M bring us that meaning? The letter A (Aleph) brings the meaning of guiding and strong. It can also represent humanity.

It could be saying that humanity (A) is being led to a time of testing (M) – which is our time on earth. It's this time of testing which builds trust – which is the glue which binds our relationship with God. So, the physical meaning is to bind together – which illustrates the spiritual meaning of building trust through testing in a time of unknown. Perhaps our time on earth is akin to growing in the mother's womb. At some point we'll be birthed into our eternal life.

---

[1] Strong's 517
[2] AYM Strong's 518
[3] AMH Strong's 519, 520, 521

B – Bayt – House

*Genesis 7:1 The LORD then said to Noah, "Go into the ark, you and your whole **family (BYT[1])**, because I have found you righteous in this generation."*

The letter B is the first letter in the Bible and with good reason. It could be the most important letter in the whole of history and the universe!

The letter B has the name spelt BYT[2] which means, 'family in the house' and relationship.

The first phrase in the Bible is 'In the beginning'. This is written as B RAShYT ܒܪܐܫܝܬ. In this context, B means 'in'. The word RAShYT[3] means 'beginning' and much more. It's from the root RSh[4] which means 'head' and most important. It's also saying that the most important thing is at the beginning – family dwelling in the house of the Father! This is the whole purpose of creating humanity.

The first phrase goes on to say 'In the beginning God...' God is in the beginning of everything including the first letter of the Bible. We could expect that the letter B also tells us something about God. It certainly tells me that God is about relationship and family.

The letter B was written with the symbol of a house – 4 walls and an opening for a door. It has the name spelt BYT – in modern Semitic languages pronounced as 'bayt'. The three meanings of this word are,
- 'house' (visible physical meaning)
- 'family' (abstract spiritual meaning),
- 'to be in' (the directional, verb meaning).

---

[1][2] Strong's 1004
[2] BYT Strong's 1004 Often translated as 'house' in the KJV and 'family' in NIV
[3] RAShYT Strong's 7225
[4] RASh Strong's 7219

So, when we put all this together, we get the meaning 'family dwelling in the house.'

The letter B is the second letter in the alphabet so has the numerical meaning of 2. Many numbers in Proto-Semitic have meanings associated with them and we could expect that the numerical meaning is connected to the word meaning. I can see at least two connections with 2 and 'family dwelling in the house'.

Firstly, relationship starts with two or more persons. Relationship is central to family.

Secondly, God's divine family which starts with Father and Son, consists of two persons, but it's more than about the number – it's about there being both human and divine. Two also talks about God's dual nature as mentioned previously.

I've heard of discussion among Rabbis as to why the letter B should be the first letter in the Torah (Bible). They reason that surely the letter A should be the first letter because it represents the name of God – spelt AL.

My view is that it's there because it shows us our destination and God's purpose. We need to see our destination right from the first step, and where else could He show us that purpose than right at the very first letter? Sure, we can find it as we read through the Bible, but you can get all different angles depending on which of the many thousands of angles you read the Bible from – and where you stop reading it. Do you read just the Old Testament, or do you continue through to the New Testament also?

The word AWT meaning, 'God's communication to humanity' is a clear pointer to us. As we've observed, it gives us the picture of the plough marker – which must be focussed on, right from the first step.

Our destination is to be a family dwelling in the house. That sounds simple enough – most of us do that anyway. There's much more to it – we're looking at our ultimate destination – the ultimate purpose for all human history. Our natural biological family is just a training ground for our ultimate spiritual, eternal family.

Let's take a closer look at the word spelt BYT – the name for the letter B.

The first two letters BY are the ancient Semitic way of writing the number 12. This number is used in the Bible to refer to God's family – first the 12 tribes of Israel and then the 12 disciples of Jesus. The 12 tribes were God's physical family, and the 12 disciples represent the foundation of God's spiritual family. Both are part of His purpose and family. The latter doesn't supersede the first. They are in reflective symmetry with each other.

The disciples of Jesus and subsequent believers in Jesus (Christians) are a continuation of God's family – not a replacement of Israel as God's family. Bayt includes both Israel and Christians. It is misleading to introduce a new name such as ecclesia or church because it suggests a new entity which is separate from Israel. For similar reason, it was misleading to introduce a new name for Jesus. If the name Joshua (Anglicized version of Yeshua) was retained, there would have been a more obvious link back to the Joshua who led the people into the promised land through faith – as Jesus leads his people into eternal life through faith.

How does the number 12 talk about God's family? The number 2 and letter B represents family. The letter Y has the value of 10 which tells us about God (Yahweh) (this is explained in more detail in the chapter on the letter Y). So, B and Y equate to God's family.

Back to the word BYT. We've seen that the letters BY talk about 12 – God's divine family made up of both the human and divine. The letter T is the last letter in the alphabet and talks about the ultimate destination – it's linking God's family with the ultimate destination – plain enough!

But there's more, the name for the letter T – Taw, talks about the completion of a contract – in this case a marriage contract. The means for humanity to enter God's family is through a marriage contract with the Son Jesus.

The root of BYT is BT; The word spelt BT[1] [bet] means 'measure' – translated as 'bath' in the KJV Bible. The modern Hebrew pronunciation of BT is [bath]. Could this be the origin of the English word 'bath'?

---

[1] Strong's 1324

We see it used in the context of measuring wine or oil. Presumably this is because it's measuring something in a vessel. BT seems to have the underlying meaning of something in a container – related to the idea of a family in a house. So how is BT connected to the idea of a measure? The letter B is clearly about a vessel. The letter T talks about a completion or purpose. So perhaps BT is talking about a measure being a complete fill of the vessel – the bath. A measuring instrument must be full to give an accurate measure. That's the physical meaning of BT. What does that tell us about the spiritual meaning? Perhaps it's talking about the full measure of God's purpose – which is family.

What dynamic does the combination of B and T bring and in that order? It appears to be saying that family leads to God's destination. Family is the path and the destination.

What does the opposite order of TB tell us? TB means to long for something. Is this talking about the family going away from God's purpose? This truly will bring about a sense of emptiness and longing.

The letters B-Y-T tell a story. B means family, Y (throwing arm) is about destining something, T is about the destination. So put together it says, the family destined for completion.

In the Book of Revelation, we see the physical family of Israel and the spiritual family of Jesus' disciples coming together in the one city of the New Jerusalem. The twelve disciples are the 12 foundations of the city, and the 12 tribes are the 12 gates of the city.

We can see the 12 tribes and 12 disciples (God's spiritual family) working together in the 144000 in Revelation. 12 x 12 = 144. Multiplication talks about one value acting on another value. In comparison, addition is about joining one thing to another. So, the number 144 likely talks about people from the 12 tribes of Israel being acted upon by the 12 disciples of Jesus and vice versa. It's likely talking about Israelites becoming followers of Jesus. Now we multiply 144 by 1000 to get 144000.

A thousand is used Biblically to talk about God's leading through the generations. That equates to 144000 Messianic Jews being led by God.

Each of these has both the name of the Father (God) and the Son (Jesus the Lamb) written on their foreheads.

> *Revelation 14:1-5 Then I looked, and there before me was the* **Lamb***, standing on Mount Zion, and with him 144,000 who had* **his name** *and* **his Father's name** *written on their foreheads. And I heard a sound from heaven like the roar of rushing waters and like a loud peal of thunder. The sound I heard was like that of harpists playing their harps.*
>
> *And they sang a new song before the throne and before the four living creatures and the elders. No-one could learn the song except the 144,000 who had been redeemed from the earth. These are those who did not defile themselves with women, for they kept themselves pure. They follow the Lamb wherever he goes. They were purchased from among men and offered as first fruits to God and the Lamb. No lie was found in their mouths; they are blameless.*

On This Foundation I Will Build My Family

> *Matthew 16:18 "On this Rock I will build my* **church***."*

Jesus would have spoken those words in his native tongue of Aramaic, but we don't have a record of his original words, which were translated into Greek. The word, 'church' is old English – not Aramaic. The word, 'church' comes from the same family of words as circle and circus. The ancient English places of worship were round, so the name was applied to the Christian places of worship also. The word was really about a place and that has largely stuck to this day. Over time, the word "church" has come to mean a building, but is God really so concerned about a building made of brick and wood? I believe it's more about family.

So, what word did Jesus most likely use instead of 'church'? There is a Hebrew word which fits the context perfectly and better than any other word – BYT. It means both 'house' and 'family'. 'House' is the physical meaning, and 'family' is the spiritual meaning. Let's see how well it fits into this context of Matthew 16:18:

*On this rock (foundation), I will build my **house**.*

The physical picture is illustrating a spiritual truth. The spiritual meaning reads like this:

This confession that Jesus is the Messiah, the Son of the Living God, will be the basis of my family.

The physical is only a shadow or illustration of what God wants. Let's not think that the physical building is at all important. Relationship leading to eternal family is the reality here.

What does family look like?

So, since we're on a journey towards family, what does that journey look like? I believe that if we don't walk the journey of family, we won't arrive at the destination of family. Every step we take on the journey is a step towards family – and should be a step which builds God's family. Our expression of love for one another is an expression of love for our groom and Father.

Church needs to be family. Well, we should just do away with the word 'church' and say "Let's do family". There's no need to say, "Let's go to family on Sunday morning". Family is a lifestyle – not a place and time.

One thing we can retain from the word 'church' is the idea of a circular gathering. This would be an improvement on the classic lines of pews and a stage up front. A circle invites participation from all in an equal manner.

If we do family in a building on a Sunday morning, let's not sit in straight lines watching a stage show up front where only a handful of people can participate. After one hour of looking at the back of the person in front of us, we may share a brief drink and snack and then leave, never to see those people again for a week. If we don't come again next week, will anyone notice? If we walk into a building with 200 people and we're completely new – will anyone notice? Everyone thinks it's someone else's or the pastor's job to follow up on a new person or absent person. If God's people settle for this, then in my view, this is one of the greatest robberies of God's people in history. This is not family!

Church can be like a slot machine. Put in your Sunday morning and some coins and out comes a sense of personal satisfaction. Family is not about personal satisfaction and getting a spiritual buzz – which is about self. Family is about being a group of people relating to each other in a caring way.

I observe that for the majority of people, Sunday morning attendance at 'church' is an inoculation against the real thing. They get just enough spirituality to make them feel they've done their 'church', and then the rest of the week and their lifestyle is largely void of spiritual family.

Family share everything in common. Family is the opposite to self-obsession. Family is all about relationship and connection. This is not something we do some of the time when it suits. Family is life and our whole existence. Relationship brings meaning. If we are an island and have no concern for relationship, where is our meaning?

Family is the whole of life. It's lifestyle.

What's the significance of family being represented by the number 12?

A good size group for quality family relationships is about 12. Sure, family will work fine when there are slightly more or less, but more decreases the quality of time together. Less reduces the diversity and richness which comes with bigger numbers. 12 is a good balance to aim for.

Within the twelve disciples of Jesus, there was a smaller number of two or three who were closer to Jesus. There was also one at the other extreme who ended up being a drop-out. Though he was chosen by Jesus, he ultimately had his own agenda.

In the book of Acts, we read of 120 believers gathered in an upper room. This illustrates that beyond the daily interaction of a group of 12, we also need to be part of a larger community of believers who may connect on a weekly basis – perhaps for a shared meal as the early believers did. These numbers are not a prescription or magical number but give us an idea of the relationship dynamics we need. Jesus would have likely seen his 12 disciples on a daily basis, as they travelled with him. They would have been like his nuclear family. It's less likely that he saw 120 of the same believers each day, but they would have been familiar faces to him – much like his tribe – people who share a loyalty to one another and feel related. Like a tribe, they would share their resources in common as people needed.

If the whole of humanity lived as a family and tribe, there would be far less degradation of the earth's resources. There would be no exploitation of others and natural resources. Of course, there would be no wars. People would share resources rather than fight for them.

In my time working with sustainability, in poor countries and in more affluent countries, many people had a focus on being able to grow food and use resources sustainably. But I came to see that the real key to sustainability is being a family. If we share resources, then those resources will not be anywhere near challenged. Many Humanists believe that the best way to solve the world's resource and pollution problems is to reduce the population. But those same people generally live in the West and use 8 times as many resources as a poor Indian family of 8 persons. I believe God loves people and doesn't want to reduce the population. The real answer God would like to see, is the change in human character, so that resources are shared, with no greedy exploitation of resources and people.

A lifestyle of family would not require large-scale monocultures which turn the land into deserts. People would not exploit the lands of others for luxuries. They would grow food in their own communities. Those farms would operate on the model of permaculture – which is about the maximum diversity of species which all support each other and keep each other in balance.

But realistically, that's not going to happen as long as we turn our back on God and His purpose for family. A time will come soon when God will intervene because humanity is going in the opposite direction.

What does a lifestyle as God's family (BYT) look like?

Firstly, since we're talking about God's ultimate plan for family – God Himself needs to be the centre pole. The word AB means both Father and tent pole – the centre pole which supports the roof. What does this mean in everyday life? It means trusting our Father in everything. This is a spiritual task, but it does affect our lives in tangible ways. We need to quietly listen to Him.

But to enter into God's family, and come under His protection, we need to be married into that family by accepting the marriage proposal of His Son. What does that involve? I see that it must relate to what Peter said to Jesus, "You are the Messiah, the Son of the living God." Jesus replied, "On this rock (foundation) I will build my family."

What does that statement really mean – "You are the Messiah, the Son of the Living God"?

The word, 'Messiah' is from the Hebrew word spelt MShYX [1] ܡܫܝܚܐ [mashiyakh], which is used 38 times in the Old Testament. It means to be anointed with oil and set apart for a special purpose.

I understand that in the Bible, and especially for the disciples, the term, 'Messiah' spoke about the promised saviour of Israel, chosen by God for this task. So, this would easily equate to the man whom a woman sought for marriage. Accepting Jesus as the Messiah equates to accepting Him as our groom.

The word MShYX comes from the root MShX, which in turn likely comes from the root ShX, which has the underlying meaning of being low. This root brings us the word ShXH which means to worship, which is about bringing oneself low and bowing down before someone in humility. This is certainly a key expression of trust in another, which is essential for the woman as an expression of her trust in her man. I'm not saying that a woman should literally bow down to her man, but we certainly do need to humble ourselves before Jesus, our groom. Humility is key to the relationship of trust between a man and wife – going both ways.

A person who dwells in the family is not out to look for their own interests. In humility, they act as part of a group. Everything they do is for the family – which does include benefit to themselves. In fact, they will do

---

[1] MShYX Strong's 4899

themselves better by looking to the needs of the family. But for that to work, the leaders must also be serving the interests of the family. If they exploit the members of the family for their own benefit, then it all falls down. Jesus told us that the greatest among us should not put themselves in the most privileged position at the head of the table but should put themselves at the lowest position to serve – to lead by example.

> *Luke 14:10,11 But when you are invited, take the lowest place, so that when your host comes, he will say to you, 'Friend, move up to a better place.' Then you will be honoured in the presence of all your fellow guests. For everyone who exalts himself will be humbled, and he who humbles himself will be exalted.*
>
> *Matt 20:25-28 Jesus called them together and said, "You know that the rulers of the Gentiles lord it over them, and their high officials exercise authority over them. Not so with you. Instead, whoever wants to become great among you must be your servant, and whoever wants to be first must be your slave – just as the Son of Man did not come to be served, but to serve, and to give his life as a ransom for many.*

Many churches have the idea that they need a leader who will attract people by their skill and personality. But perhaps we should turn this upside down (as Jesus was prone to do) and instead, attract people by the evidence that every person is valued and given opportunity to participate, share, and develop their talents and giftings. They don't just turn up to watch someone else but instead, are themselves engaged. It's not about the leader, it's about each person finding their place as part of the body.

Some will say that we need signs and wonders to attract people to our community, but as Paul says[1], we may have the ability to perform signs and wonders, but if we have not love, we gain nothing. Sure, signs and wonders will attract a crowd as was the case for Jesus, but what do you then do with the crowd? What will the crowd become? Love is what will build them into a family. I believe we attract more people by love than by signs and wonders

---

[1] 1 Corinthians 13:1-4

or a stage show of amazing preaching or music. This will then build a stronger family. People will be attracted like moths to a light, but they themselves need to live a life of love and family, not just be one of a crowd of moths around a light.

BN – Son

*Isaiah 9:6 For to us a child is born, to us a **son** (BN) is given, and the government will be on his shoulders. And he will be called Wonderful Counselor, Mighty God, Everlasting Father, Prince of Peace.*

The word pronounced [bin] is from the root BN whose children include:
BN ◡ [bun] tent panel,
BN[1] [bin] son,
TBN[2] [tibin] straw (used to make mud bricks)
BNH[3] [binah] build,
ABN[4] [abin] stone,
BWN[5] plan, intelligence (design?),
BYN[6] [bayin] between (noun), understand (verb).

From the children of BN, we can see that the meaning which the parents (root) talk about has to do with the continuation of a design. For example, the tent panel is about the continuation of the design of the tent. Worn and damaged panels are replaced, while maintaining the overall design of the tent.

A son is the continuation of the genetic design of the family.

---

[1] BN Strong's 1121, 1123, 1247
[2] TBN Strong's 8401
[3] BNH Strong's 1124, 1129
[4] ABN Strong's 68, 69, 70
[5] BWN Strong's 8394
[6] BYN noun Strong's 996, 997, 1143. BYN verb Strong's 995

Note that the letter B works well for both the tent and the family because the name for B, (Bayt) means both house (tent) and family.

The letter N (sprouting seed) talks about genetic design because the seed is essentially all about the information for the construction of a new plant. That is its primary purpose, though it does carry some added packaging to help it to be dispersed in the best way and to provide nutrient to start its growth. The sprouting action of the seed shows that it's not dead but is actively progressing in its task of continuing the design.

Jesus is called the Son of God because he is the continuation of God's family. He is the means by which God's family will grow. How does He do that? The letters BN tell us how:

The letter B as we know is all about the family. The letter N has the numerical value of 50, which is used in the Bible to talk about the year of Jubilee, when all the slaves were to be released and debts forgiven – allowing the continuation of life. Jesus is all about forgiveness. Humanity was once in God's family when Adam and Eve walked with God in the garden. But they chose self-gain over relationship and trust in God, so they became separated from God and His family. Now, those who choose to look beyond themselves and humbly accept and trust in the forgiveness which Jesus offers us, can once again come back into God's family. By accepting Jesus, the Son, we are essentially accepting His hand in marriage, so in that way, we will enter into God's family. We will finally dwell in the room which the Son has prepared in His Father's house. This is the practice today in many Semitic homes – the son will build a room onto his father's house. He will call that room his bayt (house) – a house within a house because that room is where his family lives. In many modern communities a husband will sleep in that room with his wife and children but will share the common rooms of the house with the wider family such as lounge, kitchen and bathroom.

A word which is derived from the root BN is spelt BNT[1] [bint], which means, 'daughter' but can also be used for the daughter-in-law. Those who come into the house of our Father God are his BNT. The letter T added to

---

[1] BNT Strong's 1323. BT [bath] is also translated as 'daughter' e.g. Bathsheba

BN means completion and especially in this context, the completion of a marriage contract – the means by which we enter into the father's house. The Hebrew word for 'bride' is KLLH[1] ܝܠܠܗ [kallah] which is from the root KL meaning, 'complete'. We are made complete through the marriage contract.

The letters K and L are the 11th and 12th letters of the alphabet which relate to the 11th and 12th sons of Israel (Jacob) – the completion of his family, son's born to his first love Rachel through promise.

It's not by chance that Jesus was a carpenter, a builder of a house in His physical life. His foster father (Joseph) was a builder and so it was the custom of the time that a son continued the trade of his father.

Jesus said to Peter, "On this rock I will build (BNH) my church (house/family) BYT". The use of the word BNH lends to the idea that God's family will be built through the forgiveness that Jesus brings to his beloved.

I also, the author of this book, am a physical builder of houses, and I also view building God's family as my number one calling. At age thirteen, I made a conscious decision to accept Jesus' proposal and to trust in Him. When I left school, and after a year or two of farming, I went to house building for a few years. Then went to Bible college where I found my life's mission to plant churches (build God's family), which evolved into planting churches in unreached people groups, which then developed into Bible translation. And now, the final mode of that is to focus on building God's family by actually doing it, not by starting churches in its traditional mould, with buildings and pews in a row, but by helping to bring people together who support one another in every aspect of life. Also, I have a role in bringing God's written word about the importance of His family to others. I hope this book will be effective in that.

Another gem to note is that BN comprises the first letter in the Bible, B, and the last letter of the Bible, N, from Amen. This word effectively

---

[1] KLLH Strong's 3618

THE ETERNAL FAMILY IN THE HEBREW ALPHABET

BRA – Create

*Genesis 1:1 In the beginning (B RAShYT), God **created** (BRA) the heavens and the earth.*

In ancient texts, there were no spaces between words. There was just a continuous string of letters. So, in reading the Bible, the first three letters were BRA. But someone who knows the language would know that there is a word break between the first letter B and the next word RAShYT. However, the word BRA does appear in the first sentence of the Bible.

BRA[1] [bara] (to create) is from the root BR.

Other children of the root BR include:
BR 𐤁𐤓 [bar] (grain, soap, clean),
BRBWR 𐤁𐤓𐤁𐤅𐤓 [brabuur] (fowl),
ABR 𐤀𐤁𐤓 [abar] (wing),
ABYR 𐤀𐤁𐤉𐤓 [abiir] (strong),
BRYA 𐤁𐤓𐤉𐤀 [bariia] (fat),
BRYAH 𐤁𐤓𐤉𐤀𐤄 [bariiyah] (fill),
HBR 𐤄𐤁𐤓 [habar] (astrologer),
BHRT 𐤁𐤄𐤓𐤕 [bahret] (blister),
BHYR 𐤁𐤄𐤉𐤓 [bahiir] (bright),
BYRYH 𐤁𐤉𐤓𐤉𐤄 [biiriih] (meat),
BYRH 𐤁𐤉𐤓𐤄 [biirah] (palace),
BYRNYT 𐤁𐤉𐤓𐤍𐤉𐤕 [biirniit] (castle).

It's difficult to see what these children share in common. There appears to be a common theme of choice, the best, opulent. It is an important word

---

[1] BRA Strong's 1254

talking about the creation of the world - which is well worth trying to understand.

In the Mehri language of Southern Arabia, the word BR is used as part of the name of tribes, for example my adopted tribe was BR Haydirah. BR here seems to be used to talk about the children or descendants of Haydirah. The name Haydirah may have its origins in the ancient Hebrew word HDRH (beauty, honour). Arabic speaking tribes use the term Bin, meaning son of. Mehri is not Arabic but is more closely related to ancient Aramaic and Hebrew.

We seem to be building a picture of BR talking about the manifestation, outworking, filling out of a central purpose or entity.

This may tell us more about the concept of family. Perhaps family is essentially about the manifestation or outworking of God's central purpose.

Creation is all about bringing into being a family (B) which gathers around and is a manifestation of God's ultimate (R) purpose.

The physical creation is only the stage for humanity to build a relationship of trust in the Creator. God doesn't create His family, that's left to each person to choose. I hear atheists often reason that the universe is so incredibly huge and that man is so tiny and insignificant in comparison. Are they trying to say that there can be no God because humanity is so insignificant? I believe the opposite – that the created universe is but a passing flower and that the importance of God's relationship with humanity is unspeakably huge.

> *Isaiah 34:4 All the stars of the heavens will be dissolved and the sky rolled up like a scroll; all the starry host will fall like withered leaves from the vine, like shrivelled figs from the fig tree.*

BRA has 54 occurrences in the Bible of which about 50 relate to God creating. About 4 uses appear to have nothing to do with creating; in fact, they're quite opposite. These 4 are all used in relation to people cutting something down. There is one instance (Ezekiel 21:19) where it's used to talk about a person making something – but at the instruction of God.

The second word of the Bible RAShYT [1] [rashiit] is translated as 'beginning', but the root of the word is RSh meaning 'head', which also brings the meaning of 'most important'. We could read, "In the beginning is the most important." The first letter at the beginning of the Bible is the letter B, which talks about family dwelling in the house. This is the most important task God has in mind for creation. All relationships in the process of creation leads to what is most important.

Science and Creation

The topic of creation, as we know, has a lot of disagreement. And the disagreement doesn't necessarily follow the line of those who believe God and those who don't. For example, my father believed in God but also believed that science was indisputable and that therefore, evolution and God can exist side by side. He had the view that creation could have happened over millions of years. One problem he wasn't aware of, or had overlooked, is that the account of creation has the sun being created on the fourth day and plants on the third day. Plants can't evolve without sunlight.

This brings us to the truth value of 'scientific studies'. There are scientists who believe that they can demonstrate evolution very clearly, and there are scientists who believe that they can show creation very clearly. Sure, physical, visible facts must be true. However, these facts are like dots on a page; we can connect these dots in whatever way we believe the final picture should look. We can even ignore some dots which we believe don't fit the picture.

Regarding creation, I see that there's some very important dots which have been laid aside because they sabotage the view that there cannot be a Creator.

---

[1] RAShYT Strong's 7225

Here are some of those dots:

Irreducible Complexity

This concept can be illustrated with a mouse trap. Without any one part of the trap, the trap will not work. We can consider the human eye which is extremely complex. If it were to have evolved to its current state, that would mean that there are billions of years where it would not function because all the parts weren't ready. Why would something remain in place if there were no function for it? The creature with that eye would die out very quickly and stop that evolution path.

Linking forms

If evolution is true, we should see, for example, many forms which are somewhere between a human and a monkey. And these forms should exist in the current time and in archaeology. But they don't. There is a scant selection of bones which appear to make the link. But these bones are far from complete and usually only a very small fragment, which, if you wanted to, can be slotted into an evolution story. There should be far more evidence and there should be living evidence, but there isn't. Charles Darwin in his late years, realised this flaw in his theory, but by that time, it was too late; 'Science' had already run with it because it suited their 'fine without God' world view.

Chance

Evolution claims that new forms come about through at least three factors – chance, time and what works. New forms come about by chance and any new forms that work will stand the test of time.

However, when we consider highly complex and finely balanced systems, the chances of that working are extremely small – to the point of being absurd. And those evolution paths have even less chance of continuing if they are not fully functional. The leaps from chance to functional forms would have to be extremely large. Consider, for example, the earth. It can only sustain life because it's positioned in exactly the right distance from the sun. It also has just the right collection of minerals to form life as we know it. In all the billions of space objects we've observed, there's nothing which comes close to what earth has.

BThX – Trust

> *Psalm 143:8 Let the morning bring me word of your unfailing love, for I have put my **trust** (BThX) in you. Show me the way I should go, for to you I lift up my soul.*

BThX[1] [bathakh] has the verb meaning of 'to cling', and the spiritual meaning of 'security'.

The letter B talks about a relationship.

The letter Th was drawn with the symbol of a basket which was used to store precious things high up on the tent pole away from children and animals. It effectively clung to the pole.

Note that the word for 'pole' is AB – which also means 'father'. Our ultimate trust and security are found by clinging to our heavenly Father.

The letter X is the wall, which speaks of something hidden behind the immediately physically visible. An important part of trust is being able to let go of reliance on your own faculties and abilities and to trust beyond that.

Who Do You Trust?

Someone asked me how do you know who to trust? There's a lot to that question, but one measure – which is not entirely waterproof – is that I

[1] Strong's 982

would rather trust someone who has made a claim at cost to themselves than one who is standing to get financial gain or control. For this reason, the ones I trust least are those in government and large corporations. This brings us onto the subject of conspiracies – which is defined largely as a plot by someone to pull the wool over someone else's eyes so that they can exploit the person or situation for their own ends – that may be finance, control, ideology or all of those. This is normally done by a person with greater power over a person with less power. It's normally harmful to the person being exploited. The person who's pushing their own agenda or ideology may justify it as being of benefit to humanity as a whole – for example Nazi (the ideology of a superior race derived from Darwinian evolution), communism or humanism. This justification is like the sheep's clothing on the wolf – it's a front hiding a harmful intent. The wolf thinks that any means, including deception, justifies the end.

The mainstream media labels anything which is not in line with their agenda as 'conspiracy theory'. They say that to identify a conspiracy theory you must think scientifically and logically. But science and logic don't define conspiracy. The definition of a conspiracy is 'a secret plan to do something unlawful or harmful'. It's all about uncovering something which is considered to be harmful to myself and society. A society which ridicules conspiracy theorists is a dangerous society indeed.

A conspiracy has nothing to do with a flat-earth theory, as it's been labelled and associated with, in an effort to redefine the word 'conspiracy'.

At the core is the question of who do you trust? From my view, I would trust less the person who will gain money and power from their agenda. They are being deceitful because they are wanting to exploit another because exploitation is all about gaining money and power.

In times past, people exploited others by force such as by war or kidnapping slaves. But today, it's done more by deceit.

Today, exploitation usually requires another to be absorbed into your plan without them knowing the final outcome. I have seen first-hand a good dose of exploitation from high levels. I am less naïve now. Those who rely on mainstream mass media as their source of truth, receive a whitewashed version of the world and therefore become naïve to the actions of their own governments.

I would trust more the person who is sacrificing money and prestige to expose a truth. I would trust more the person on the street – the people.

To deny the possibility of conspiracy is being very naïve of human behaviour and its thirst for power and control – the drive for self-gain. The time of Hitler should teach us that every citizen needs to take responsibility for truth and not just follow a single leader. No individual should be silenced or denied a voice. Every life is sacred and must be allowed to contribute their view of truth to the whole.

A society which ridicules those who question the government is a very dangerous society indeed.

Those who claim to be the only source of truth should not be trusted. They smell of cult.

Conspiracy theorists are not hiding anything – on the contrary they're bringing it out into the open. They're practicing freedom of speech. We should be more concerned about those who say nothing while wielding power. In fact, those who have the money, have the power to control the mainstream media.

There was a time when governments used religion as a sheep's clothing to whitewash their corruption. But now that religion is out of fashion, another sheep's clothing is being used – global warming and health. These are the trojan horses being used to bring in sweeping changes which we would never have accepted otherwise.

A note on climate change: We are being shown that there is a close correlation between carbon dioxide and global warming. It is said that the increase in carbon dioxide is causing global warming. But I've seen a study[1] of historical data going back thousands of years which show that global warming is the cause of the increase in carbon dioxide levels. The causality is switched around. There have been many cycles of global warming and

---

[1] Studies from Prof. Ian Clark of the University of Ottawa. He features in a UK television documentary, 'The Great Global Warming Swindle'.

cooling in the earth's history. The ocean is the main emitter of carbon dioxide. Because of its immense volume, it takes hundreds of years to change temperature, but it's increase in temperature causes an increase in its emitting of carbon dioxide ($CO2$). $CO2$ is not a poison to the earth, it's part of what drives all living things.

A Government should never be the one source of truth. We need to take lessons from the Jews on the cattle trains in Nazi Germany. They were told one thing by their government, but the reality was another thing indeed. Many Jews could not imagine the atrocities that their government was planning, therefore they showed more optimism than was safe for them. They thought they were living in one of the most advanced and civilised societies.

Is this anti-government talk or hate speech? No, it's every person using their own instinct and intellect to know for themselves what is right. We shouldn't farm out our intellect and conscience to any human institution or government. Though there are many who are too distracted with peripherals and entertainment to think about what's really happening. One example is our mainstream news which has more entertainment than real news. We will hear all about the sports and celebrities but not hear about monumental injustices in Africa or Yemen, for example. We are being led to believe that we live in a world where everything is being handled just fine by humanity.

The Biblical Daniel served the government but when the government crossed the line of his conscience and spirituality, he had to lay his life on the line to be true to what he knew to be right – to worship God before the state.

BT – Daughter

*2 Samuel 11:3 and David sent someone to find out about her. The man said, "Isn't this **Bath**sheba (**BT**ShBʕ), the **daughter** (BT) of Eliam and the wife of Uriah the Hittite?"*

The name Bathsheba is comprised of two words, bath (BT) and sheba (ShBʕ). Does the name of Bathsheba tell us anything about her role in history?

The word spelt BT is a variation of BNT which is from the root BN, meaning 'son'. The letter T is commonly put on the end of a word to make it a feminine noun. The letter T likely serves this purpose because it talks about the completion of a marriage contract. Humanity as the betrothed daughter in law, becomes part of God's family through the marriage contract. Without it we come to a dead end.

The word ShBʕ ⊙◻︎〰︎ means both sabbath and oath. The thing which brings sabbath and oath together is that the sabbath is an agreement or oath to rest on the seventh day. This is a physical picture of the spiritual concept to cease from physical striving and trying to please God and to come into the rest which is simply trusting in God and promise of marriage.

David and Bathsheba significantly did break a marriage oath when the two of them lay together outside of their existing marriage oath. Under the law, this was punishable by death. And David took it further. Because Bathsheba became pregnant from the encounter, David arranged for her husband to be sent to the front line of a battle at the most dangerous point where he died. This certainly displeased God.

This talks about a significant struggle most of us have in life. As humans, we are born with a strong connection to the physical. One of our strongest drives is our attraction to the opposite sex. We also have a strong appreciation of our own bodies which helps us to be attractive to others. We may also appreciate the physical attractiveness of others in our own sex at varying levels. But there's a point where we need to control that drive and think about our ultimate direction and relationships. If we are led merely by our physical drives, we cease to be responsible for the destiny of our lives and the lives of others. To be attracted to someone or 'be in love' with someone is not reason enough to put aside the ability to choose our path responsibly.

There's a good chance that Bathsheba was well aware of her attractive form and enjoyed bathing where she could be seen by the king. But the power that the king had was a key element in bringing the two of them together.

The physical attraction we have for others starts early. The subject is something which we try to conceal away.

I think I was about 9 years old when I found myself glued to the beauty of a girl in my class. She was wearing a low-cut shirt so that I could see her clavicle bones below her neck. I must have been staring and totally oblivious to everything else because she asked what I was looking at. From around that time I was totally awestruck by girls and couldn't even talk to them. The appreciation of the female form and personality only grew stronger in the teen years. It got to the point where I could no longer watch tv with my parents, but had to stay in my room. I had to do everything I could to feed my mind with things such as Scripture and music to keep myself from derailing.

For David, seeing a vision of beauty bathing in the light of the moon would have been the ultimate challenge. That, combined with his ability as king to make things happen, was more than his ability to resist.

Sometimes, when I'm struggling with the tug of war that's going on inside, I wonder why God created us with these urges. I think that the appreciation of beauty is a gift. What would life be like if we had no appreciation of physical beauty such as the grandeur and subtleties of nature? Because other humans are very much a part of our lives, it goes without saying that other humans are significant in our appreciation of beauty.

But if we divorce that gift from our spirits, hearts and relationships, then we can bring much pain to ourselves and others. I think it's all part of the test we are placed in. Given the choice, would we be better off without our appreciation of beauty? Would there be any quality of life without the appreciation of beauty which comes from the physical senses? I don't think so.

Should God not have put the tree of knowledge of good and bad in the garden of Eden?

I think ultimately, it will aid in our appreciation of the beauty of Jesus – our betrothed. It is important in the process of building our trust in God. It's a bit like resistance training to build our muscles.

Our ability to make and keep an oath – to set a course for ourselves and stay on that path in relationship with others is surely one of the most important aspects in being free humans. We are not just physical organisms directed by our environment. We have a spirit and will which enable us to determine a course and destiny. This is an important way in which we are in the image of God, which sets us up to be part of His eternal family.

G – Gimel – Foot

The letter G was written with the symbol of a foot. It's the third letter in the alphabet so has the numerical value of three. The foot can bring various ideas depending on context. It could talk about walking, and sometimes even going in a circle.

The foot also tells the story of humility. This is in direct contrast and in reflective symmetry to the third from last letter of the alphabet, which is the letter R, meaning head.

The first three letters show us the tri-nature of Jesus the human. The universal tri-nature pattern is direction, relationship and physical manifestation. The letter A (ox) talks about the direction nature – being led.

The letter B talks about relationship. The letter G talks about the physical nature – being a humble human.

Jesus was both divine and human. His human nature expresses humility – being lower than the angels and lower than God.

> *Hebrews 2:7-9 "You made him a little lower than the angels; you crowned him with glory and honor and put everything under his feet." In putting everything under him, God left nothing that is not subject to him. Yet at present we do not see everything subject to him. But we see Jesus, who was made a little lower than the angels, now crowned with glory and honor because he suffered death, so that by the grace of God he might taste death for everyone.*

Here we see that Jesus is both humility (at the foot) and headship (the head) where everything is under Him.

His humility goes hand in hand with Him serving others.

John 13:5 After that, he poured water into a basin and began to wash his disciples' feet, drying them with the towel that was wrapped around him.

Psalm 119 takes us through each letter of the alphabet in order. In the Hebrew script, the first words in each sentence of each section start with the relevant letter of the alphabet. Note that the first word in the original Hebrew writing may not necessarily translate to being the first word in an English translation.

Here's the section related to the letter G:

*17 **Do good** (GML) to your servant, and I will live; I will obey your word.*

*18 **Open** (GLH) my eyes that I may see wonderful things in your law.*

*19 **I am a stranger** (GR) on earth; do not hide your commands from me.*

*20 My soul is **consumed** (GRSh) with longing for your laws at all times.*

*21 You **rebuke** (GʕR) the arrogant, who are cursed and who stray from your commands.*

*22 **Remove** (GL) from me scorn and contempt, for I keep your statutes.*

*23 **Though** (GM) rulers sit together and slander me, your servant will meditate on your decrees.*

24 Also (GM) your statutes are my delight; they are my counselors.

Many of the words and verses appear to share a theme relating to the humility of the human existence.

ARGMN – Purple

The colour purple is spelt ARGMN[1] [argamawn]. Purple is not a colour in its own right in the colour spectrum but is made up of the combination of the colours at the opposite ends of the spectrum – red and blue (or violet). This word is prophetic of the human and divine nature of Jesus. The red is associated with the beginning of the alphabet. The first letter A is the first letter in the word ADM meaning red and man. That at first seems like a weak link to make, but the pattern is strengthened when we see that three other colours also have their first letter aligning perfectly to the same position in the colour spectrum as in the alphabet and are spaced at the start, end and at two thirds: Red, yellow (gold), sapphire and violet.

ADM is from the root DM meaning blood. So red is linked to the blood of humanity.

At the other end of the alphabet and colour spectrum is the colour violet. The colour violet is spelt TKLT ✝∠⑭✝ [tekalet] – which is from the root KL meaning, 'complete'.

The word ARGMN is from the root RG which has the underlying meaning of 'weave'. Purple is the weaving together of the two colours red and violet. That's the physical meaning, which is a picture of the spiritual meaning – which is the weaving together of humble humanity and ruling divinity. The R (head) is about the divine rule. The G (foot) is all about the humility of being a human to serve.

Notice how the letters R and G as seen in the root RG, are not in the same order they appear in the alphabet – which should be GR. They have been crossed over – woven. It also seems that spiritually, God has switched around the roles – almighty God becomes humble human Jesus as a baby

---

[1] ARGWN Strong's 713. It's also written as ARGMN

born in an animal barn and humble human Jesus later becomes the King of all.

GB ~ Pride

Psalm 10:4 In his pride (GBH) the wicked does not seek him; in all his thoughts there is no room for God.

The word GBH[1] 𐤇𐤏𐤁𐤂 [gobah] means 'pride' and is from the root GB which appears to talk about an arch, which can stand high upright or be arched down like a depression dug in the ground. Perhaps the idea of the arch is brought by the arch of the foot which represents the letter G. Not sure how the B comes into it. Could it relate to what's coming to the relationship, or the arch of a house?

But for sure, pride relates to a person putting themselves up high. When people put themselves up high, they are putting themselves before relationship which is perhaps why G comes before B. There is no room for God or God's family when a person places himself high.

Pride has a lot to do with why the leaders of Judaism didn't accept Jesus as the Messiah of Israel.

In short, there were some fundamental mismatches between what Jesus was presenting and what the leaders were expecting. And Jesus deliberately reinforced these mismatches to filter out those who were living by pride in their own attainment and who could not look beyond the physical to a spiritual kingdom.

The first mismatch relates to the manner of his relationship with humanity and the ultimate purpose of his coming – to build an eternal family.

---

[1] GBH Strong's 1363

Jesus came in the manner of a groom courting his bride. This involved making a first visit to affirm his love for his bride to be and pay the bride price (by his death on the cross). After doing so, it was customary for the groom to leave and prepare a bayt (room or house) for his bride. Once finished, he would return to take his betrothed to join him in his house and so complete the marriage.

The leaders of Judaism at the time were expecting a Messiah who would become a king and reestablish the Kingdom of Israel before their eyes in their time. They weren't expecting a king who would avoid public fame and instead die and return at an unknown time to become a ruling earthly king.

The second mismatch connecting to the first was relating to spirituality versus a physical visible King.

Jesus knew full well that the people were looking for a physical king, but he deliberately avoided playing into that expectation. The people wanted to make him king when he fed the 5000.

John 6:15 Jesus, knowing that they intended to come and make him king by force, withdrew again to a mountain by himself.

Jesus could have become King and Messiah of Israel at that time, but he hid from them. He didn't want subjects who make him king on the basis of physical blessings. Instead, he wanted subjects for his kingdom who understood his spiritual significance. Even his close disciples struggled to understand the spiritual nature of his Kingdom. It's an ongoing challenge we must all pursue if we want to break through into eternal life.

This fundamental mismatch ultimately relates to the kind of relationship he wants with his people. He doesn't want the focus to be on physical benefit which is really about self-satisfaction. Instead, he wants a spiritual relationship which is about looking beyond self to what's between us. He very much taught about looking beyond self and the pride of self-attainment in fulfilling the law.

We can take it right back to Adam and Eve eating from the tree. They ate from the tree for reasons of personal satisfaction – to gain knowledge and instant bodily pleasure. They could have chosen to obey God, walking in relationship and trust in future provision.

So, if Jesus is true to his actions while on earth 2000 years ago, then we can expect that he will not return to be king of the earth in a physical manner until Israel accepts Jesus in a spiritual manner. To do this Israel must put aside it's pride. This needs to happen by choice rather than by force. He's waiting for Israel to accept his proposal of marriage.

GAL – Kinsman-Redeemer

> Ruth 4:14 *The women said to Naomi: "Praise be to the LORD, who this day has not left you without a **kinsman-redeemer**. May he become famous throughout Israel!"*

The Hebrew word spelt GAL[1] [gaal] is translated as 'kinsman' in the King James Bible and 'kinsman-redeemer' in the NIV version. The dictionary meaning of this word is 'redeem'. It's from the parent root GL which has the meaning of rolling round. I'm not sure how the letter G (foot) brings the idea of going around, but this letter is often used in the context of a circle. Perhaps it relates to walking in a circle such as a dance. Perhaps it relates to the curved shape of the foot. The Arabic word GWLA [gowla] means a roundabout on a road.

The letter L (shepherds' staff) talks about a direction.

Interestingly the place where Jesus was crucified was called Golgotha, which is a word of Aramaic origin. The word means, 'skull'. The Hebrew word is very similar – spelt GLGLT ✝∠∧∠∧ [gulgo'let] which is from the same root GL.

---

[1] GAL Strong's 1350

It's no coincidence that Jesus redeemed humanity on the place which has its meaning connected to redemption. He is our kinsman-redeemer for two reasons. Firstly, He shares the same human blood as us so is physically related. Secondly, He redeemed us by paying the bride price with His life on the cross. The root GL means to roll. The act of redeeming is about rolling us back to our original place in relationship with God, as we were in the garden of Eden. We can come full circle.

In the word GLGLT, the final letter T is usually added to a Hebrew word to form a feminine noun. In this instance it's very appropriate because the letter T talks about reaching the completion of a contract. It's also appropriate because it's at the end of the word signalling the end and completion of the story. Golgotha was certainly the place of the completion of the marriage contract by the payment of the bride price.

GN – Garden

*Genesis 2:8 Now the LORD God had planted a **garden** in the east, in Eden; and there he put the man he had formed.*

It's likely that God planted a garden with especially chosen plants which would support Adam and Eve. They shared the garden with many animals also. You can see many jungles and landscapes today where a person would find it difficult to find food.

The word translated as 'garden' is from the Hebrew word spelt GN[1] [gan]. Children of this root include:

GN ↶↥ (garden),

MGN[2] ↶↥〰 [meginaw] (shield),

---

[1] GN Strong's 1588
[2] MGN Strong's 4043

AGN[1] ﬤﬥﬦ [aggan] (basin).

It appears that a garden is something which is protected by a surrounding enclosure. The context of use consistently shows that it contains special plants which need to be protected. The context also shows that a garden has water running through it. In ancient times before they had pipes, a garden in the dry regions of the Middle East could only exist where there was a flowing supply of water. The water source was the foundation of the garden. We read in the Bible that when Adam was in the garden, water came up from the ground like a spring.[2]

A garden in the dry Middle East is also mostly situated in a basin-like earthworks so that it collects and holds the water from the rain when it comes. Many gardens in the desert regions are even constructed with an earth mound all around so that when it rains, water is diverted into the enclosure so that it forms a pool up to one meter deep. This water will then soak into the ground where it will continue feeding the plants for months, which is enough to bring a crop of sorghum to full maturity. Date palms are also grown in these gardens, and they will survive and fruit with just this one good watering each year.

The arch of the foot (G) may well be talking about the arch like depression in the ground. The depression collecting water to water the plant (N). Since the water came up from the ground, it would make sense that there would be more water in lower areas such as a depression than in higher areas, because water would drain rapidly from the elevated areas. The letter N means, 'sprouting seed'.

It may not be chance that the English word, 'garden' has some resemblance to the Hebrew root GN. A Hebrew word spelt GDR means 'enclosure'. The old origins of the word 'garden' likely come through a vulgar[3] Latin phrase 'hortus gardenus' where 'hortus' refers to plants and 'gardenus' to an enclosure.

---

[1] AGN Strong's 101
[2] Bible, Genesis 1:6
[3] **Vulgar Latin** was the spoken form of **Latin** that evolved into the Romance languages. It differed from Classical **Latin** in pronunciation, grammar, and vocabulary, and was influenced by local languages and cultures.

It could alternatively be that the G (foot) relates to how the garden is irrigated, though I doubt that the garden of Eden was irrigated like this, and judging by what God spoke about in the promised land, there would be no irrigation by foot. I imagine foot irrigation was especially used in Egypt where water was diverted from the Nile into canals, which diminished in size until they became small canals which were opened and closed by pushing soil with the foot. I saw this method of irrigation being used in the Middle East where water was diverted from a river or brought up from a well.

> *Deuteronomy 11:10 The land you are entering to take over is not like the land of Egypt, from which you have come, where you planted your seed and irrigated it by foot as in a vegetable garden.*

The letter G often brings the idea of a circular formation, perhaps from the idea of walking around. So, the G may refer to an enclosure.

One distinctive feature of the Garden of Eden is that it was most likely a permaculture garden with a natural balance of plants and animals. When humanity was put out of the Garden, God determined or foresaw that humanity would have to work by the sweat of their brow to grow food and that their crops would have weeds. Both these problems occur when monoculture is practiced, that is having gardens where only one crop is grown in a large block. As a result, there is an imbalance and people must work harder to prevent other plants (weeds), disease, animals and insects from taking over.

Monoculture agriculture came into place early when people started to build protected cities which were required to protect themselves from raiders who were driven by selfishness and greed.

> *Song of Solomon 4:16 Awake, north wind, and come, south wind! Blow on my garden, that its fragrance may spread abroad. Let my lover come into his garden and taste its choice fruits.*

D – Dalet – Door

The letter D was written with the symbol of a door – in the form of a hanging tent curtain.

It's not difficult to see how it came to be written later as the modern letter D.

It has the numerical value of 4. The word, 'dalet' means 'door' and is from the root DL which has the underlying meaning of something which hangs down passively and moves back and forth. It's often used to bring the idea of reciprocity.

Dalet is the origin of the Greek word, 'delta' which is the opening or doorway between the river and sea, and which has been borrowed into English. The tide is also reciprocal as it comes in and out at this point. In a delta, there is a noticeable change in current at the change in tides – more so than at an open beach.

DM – Blood

*Exodus 12:13 The **blood** will be a sign for you on the houses where you are; and when I see the **blood**, I will pass over you. No destructive plague will touch you when I strike Egypt.*

It's not so easy to pin-point the underlying meaning of this root. The children include DM[1] [dawm] (Blood), DMM[2] [damam] (silent)

---

[1] DM Strong's 1818
[2] DMM Strong's 1826

D – DALET – DOOR

(could this be the origin of the English word 'dumb'?), ADM[1] 𐤌𐤃𐤀 (red, man), ADMH[2] 𐤄𐤌𐤃𐤀 [adamah] (ground), AWDM[3] 𐤌𐤃𐤅𐤀 [awdome] (ruby – from the red colour). Perhaps an animal becomes silent when it bleeds. The root seems to bring a predominant theme of red. The ground can also be red in some areas.

There seems to be different angles you can go with this.

The letter D is likely talking about the backwards and forwards motion of the blood in the body going to and from the heart. Also, in an abstract sense, the door often talks about a passive nature – which would account for the meaning of 'silent'.

The letter M in a physical sense is likely talking about the fluid nature of blood. In an abstract sense, M (ocean) talks about a great unknown. M is used in relation to the mortal nature of humanity – which is a life of unknowns which is man's test.

The colour red and blood has a strong Biblical connection to the saving of humanity. The first spilling of blood mentioned in the Bible is inferred from God providing skin clothing to Adam and Eve after they were ashamed of being naked[4]. They were hiding from God. This is a picture of what Jesus did on the cross. He spilt blood and died on the cross to provide a spiritual covering for humanity to cover their shame[5].

The Israelites were instructed to paint blood over their door lintel and posts so they would be saved from the angel of death coming to take the lives of the first-born of Egypt[6].

The prostitute Rahab was asked to hang a red cloth out of her window to mark her household as one to be saved when Joshua attacked the city[7].

---

[1] ADM Strong's 119, 120
[2] ADMH Strong's 127
[3] AWDM Strong's 124
[4] Genesis 3:21
[5] Hebrews 9:12-25
[6] Exodus 12:23
[7] Joshua 2:18

ADM – Red, Man

*Genesis 1:26 Then God said, "Let us make **man** (ADM) in our image, in our likeness, and let them rule over the fish of the sea and the birds of the air, over the livestock, over all the earth, and over all the creatures that move along the ground."*

The root DM gives birth to the word ADM[1] meaning, 'red' and 'man', and is used as the name for the first man, Adam. It's hard to know whether it was given to him as a personal name or as a description of who he is – the first person representing humanity

The letter A is drawn with the symbol of an ox head. The name of the letter is 'Aleph' which means, 'to guide'. So, the physical picture is all about the ox being led. But spiritually, God is more interested in leading humanity than an ox! So, it seems that A is talking about humanity being led. The word aleph is likely derived from the more basic root AL – which means to guide, and the name translated as, 'God' – the one who guides humanity.

The letter D (door) often talks about a coming and going. We see that one of the children of DM is DMWT which talks about comparing and likeness. Comparing is a process of looking backwards and forwards between two or more entities. Man was created in the image and likeness of God.

In the context of humanity, could the letter D also be talking about a reciprocal relationship? God created man with a very special purpose – in God's own image for the purpose of having a relationship with God for eternity – to be joined as one in the same family. Let's not lose sight of this very special destiny we have as we struggle with day-to-day existence in this current life.

The word ADM (humanity) is contrasted clearly with the word ANSh (male man) in Genesis 2:23:

---

[1] ADM Strong's 120 Translated as both 'man' and 'Adam'.

The man (ADM) said, "This is now bone of my bones and flesh of my flesh; she shall be called 'woman', for she was taken out of man (ANSh)."

Notice previously that the woman wasn't created for the male man (ANSh), but for humanity (ADM). The author has chosen his words with purpose:

Genesis 2:18 The LORD God said, "It is not good for the man (ADM) to be alone. I will make a helper suitable for him."

Curiously, also, the noun ?ZR[1] (translated as 'helper') is only used elsewhere to refer to God as our helper. The only exceptions to this are where help is expected from a human but doesn't eventuate. The verb 'to help' is used widely to include help given by humans.

From the English translation, I had always thought that Genesis 2:18 was talking about the female being a help so that the male wouldn't be alone, but it appears from the Hebrew words that the help is referring to divine help given to humanity. What help could that be? Without the birth of the first woman, humanity wouldn't receive the Messiah to bring humanity back to God. With the help of the Messiah, humanity wouldn't be separated and alone from God.

DMWT – Compare, Likeness

+Y𐤌ᴅ

*Genesis 1:26 Then God said, "Let us make man (ADM) in our image, in our **likeness** (DMWT)..."*

The word DMWT[2] [damawt] is from the same root (DM) as ADM. This indicates a close relationship in meaning between the two words.

Man (ADM) was created in the likeness (DMWT) of God. The English word, 'man' may also have in its origin the idea of likeness. It may originate

---

[1] ?ZR Strong's 5828
[2] DMWT Strong's 1823. Look also at DMH 1819, 1820, 1821

from the Hebrew word MN meaning 'from' and answers the question from where? He is from the likeness of God. MN then evolved through the Indo-European languages where it meant, 'humanity' through to the word 'man' in the Germanic and English languages.

The meaning of 'likeness' is shown in the letters. D means a going back and forth – which we do when comparing a likeness between two or more items. It could also say that there's something reciprocal between the two entities being compared. The letter M (ocean) brings the idea of an unknown or a question – which we answer when we look at what is shared between the two.

What is the likeness shared between God and humanity?

Since the Bible says that we're created in God's image, the next question is, in what way are we created in His image? I see that it is our tri-nature. God is Father, Son and Spirit. Father is essentially the will of God – the aspect of God which sets the order and direction. This is like the will of a human person. The Son is the physical manifestation of God. A human person also has a physical manifestation – his body.

The Spirit is like our spirit. Spirit is not a person but is part of our person. It has to do with relationship – the invisible yet powerful connection we have with others.

We are also similar to God in that we have a kind of dual nature. God is two persons, the divine father and the physical son. They share one spirit between them. A human is similar in that we are also kind of two persons sharing one spirit. We have our spiritual person which is directed by our will. We also have a physical person which is directed by our physical brain and body. The physical functions of our body do a lot to direct us – our hormones, our stomach, our physical heart, and even our genes bring behaviour and physical traits from previous generations. People who don't recognise the spiritual, see only the physical person and are led by it. However, our physical person will cease to exist at some point, and we'll be left only with the spiritual person.

We feed our physical person with physical things, and we feed our spiritual person with relationship. Spirit is relationship. We couldn't say that relationship is spirit because there is also a relationship between physical entities. See my writing about the Universal Fractal of Life where we see three different layers.

However, the word 'God' is spelt AL – which talks about the possibility of God leading us – if we choose with our will. Our will and spirit are the two aspects of our being which will last for eternity. We may well have another physical manifestation of that person after our current earthly body has ceased. The Bible says we will have a spiritual body – which we can't understand at this point.

Paul points to us having two directions pulling us. One part of us wants to be led by physical things and the other part wants to be led by the spiritual.

Romans 7: 15-25 I do not understand what I do. For what I want to do I do not do, but what I hate I do. And if I do what I do not want to do, I agree that the law is good. As it is, it is no longer I myself who do it, but it is sin living in me. I know that nothing good lives in me, that is, in my sinful nature. For I have the desire to do what is good, but I cannot carry it out. For what I do is not the good I want to do; no, the evil I do not want to do-- this I keep on doing. Now if I do what I do not want to do, it is no longer I who do it, but it is sin living in me that does it. So I find this law at work: When I want to do good, evil is right there with me. For in my inner being I delight in God's law; but I see another law at work in the members of my body, waging war against the law of my mind and making me a prisoner of the law of sin at work within my members. What a wretched man I am! Who will rescue me from this body of death? Thanks be to God-- through Jesus Christ our Lord! So then, I myself in my mind am a slave to God's law, but in the sinful nature a slave to the law of sin.

DMM – Quiet

ᴍ ᴍ D

*Psalm 131:2 But I have stilled (ShWH) and **quieted (DMM)** my soul; like a weaned child with its mother, like a weaned child is my soul within me.*

This verse was a lifeline for me when I was undergoing a time of anguish at the break up of my first marriage. I certainly felt like someone who had nothing left – like a weaned child. But in that place of simplicity, I was able to be still and quiet with my parent God.

DMM[1] [damam] is from the root DM. Being still and quietening our soul is a key part of trusting in God, and the act of being at rest in that way is a very healthy part of our being and health. It's free of striving.

What does the root DM bring to this meaning?

The letter D (door) is often used to bring the idea of being passive. It rests and is only moved when others move it one way or the other. The letter M (ocean) brings the idea of a great unknown. So together D and M bring the idea of great humility and trust extended beyond our own person. It's akin to the word meaning, 'worship' ShXH[2] [shakhah] which talks about humbling ourselves before God's awesomeness.

DBR – Word

*Psalm 119:105 Your **word** DBR is a lamp to my feet and a light for my path.*

---

[1] DMM Strong's 1826
[2] ShXH Strong's 7812

D – DALET – DOOR

The underlying meaning of the root DBR[1] [dabar] talks about order. This relates to the Father – who is the aspect of God who brings order and direction.

The letter D (door) may bring the idea of an entrance or a reciprocal understanding.

This is followed by the letter B meaning house or relationship.

So, D followed by B may be talking about entering into the house, family or relationship.

Another similar root DB has the meaning of quiet rest and a slowing down – perhaps referring to entering into the house where there's quiet from the world outside.

Jesus describes Himself as the door to the father – the door to God's family. And Jesus is also described as the Word. A word is the manifestation of the will – it's the tangible expression or communication of God's will.

The letter R (head) talks about headship and importance. God's word leads us to the head – the most important.

I think we need to move on from the idea that a word is just writing or a sound – or even a sign language. Perhaps a word is even more than a concept or information.

Could it be that a word is something which brings direction in a relationship. It brings order. Jesus the Word, is the manifestation and outworking of God's purpose.

The word DBR can be used in relation to a person saying a word, but it's especially pertinent to God's word. To accept His word, we must enter into His house where there is rest. There we meet God – the head and what is most important.

> *John 1:1-3 In the beginning was the **Word**, and the **Word** was with God, and the **Word** was God. The same was in the*

---

[1] DBR Strong's 1697

beginning with God. All things were made by him; and without him was not anything made that was made.

*Psalm 33:6 By the **word** of the LORD were the heavens made; and all the host of them by the breath of his mouth.*

The word DBR is a very important word which can benefit from greater in-depth examination. There's far more to this word than the English translation 'word'.

Let's look at the children of the root DBR:

They have the meanings of

speak[1], word[2], thing[3], plague[4], DBR ߆ߐߐ

bee[5], DBWRH ߆ߐߐߐ

order[6], DYBRH ߆ߐߐߐߐ

wilderness[7], DWBR ߆ߐߐߐ

manner[8].

How does a plague fit with the other meanings? Plagues were God's communication of warning to Pharoah.

A common theme which seems to be coming through with all words is the idea of order. The wilderness is a place where we can see everything clearly. A bee lives with complex order.

The word DBR quite likely comes from the simpler root of DR which has the meaning of circle or wide area.

D with the literal meaning of Door could have many meanings depending on the context. It often brings the idea of reciprocal – a two-way

---

[1] Strong's 1696
[2] Strong's 1697
[3] Strong's 1697 (Gen 18:14 – any thing)
[4] Strong's 1698 (Deut 28:21 - pestilence -in the sense of destroying)
[5] Strong's 1682 (Deut 1:44 - ordered movement)
[6] ? couldn't find this one.
[7] Strong's 4057 (midbawr – open field, by implication, a desert)
[8] Strong's 1700 (Psalms 110:4)

communication – going in and out. One example is the word ʕD[1] [ʕaD] which means a witness between us.

Creation was a process of ordering - starting with the most fundamental of dividing light and finishing with the more complex.

The letter B is the first letter in the Bible. It's worth noting that we are told that the Word was in the beginning. The letter B talks about relationship and family. A word is also very much about a relationship.

The letter R has the literal meaning of head. It generally talks about something very important. It's used in the second word of the Bible – RAShYT which is translated as beginning but also carries the meaning of most important. The root of RAShYT is RSh – meaning head.

So, DBR seems to be telling us about something of utmost importance which is shared between us. This requires reciprocal communication.

So, what' the most important thing which is shared between us? According to the first words in the Bible, B RAShYT, at the beginning is the most important – that is, His family and relationship. This is what's shared between us. This is His perfect order. This was in place in the Garden of Eden and will be again at the completion of all things.

So, if things seem out of order in this current world – be assured, God's order will prevail in the end. And it's best if we're part of it. If anything comes against God's family in any form at all – look carefully!

Let God's Word be a light to our feet. Make building God's family the first thing in our lives.

---

[1] ʕD Strong's 5707 The letter ʕ is a voiced pharyngeal fricative which sounds much like a camel moo.

ADNY – My Lord, Adonai

*Psalm 8:1 O LORD (YHWH), our **Lord** (ADNY), how majestic is your name in all the earth! You have set your glory above the heavens.*

The word spelt ADNY[1] [aw-dony - often pronounced as Adonai] is from the root DN.

The letter D (door) talks about a backwards and forwards movement, in this case, between two or more persons.

The letter N (seed) talks about information.

So DN talks about the exchange of information between persons. The flow back and forwards results in information.

Children of DN include DN (quarrel, perhaps the origin of the English word 'din'?), ADN (base, Lord), DYN (judge – judgement resulting from the backwards and forwards flow of information), MDYNH (Province). Medina is the Arabic word for city. A province or city is likely defined as an area under a particular judge or lord).

The opposite order of ND talks about something being moved away. The door isn't moving both ways but only swinging one way, so children of ND include nod (likely origin of the English word nod), toss, mound (tossed onto mound), NYDH removal.

In Genesis 15:2 the phrase, ADNY YHWH, is incorrectly translated as, 'Sovereign Lord'. ADNY means, Lord, but YHWH doesn't actually mean, 'sovereign'.

---

[1] ADNY Strong's 136

D – DALET – DOOR

Dʕ ~ Knowledge

👁𐤅

*Genesis 2:17 but you must not eat from the tree of the **knowledge** (DʕT) of good and evil, for when you eat of it you will surely die."*

The root of DʕT[1] +👁𐤅 [daʕat] is Dʕ which includes the meanings of 'to know or perceive'.

In the Bible context, knowledge is a function of the heart, spelt in Hebrew as LB. We should note that the Hebrew word LB has nothing to do with the pumping heart in our body. It's an aspect of our person which leads us in relationship.

The letter D (door) talks about something which goes two ways or is reciprocal. It could also talk about an opening.

The letter ʕ (eye 👁) talks about seeing. If this is the first time you've come across the sound ʕ, it's a voiced pharyngeal fricative. Without explaining the technicalities too much, it sounds like a camel moo. This sound is found in most if not all Semitic languages.

The ideas of seeing and an opening come together in Genesis 3:5 where we see the first mention of the word meaning, 'eye'. Spoken by the Serpent:

*"For God knows that when you eat of it your **eyes** will be **opened**, and you will be like God, **knowing** good and evil."*

The verse brings us a total equation of:

D (door) + ʕ (eye) = Dʕ (know, perceive).

The opposite order of letters ʕD talks about an agreement or witness (eye) between two persons (D reciprocal). The witness is between two persons.

---

[1] DʕT Strong's 1847

But with D? the reciprocation (D) is going to the eye (?) or perception... What does that mean?... Is knowledge something which requires a mutual understanding? Without that mutual understanding it's not knowledge?

Adam and Eve were permitted to eat from any other tree including the tree of life. It seems that they had no need of the knowledge of good and evil while they had the tree of life. Could it be that the knowledge of good and evil is akin to the law. Following the Law doesn't bring us into relationship with God, *trust* in Him does. Law is there to show us our need for relationship, because being good in ourselves doesn't necessarily bring us to relationship.

It seems there is an opposing contrast between life and knowledge. So, to understand knowledge more, it would be useful to understand more about life.

The word translated as 'life' is from the Hebrew word spelt XY[1] ⊃JH [khay].

> *Genesis 2:9 And the LORD God made all kinds of trees grow out of the ground - trees that were pleasing to the eye and good for food. In the middle of the garden were the tree of* **life** *and the tree of the knowledge of good and evil.*

At first glance, the letter X (wall) is talking about something unseen and beyond the physical. It's talking about the spiritual. This is perhaps in contrast to the law (knowledge of good and evil) which may relate to the physical 'do this and don't do that'. The spiritual is all about trust in what we can't see – a relationship.

The letter Y (throwing arm) talks about destiny. Could it be saying that the spiritual and relationship is our destiny? Destiny is also about the future.

When Adam and Eve ate from the forbidden tree, their motives were all about self-gain and the physical benefits in the now. It wasn't about trust and relationship and the future consequences or destiny.

---

[1] XY Strong's 2416

H – Hey – Behold

The letter H was written with the symbol of a person with hands raised. It means, 'behold' and 'exist'. It can bring the meaning of the existence of a person – divine or human.

It often brings the idea of 'wow' and 'awesome', signalling something significant.

The letter H is used by itself as a word to mean, 'the', pronounced 'ha'. But it can't be used with any old noun. You can't say Ha cat. It's only used to mark something important, such as, Ha Shem (The Name) – the name Judaism uses as a substitute for saying YHWH (God's given name), or Ha Adam (the human)

The letter H is used to indicate a question. This is apart from the use of the letter M which usually starts a question word such as 'whose?'. H works in a similar way to the English word 'is' – as in 'is he ready?' H is used in this context because it talks about the existence or state of something or someone.

Could Hey be the origin of the English word 'hey' – a word which signals another to pay attention to something significant?

Hey has the numerical value of 5. It's often used in the context of two persons joining to make one, or the spiritual person joining the human person. The whole is 10.

Examples are the Ten commandments, where the first 5 commandments relate to our relationship with God and the second 5 relate to our relationship with other humans. The fifth commandment is about obeying your mother and father, so it could relate to relationship with fellow humans, but I think we can include it also in our relationship with God because our earthly parents are a physical picture of our spiritual Father.

HYH – I Am

ℲⵆℲ

Exodus 3:13-15 Moses said to God (ALHYM), "Suppose I go to the Israelites and say to them, 'The God of your fathers has sent me to you,' and they ask me, 'What is his name?' Then what shall I tell them?"

God said to Moses, "I (A) AM (HYH) WHO (AShR) I (A) AM (HYH). This is what you are to say to the Israelites: **I AM (HYH)** *has sent me to you." God also said to Moses, "Say to the Israelites, 'The LORD (YHWH), the God of your fathers-- the God of Abraham, the God of Isaac and the God of Jacob-- has sent me to you.' This is my name forever, the name by which I am to be remembered from generation to generation."*

God makes Himself known to the Israelites with the name AHYH[1] [ahayah]. AHYH can be translated into two parts: 'A' means, 'I', and HYH means 'to exist'. In the same scene He also tells us His name, spelt YHWH[2], pronounced 'Yahweh', and translated as LORD (small caps). It's usually anglicized as 'Jehovah'. YHWH means, 'the existing one'. You could also read it to mean, 'He exists'.

Both HYH and YHWH come from the same root HH.

Let's bring attention to the command that the name spelt HYH and YHWH is the name by which God is to be known from generation to generation. We don't use that name. Perhaps we should! Is it enough to use a translated name such as 'God', or should we be using the name Yahweh (He exists)? Judaism has the tradition which says that no one should use that name because it's too holy. However, God did instruct Moses to tell them this name if they asked who had sent him.

---

[1] HYH Strong's 1961
[2] YHWH Strong's 3068

The interesting thing here is how the word HYH and YHWH both have two H's. I understand this to indicate that God is two persons - a divine person and a human person, combining to make one complete whole. We can see this again in the letters which go with each H.

The first set is YH. The letter Y has the value of 10 which is understood to bring the meaning of completion by the joining of two persons, 5 + 5 = 10. Y is also understood in Judaism to indicate divinity – probably because it's the first letter of God's sacred name YHWH. So YH appears to indicate the divine person.

The second set is WH. The letter W has the value of 6 which is understood to talk about humanity – who was created on the sixth day. The W also has the underlying meaning of, 'to connect'. This is the role of Jesus – to connect divinity to humanity. Notice how the W is between the two H's – to connect the two persons together.

God appears to understand that for a human, it's hard to believe in the existence of a seemingly invisible God. It's probably the elephant in the room for the relationship between God and humanity. Yet His name meaning, 'I exist' addresses that elephant directly. But just saying that He exists isn't sufficient – there must be more to it! Does the name HYH and YHWH tell us anything which is tangible to us physical humans?

The double H tells us that there are two aspects to His existence – spiritual and physical. The spiritual is eternal, and the physical is visible and tangible – but fleeting. Both are important for existence. God gave us a physical display of His existence when He sent Jesus to earth. Many accepted His existence as God, and many didn't – though they had hard evidence in front of them. They couldn't get past their own pride. And pride is ultimately the barrier to accepting God at any time – whether He's visible in front of our eyes or not visible. On the other hand, humility will open the door to trusting God and going beyond our own abilities – as the word BThX ⌂⊕H [bathakh] (trust) shows us.

We struggle to accept God's spiritual existence, but we must also strive to recognise our own spiritual existence because this is not only our eternal existence, but it actually does drive our relationships in the present. We are spiritual beings.

Here's an interesting observation. The first time God's name Elohiim is used is in Genesis 1:1, talking about God creating the heavens and earth. The first time the name YHWH is used is in Genesis 2:4, also in relation to creating the heavens and the earth. YHWH is joined to the name Elohiim. Why use a different name in relation to the same action? What's the difference? Could it be because the second use in Genesis 2 relates more to the story of the creation of humanity. It doesn't talk so much about the entire creation, but provides a setting for the entrance of humanity. The name YHWH perhaps has a special connection between God and humanity, talking about the existence of God in answer to the query of humanity about his existence.

> *Genesis 2:4 This is the account of the heavens and the earth when they were created. When the LORD God (YHWH elohiim) made the earth and the heavens--*

The word YHWH comes from the root HH whose children include:
HH ᏇᏇ (breath, woe – heavy breath),
HWH ᏇᎩᏇ (exist),
HYH ᏇᗽᏇ (exist).

So, what is the relationship or what's happening between H and H? Both letters talk about the existence of a person. It seems that it's telling us that existence and meaning comes when there is a relationship between two persons. If there's only one person, can there really be meaning and existence?

In the word YHWH, there are two pairings. The first pair is YH and the second WH. I see the first as relating to the spiritual and divine aspect of God – the Father. The Y (arm) relates to destining something. The Father is all about directing. So, the first pair YH talks about the directing Father.

The second pair WH relates to the physical person of God – shown to us as the person Jesus. The letter W (tent peg) brings the idea of connection. Jesus is the physical interface and connection between God and humanity. The word YHWH forms a mathematical equation:

$10 = 5 + 5.$
$Y(10) = H(5) W(+) H(5)$

This says to me, 'The completion of God (Y 10) is the result of and consists of two persons: the divine Father, who is the whole, and the physical person, Jesus. The complete is made up of the two existing persons. There can be no existence without two. One alone has no meaning or purpose.

Can this oneness made of two persons be mirrored in a human relationship between a man and a woman? The Bible tells us that when a man and a woman join together in marriage, the two become one. The Bible does tell us that the man should be the leader – like the Father God who is all about direction. The woman has usually been the one who is all about the expression of physical nurturing. Sure, a man and a woman are capable in themselves of both direction and physical expression, but perhaps those unique roles are best expressed in the context of a marriage and family. Often the man doesn't lead responsibly, or the woman express physical nurture so well, but the model God sets for us is a good one. There is plenty of room for abuse of that model if it becomes unbalanced and overbearing, but when the best for the relationship is sought – putting aside personal interest, loving the other as we love ourselves, then it should work.

HL – Hallelujah

Revelation 19:1 After this I heard what sounded like the roar of a great multitude in heaven shouting: "**Hallelujah**! *Salvation and glory and power belong to our God."*

The word, 'Hallelujah[1]' is only found in the New Testament, in the book of Revelation.

---

[1] Hallelujah Strong's Greek 239

I understand it to be made up of three parts: HLL – L – YH. The three parts pretty well make up the phrase shown in Revelation 19:1 – Glory to our God – as if it were a rephrasing or translation of Hallelujah.

HLL [halal] talks about beholding something amazing.

The letter L alone points to something, telling us what is amazing. Similar to the English word 'to'.

The word YH is likely short for the word YHWH – God.

HLL[1] [halal] comes from the root HL which has the underlying meaning of 'look there, it's amazing!' The letter H means, behold and wow. The letter L (shepherd's staff) brings the idea of our attention being drawn or led to something.

The children of HL sing a story.
HLW 𐤉𐤋𐤄 (behold).
HLA 𐤀𐤋𐤄 (distant),
HLL 𐤋𐤋𐤄 (shine)'.
HYLL 𐤋𐤋𐤉𐤄 (star).

This appears to be telling us the story of the wise men who beheld the shining star in the distant east and followed it to their king Jesus.

HB – Give, Love

*Deuteronomy 6:5 **Love** the LORD your God with all your heart and with all your soul and with all your strength.*

The letters H and B tell us the story of a person or something amazing coming to the house, family or relationship

---

[1] HLL Strong's 1984

The children of the root HB are
HB[1] פה [hib] (gift) and
AHB[2] פהא [ahib] (to love).

If we reverse the order of letters to make BH [buh], we get the opposite meaning of an empty vessel. Life has gone out of the relationship or house.

What does it mean to love God? If we look at the word meaning, 'love' AHB [ahib], it's talking about a person going to the family. We give our person to God's family. That's our everything – heart, soul and strength.

When we love another human, we also give our person and existence to that relationship.

What does it mean to give our heart, soul and strength?

The word translated as; 'heart' is from the Hebrew word spelt LBB [lebab]. It has nothing at all to do with the organ which pumps blood. It's from the root LB [lab]. The letter L is the shepherd's staff which talks about leading. The letter B talks about house, family and relationship. So, LB would seem to be talking about something which leads us in or to relationship. It guides us in giving (HB) ourselves to the relationship.

The word translated as; 'soul' is from the Hebrew word spelt NPSh [nephesh]. In Arabic, this word is written as NFS and means, 'self'. Many understand the soul to be talking about the part of us which has to do with eternal existence, but I don't see that in the use of the Hebrew word NPSh. The word applies to anything with the breath of life – which can include any animal or fish for example. So, when we are commanded to love the Lord with our NPSh, it would appear to be saying to give our living breath to Him – our physical existence.

Love is perhaps the fundamental difference between ideologies such as Communism and Christianity. In its pure form, Christianity has a practice of sharing all things in common. Communism has at its core the practice of sharing communal property. They're very similar at a quick external glance, but one is done by force and the other is done by free choice – sharing as a

---

[1] HB Strong's 1890
[2] AHB Strong's 157

gift given with love. When sharing is forced, there is no love and there is a greatly reduced respect for the care of the resources.

Communism and other emerging versions of it in our current times are enforced by an elite group. It's a purely physical act. Christian sharing in contrast is a personal choice. It's essentially spiritual.

In the present times, we need to beware of global initiatives to control health and climate outcomes. This is the new face of communism and humanism in its effort to 'save' humanity and the earth by replacing personal choice with global controls.

HSH – Silent

*Habakkuk 2:20 "But the LORD is in his holy temple; let all the earth be **silent** before him."*

HSH[1] [hasah] is from the root HS which has the underlying meaning of holding onto awe. We have the picture of someone standing with jaw open in complete awe at something – speechless. Could the English word, 'hush', have its origins in this word?

The letter H brings the idea of awe. The letter S (thorn) brings the idea of holding onto something.

It's translated as, 'silent' and 'quiet' but there are other words which are also translated as silent and quiet. So, what's the unique character of HSH? Look at these contexts:

*Zephaniah 1:7 Be **silent** before the Sovereign LORD, for the day of the LORD is near. The LORD has prepared a sacrifice; he has consecrated those he has invited.*

---

[1] HSH Strong's 2013

*Zechariah 2:13 Be **still** before the LORD, all mankind, because he has roused himself from his holy dwelling.*

We are instructed to be in awe (H) of YHWH with our attention fixed (S) on him in silence as we put aside all the noise of our lives.

W – Waw – Tent Peg

There are only two words which begin with W; its name – spelt WW [waw][1], meaning 'peg', and the word meaning 'and' spelt W. This would indicate that it's not considered to be a true consonant. Linguistically, it's a semi-vowel – a kind of sound which has a foot in both camps – vowel and consonant. It identifies as a vowel because it has no mouth articulation and is vocal in some contexts. However, in other contexts it can exist to form the small rounding of the mouth which is then followed by a vowel.

It is used in many words to bring the idea of connecting two or more parts together. A peg was often used to connect two curtains together, or for connecting a tent to the ground. It may well have had a fork at the top as shown in its picture, which would have served to secure a rope at the top or stop it from pulling through a fabric. The word W, translated as 'and', is used to connect two parts of a sentence or phrase together.

So, the physical meaning is peg (or sometimes a connecting pin). The directional (verb) meaning is, 'to connect'. The abstract or spiritual meaning is also related to connection, but I think extends to the idea of spirit.

The word meaning 'spirit' is spelt RWX[2] – which is a connection between two persons. Connection is also about relationship – what's between two people or objects. In physics, there's an invisible connection between two particles – on a larger scale this is gravity. This is a physical picture of a spiritual truth.

In addition to W being a semi-vowel, it seems to me that W is not used as part of a word root because a word root is like two persons coming together to be parents to a family of words. W is not like a person – it functions as the connector between two persons. In the same way the Holy Spirit is also

---

[1] WW is pronounced [vav] in modern Hebrew
[2] RWX Strong's 7307

not a person but connects the two persons of Father and Son. The Spirit also connects God to humanity.

W has the numerical value of 6 – which relates to humanity, who was created on the 6th day. The human Jesus is all about making a tangible physical connection or interface between God and humanity.

Could the position of the letter W in the alphabet have some meaning in regards to it connecting and delineating two parts – what comes before and what comes after in the alphabet story? We do see the letter W frequently connecting the physical to the spiritual.

It could mark the end of the era of history where God leads his people by physical means – the law. The seventh letter Z marks the position of a sacrifice of the physical whereby we leave behind the physical to enter into the spiritual. This transition or crossing over not only relates to an historical era, but also relates to an era in each person's life where they choose whether or not to make the cross-over into the spiritual – to leave behind the physical. Jesus invited us to take up our cross (where our physical body is put aside) and to follow Him. We can cross over into the spiritual while we still reside in our physical bodies. Don't wait till you depart your physical body to do that because you'll be left with nothing to go on when your physical body expires Crossing over into the spiritual is also best for our earthly life.

Crossing over into the spiritual is very much about putting aside our individualistic ways where we are absorbed with our own self and to put our worth into relationship – what is between myself, God and others. This is about our connections – shown in the letter W.

Z – Zayin – Plough

The letter Z was drawn with a symbol representing an agricultural implement such as a mattock, hoe or plough. Sometimes, it's a weapon. It talks about agriculture and farming – even perhaps hard physical work. It has the numerical value of 7. The number 7 relates to the completion of the physical creation.

> *Genesis 2:2 By the seventh day, God had finished the work he had been doing; so on the seventh day, he rested from all his work.*

Zayin, spelt ZYN is most likely from the root ZN. Its children include:
ZN[1] [zan] (a kind – of species),
ZNN[2] [zanuwn] (whoredom),
AZN[3] [azan] (hearing),
AZN[4] [azen] (weapon),
AWZN[5] [ozen] (ear),
MWAZN[6] [moazan] (balance on scales),
ZWN[7] [zuwn] (food),

It's hard to see what the underlying meaning is which connect all these meanings. A strong theme is around engaging with the physical world – weight, sound, whoredom, food and flesh.

The letter N (seed) brings the idea of information and design. Different kinds/species are defined by different genetic information. All things physical have some kind of design.

---

[1] ZN Strong's 2177, 2178
[2] ZNN Strong's 2183
[3] AZN Strong's 238, 239
[4] AZN Strong's 240
[5] AWZN Strong's 241
[6] MWAZN Strong's 3976, 3977
[7] ZWN Strong's Verb 2109, 2110. Noun 2185

ZD – Proud

𐤆𐤃

*Psalm 119:51 The **arrogant (ZD)** mock me without restraint, but I do not turn from your law.*

Children of the root ZD include: ZD[1] [zed](proud), AZD 𐤆𐤃𐤀 [azad] (depart), ZWD[2] 𐤆𐤅𐤃 [zud] (boil),
The letter Z tells us that pride is about the physical efforts of self.
D (door) is about a reciprocal action back and forth - perhaps bringing the idea of comparing.
God tells us not to compare ourselves with others in pride – to say that we are better than others. Nor are we to be proud in our own strength – which doesn't lead to good relationships.

Psalm 19:13 Keep your servant also from wilful (ZD) sins; may they not rule over me. Then will I be blameless, innocent of great transgression.

ZKH – Pure

𐤆𐤊𐤇

*Psalm 119:9 How can a young man keep his way **pure** (ZKH)? By living according to your word.*

ZKH[3] [zakah] is from the root ZK[4] [zak]

The letter Z brings the idea of the physical and flesh. The K (hand) is often used to talk about taming – keeping something in hand. So ZKH is likely talking about taming the physical.

---

[1] ZD Strong's 2086
[2] ZWD Strong's 2102
[3] ZKH Strong's 2135
[4] ZK Strong's 2134

Other children of ZK include ZKK [zakak] (to refine, to make pure).

*Proverbs 20:9 Who can say, "I have kept my heart **pure**; I am clean and without sin"?*

ZHB – Gold

𐤁𐤄𐤆

*Exodus 25:11 Overlay it (the ark of the covenant) with pure **gold**, both inside and out, and make a gold molding around it.*

The word ZHB[1] [zehab] (gold) comes from the root ZB. The underlying meaning of ZB appears to be talking about the colour yellow. Other children of the root ZB include:

AZWB[2] 𐤁𐤅𐤆𐤀 (Hyssop, a yellow plant),
ZAB[3] 𐤁𐤀𐤆 [zaab] (wolf, a yellowish animal),
ZHB 𐤁𐤄𐤆 (gleam – as gold),
ZHWB[4] 𐤁𐤅𐤄𐤆 [zahowb] (yellow)

But what is the spiritual meaning? The letter Z may bring us the idea of yellow because Z is one third the way through the alphabet and yellow also is one third the way through the colour spectrum. If you drew the colour spectrum as a line on a paper, then parallel to that wrote the letters of the alphabet spaced to match the same length as the spectrum line, you would see that the first letter of four colour names line up with the same colour in the spectrum.

All these four colours are prescribed by God for use in the temple. They are prophetic colours.

---

[1] ZHB Strong's 2091
[2] AZWB Strong's 231
[3] ZAB Strong's 2061
[4] ZHWB Strong's 6669

Z – ZAYIN- PLOUGH

The first is red (ADM)[adam], then yellow (ZHB) [zahab], Sapphire – sky blue (SPR) [saphiir] and violet (TKLT) [tekelet].

Not only do they align with their colours in the spectrum, but they all serve to divide the alphabet into 3 equal parts of 7 letters each. There are 22 letters in the alphabet and the three groups of seven equal 21. That leaves a spare one at the end. That's because God guides his people for the three eras in three different ways then the 22nd is when we enter into the eternal leading of God where He leads with all three ways together – in completion. These three parts appear to relate to the three eras of God leading His people in human history. He leads His people in three different ways – in line with His tri-nature of physical, spirit and will.

The first period is the physical which is marked at the start with the letter A which represents red and physical humanity. It's the start of the human story with ADM (Adam). This period goes for 4000 years and finishes with the death of Jesus on the cross. During this period, God leads his people by the written law which is all about 'do this and don't do that' – relating to the physical body and mind.

Jesus' death is marked with the letter Z which relates to the colour gold or yellow. Jesus' death is the ultimate sacrifice (ZBX). Sacrifice is all about giving up something physical in order to gain a spiritual benefit. It can be the crossover from the physical to the spiritual, but many stop at the physical sacrifice and don't enter into the spiritual.

The second era starts with the physical death of Jesus and the giving of His spirit to lead His people. It appears that this era will last for 2000 years. I arrive at that date because it fits a pattern. As mentioned in the section on A – Aleph, the first era is 4000 years. The third era is 1000 years. So, if the second was 2000 years you see a clear pattern of the time halving each time – 4000, 2000, 1000.

I also see that God leads his people in units of 1000 years. This idea comes from the word spelt ALPh – which is the name of the first letter in the alphabet and means, 'to lead' and '1000'. The word translated as, 'God' is spelt AL, which means, 'to guide'. It's not for nothing that the word meaning, 'guide' also means, '1000'.

The second era ends when Jesus comes again to rule in person. This point is marked with the letter S representing the colour sapphire spelt SPhR. Sapphire is the colour of God's throne which is said to be sky blue.

> *Ezekiel 1:26 Above the expanse over their heads was what looked like a throne of sapphire, and high above on the throne was a figure like that of a man.*

Jesus will rule the nations with an iron sceptre from His throne for 1000 years.

> *Revelation 20:4 I saw thrones on which were seated those who had been given authority to judge. And I saw the souls of those who had been beheaded because of their testimony for Jesus and because of the word of God. They had not worshiped the beast or his image and had not received his mark on their foreheads or their hands. They came to life and reigned with Christ a* **thousand** *years.*

When the thousand years of rule has finished, God will release the Serpent who will lead humanity once again to war against God's people. This time God will completely destroy them and throw them into the abyss for eternal separation. This is the completion of the story of humanity on earth.

The full completion is when Jesus takes His bride (those who chose to follow Him) to His home. He has prepared a room in His Father's house. This point is marked with the letter T and the colour TKLT (violet). The word TKLT is from the root KL which means, 'completion'. Another child of KL is KLLH meaning, 'bride' – one who has been made complete through uniting with her husband.

ZAB – Wolf

זאב

*Isaiah 65:25 "The **wolf** and the lamb will feed together, and the lion will eat straw like the ox, but dust will be the serpent's food. They will neither harm nor destroy on all my holy mountain," says the LORD.*

Wolf is spelt ZAB and is most often associated in scripture with being ravenous. It's contrasted with the lamb which is the wolf's prey.

*John 10:12 The hired hand is not the shepherd who owns the sheep. So when he sees the wolf coming, he abandons the sheep and runs away. Then the **wolf** attacks the flock and scatters it.*

There's no Scripture talking about a wolf in sheep's clothing, but in these times, it does appear that there is a wolf attacking God's flock and he does it by disguising in sheep's clothing. The Serpent's middle name (metaphorically speaking) is Deception.

The Beast is spoken about in the Old Testament and the New in relation to something which will serve the purposes of the Serpent. We do have a Serpent in sheep's clothing.

I see the Beast and Serpent as being out to destroy humanity and to bring separation. There's three parts to this scene. The sheep's clothing – which is all about a disguise which we think is harmless and perhaps even useful – something which people don't have any issue with.

Then there's the wolf – the thing which does the devouring and brings harm.

Finally, there's the victim - things which are attacked and destroyed.

In this current time, I see the sheep's clothing (the things which appear as being good and innocent causes) as including the issues of the environment, science, public health, safety, freedom of identity, race and water. These are all things which most people agree are important issues and are held up as being of utmost importance. Society will do anything to uphold these values.

The wolf is international trade, greed, global corporations, Humanism, and universal control. These all work together to build one huge beast which is the pinnacle of human achievement. I understand that the Beast will likely be disguised as a computer or similar entity – which supposedly does away with human error and emotion and will rule 'perfectly'. There will no longer be elections or even 'foolish dictators' – all those weaknesses will be done away with.

It's being said that humans are destroying the environment and health and making foolish, unscientific decisions. In order to save the planet, we need to side-step human interference and take control. We need to act as a team – a unified community.

So, using a global, viral pandemic as a ruse, we've seen the introduction of coerced vaccinations and tracking. Those who didn't take the vaccination lost the right to travel or enter shops. Many were forced to stay at home. In 2022, the pandemic crisis had seemingly gone away, but the scene is set in people's minds to be better prepared for the inevitable return of a global pandemic.

To keep a tab on where people are and who has been vaccinated, electronic tracking may be introduced. At first, in the form of an app on your phone. Then in the form of radio frequency cards carried by people, then ultimately a chip inserted into the hand or head of every person. As the Biblical prophecy states, those who don't have the mark of the Beast (the identity marker) will not be allowed to buy or sell. The chip will have several important functions, to replace credit cards, to identify people and to act as a tracking device of movements and spending.

The Bible says that those who take the mark will not enter the Kingdom of Heaven. That's likely because trust has been given to humanism rather than God. The mainstream media accuse those who see something bad happening as being 'conspiracy theorists.' The main issue which the mainstream press cannot see and accept is the prophecy – the direction from

God not to accept the mark or to worship the Beast – that is, to be led by the Beast and to let it take control.

'Conspiracy theorist' is a label applied and defined by the mainstream press – which is the mouthpiece of the Beast and Humanism. The very qualities which are at the heart of the wolf, are what he accuses others of being. This is an effort to take attention away from his own evil intent and point the accusing finger at others. In the true sense of the word, a 'conspiracy theorist' is a person who is trying to bring to light evil intent. But such people are being mocked by the people of the wolf. The wolf has redefined the term 'conspiracy theorist' to mean someone who is misinformed or who gives misinformation. What would we say of the Jews on the train to the death camps? Would we mock them for being conspiracy theorists? Perhaps more of them should have listened to the conspiracy theorists, so that they would have taken evasive action sooner.

Those who refuse to take the chip/mark will be required to be in isolation. There will be considerable community pressure on people to comply. The worst pressure will be from family members and close friends. People will be made to think that the person who doesn't comply is being stupid and stubborn – they are not being 'scientific', or 'reasonable' they are endangering the lives of others and they are not doing their part in the 'team'. They are not being a sheep.

The victims of the wolf/beast will lose personal freedoms, the freedom of religion, the right to say what can and can't go into your own body. People will be incarcerated (at first out of the public eye) and then finally beheaded[1].

The victims are human life in different aspects. It includes the killing of unborn children who have fully developed bodies and brains (full-term abortion – already being done in NZ). Then there's the killing of people who no longer want to live (euthanasia). Then there's the lives of those who have been subjected to the introduction of the viral pandemic and other staged and very real catastrophes. There will be the lives of those who are damaged or killed through coerced vaccinations. Finally, there will be

---

[1] Revelation 20:4

outright beheading of those who speak out against the Beast. There are millions who have their lives cut short through global slavery to greedy corporations. We should not be naïve to think that humanity has improved since the atrocities of World War 2. We are being fed a diet of entertainment while the atrocities in our present time are being hidden from us. The mainstream media is entertainment for profit, not comprehensive and impartial global news. The government of New Zealand has paid the media to publish the government's ideologies – called 'public interest journalism'.

ZBX – Sacrifice

דבח

*Hosea 6:6 For I desire mercy, not **sacrifice**, and acknowledgment of God rather than burnt offerings.*

The word ZBX[1] [zabakh] means, 'sacrifice' and is likely from the two-letter root BX meaning, 'slaughter' and 'knife'.

The letter Z talks about the physical flesh and perhaps also the harvesting of that. The letter Z has the numerical value of 7 which talks about the completion of the physical.

The letter B talks about a relationship and end goal of family.

The letter X (wall) talks about going beyond the physical and immediately visible. It has the numerical value of 8 – which is the next step after the completion of the physical – going beyond the physical into the spiritual.

So, sacrifice is all about putting aside and leaving the physical (Z) and moving onto relationship (B) and the spiritual (X). The word 'spirit' is spelt RWX [ruakh].

The act of sacrificing something involves giving away something physical for a spiritual benefit.

---

[1] ZBX Strong's 2077

Z – ZAYIN – PLOUGH

Many people have stopped at the physical sacrifice and have not crossed over to the spiritual. Sacrifice for them became a means to boast in their own abilities and goodness. God desires mercy (XSD[1]). Mercy starts with the spiritual (X). The letter S (thorn) talks about grasping hold of something. The letter D (door) talks about something reciprocal between two people. It's about building a relationship, not showing how holy and pious I am.

Jesus sacrificed His life to pay a bride-price to purchase us from the curse of the physical law. We are now made acceptable and are presented as His bride to His Father.

---

[1] XSD Strong's 2617

X – Heth – wall

The letter X was written with the symbol of a wall and has the numerical value of 8. It generally talks about what is beyond the immediately visible – beyond the wall. Sometimes it talks about a journey, sometimes about something spiritual.

It's pronounced like a K but with friction – a velar fricative. So, it sounds much like gathering saliva for a spit. I've written it in this book as [kh] in the pronunciation brackets.

The number 8 is the next step beyond the physical (the physical completion of creation represented by 7).

Its original name was most likely spelt XTs – which has children meaning,
XTsH[1] ᴪᴴH [khatsah] divide,
XYTs[2] ᴴᴴH [khayits] wall,
XTs[3] ᴴH [khuts] outside,
XTsTh[4] ⊕ᴴH [khatsoth] middle,
XTsY[5] ᴴᴴH [khatsi] half.

AXD – One

ᴅHᴀ

*Deuteronomy 6:4 Hear, O Israel: The LORD our God, the LORD is **one** AXD.*

---

[1] XTsH Strong's 2673
[2] XYTs Strong's 2434
[3] XTs Strong's 2351
[4] XTsTh Strong's 2676
[5] XTsY Strong's 2677

X – HETH – WALL

The word AXD[1] [akhad], meaning 'one' is from the root XD. The children of XD include:

XD[2] 𐤏𐤇 [khad] (unit, sharp),
AXD 𐤏𐤇𐤀 [akhad] (unite, unity, one),
XDH[3] 𐤄𐤏𐤇 [khadah] (join),
XWD[4] 𐤏𐤅𐤇 [khood] (riddle, propose),
YXD[5] 𐤏𐤇𐤉 [yakhad] (together).

There's a strong theme of joining two or more entities together.

The word AXD is not about a single entity but it's about the joining together of two or more entities.

What do the letters X and D tell us?

It's interesting that the X wall and the D door are part of one structure. We start with the wall which separates out two entities – which is the beginning state. But then we have a door which opens and gives opportunity to join the two sides.

The letter A also brings the idea of 'one', being the first letter in the alphabet. But it's the root XD which brings us the core of the meaning.

The letter D (door) talks about something reciprocal – a going back and forward between two entities. It seems they are united by what's between them. What's between them is one. Perhaps that's also what the X is talking about – it's relating to something which is not the visible entities but what's between them. It's about what's joining them.

An entity in itself has no meaning or existence. Meaning and existence comes when we look at what's between two entities – the relationship. The real existence is the single relationship between the two entities/persons.

> Genesis 2:24 For this reason a man will leave his father and mother and be united to his wife, and they will become **one** flesh.

---

[1] AXD Strong's 259
[2] XD Strong's 2299
[3] XDH Strong's 2302
[4] XWD Strong's 2330
[5] YXD Strong's 3164

So, when we talk about God being one, we are really talking about what's between the two persons within God – which is the Spirit of God – spelt RWX. Note the letter X talking about what is not immediately visible.

In the Hebrew text we see an interesting pattern. Deuteronomy 6:4 is written as: Hear Israel Yahweh Elohiim Yahweh one.

There are two occurrences of Yahweh and in between them is Elohiim. As we've seen, Yahweh means 'He exists'. So, we see an existence each side of Elohiim (Almighty God). We can certainly see a pattern where two existences join together to form one God – which is between them both. I understand the two existing ones to be Father and Son – joining together to form one God. The suffix -iim on the word Elohiim has two meanings. It can mean 'almighty' and at the same time more than one, i.e., two, three or more.

XZWN – To See What Was Hidden

*Proverbs 29:18 Where there is no **vision**, the people perish: but he that keepeth the law, happy is he.*

XZWN[1] [khazown] is from the root XZ which brings the idea of seeing what was hidden beyond the present physical. Other children include:

XZ ⊐H (vision),
XZZ[2] ⊐⊐H [khaziz] (light),
XZH[3] ᛙ⊐H [khazah] (perceive).

One child AXZ ⊐Hᛘ (grip, take hold) is harder to understand how it's derived from the root. Perhaps it has the idea of what once wasn't a reality has now become a physical reality – something you can grasp hold of.

---

[1] XZWN Strong's 2377
[2] XZZ Strong's 2385
[3] XZH Strong's 2376

The letter X speaks of something which is beyond the immediately visible. Then we go beyond that to the letter Z which talks about the physical. We are seeing something seemingly tangible beyond the immediate physical realm: the spiritual realm which is the true reality.

What does that mean? The word translated as 'perish' is from the Hebrew word spelt PR?[1] ⳬ. It has the underlying meaning of to let loose or let go. Notice how it's the opposite to AXZ 'to grip'. It's a bit like being on a ship, where you get direction by seeing a tangible destination. If you don't have that vision, you are basically cut loose and lose direction and purpose. You float around in the mist, vulnerable to any danger. The law is our direction, our teacher. The use of the English word 'law' is limited. The Hebrew word Torah (translated as 'law') is ultimately talking about God's leading. Many today don't believe in following any direction outside of their own desires, so they just do whatever suits them at the time. This will ultimately lead to shipwreck, though of course, they don't see it until it's too late. God shows us that our ultimate direction is to dwell with Him as His family for eternity. Every step in the moment of today should be aiming in that direction.

XZH – Perceive

*Daniel 4:10 These are the **visions** (XZH) I saw while lying in my bed: I looked, and there before me stood a tree in the middle of the land. Its height was enormous.*

XZH[2] [khazah] is also from the root XZ so it's talking about moving from something not seen (or spiritual) to something visible.

The letter H talks about existence and something to behold in awe.

---

[1] PR? Strong's 6544
[2] XZH Strong's 2376

So, the word XZH would seem to be saying that while the vision was only in the mind, it's something which will become a tangible reality.

This word only occurs in Daniel because Daniel was the only Biblical book written in Aramaic. All occurrences of XZH relate to a vision. There would be no point in God giving Daniel a vision if it wasn't going to become a reality. This makes XZH distinct from a regular dream which has no connection to reality. XZH is prophetic.

AXZ – To Realise Something

*Psalm 139:10 even there your hand will guide me, your right hand will **hold** (AXZ) me fast.*

AXZ[1] [akhaz] is from the root XZ.

This word is often translated as 'to take hold of', but it's not only about taking hold of something tangible, it can also mean to grasp or take hold of an idea or concept. It can refer to experiencing the tangible reality of something.

*2 Samuel 1:9 ... anguish is **come upon** (AXZ) me.*

*Psalm 48:6 Trembling **seized** (AXZ) them there, pain like that of a woman in labour.*

XZQ – Courage

*Psalm 27:14 Wait on the LORD: be of good **courage** (XZQ), and he shall strengthen thine heart: wait, I say, on the LORD.*

---

[1] AXZ Strong's 270

XZQ[1] [khazaq[2]] is likely derived from the root XZ. XZQ also means 'to seize' but adds the letter Q (sun on horizon) which brings the idea of concentration or intensity, so that XZQ also means, 'strength' – taking hold of something with intensity.

We are asked to wait – which may seem to be about something intangible, but the word XZQ tells us that though we may not see the answer right now, it will be a reality – this is our courage and strength. Waiting is all about trusting – which is beyond our own strength and ability to see immediately.

*Proverbs 3:18 She (wisdom) is a tree of life to those who embrace her; those who lay **hold** (XZQ) of her will be blessed.*

XTh – Sin

*Psalm 4:4 In your anger do not **sin**; when you are on your beds, search your hearts and be silent.*

The word XThA[3] [khatha] has the verbal meaning of 'to miss', and the abstract meaning of 'sin'. It's from the root XTh.

Another child of the root XTh includes XWTh (join, cord).

We have a target which is family dwelling with God. The definition of sin is to miss that target. We will certainly miss the target if we don't aim for it!

The target is shown to us in the letter T – the target at the end of the plough field which helps us keep a straight line as we plough the ground. The letter T is often pronounced as 'th' in modern Hebrew.

It's not so obvious to me as to how the letters X and Th bring us the meaning. Perhaps the X tells us that sin is something which is beyond the

---

[1] XZQ Strong's 2388
[2] The letter Q is pronounced like a k but with the tongue root pulled back.
[3] XThA Strong's 2398

visible – it's spiritual. Perhaps it's about hiding and being separated. Adam and Eve eating the forbidden fruit was not so much a problem with eating the fruit – it was a spiritual issue of rejecting the relationship and not trusting. The X also talks about something which is hidden from immediate sight – which is a strong characteristic of sin, right from the time of Adam and Eve hiding from God in the garden. Hiding is part of separation from God.

The letter Th (basket) perhaps also talks about sin as being something which we want to conceal. Adam and Eve attempted to hide from God after disobeying Him. Perhaps sin is something precious to us and we don't want others, including those we are in relationship with, to have free knowledge of. Sin is anti-relationship. We have two persons in our being. The spiritual person wants to preserve relationship, but the physical person is all about the physical and self. Our spiritual person may have aimed at the target because it's led by the will – which is all about direction. But our physical person is not about direction, it's about what's desirable in the here and now for me, so it causes us to miss. It's not about destiny but about reacting to the physical environment in myself and around me. It's like the boulders which deflect the farmers plough as he tries to keep the plough in a straight line.

We attempt to conceal our anti-relationship behaviour, but God can still see us. Jesus provides the only effective concealment by offering to cloth ourselves in Him. He offered Himself as the skin to cover us. He is also the house which we enter into - to become part of God's family.

The law is a target and our ultimate destination. Sin is defined as missing the target and getting off track to our destination. Under the grace which Jesus provides us, we don't do away with the target, but we do find a way to reach the target outside of our own strength. That strength outside of ourselves is relationship with God – which is also expressed through our relationship with one another.

The law continues to provide us with a guide for life – the instruction manual for living in God's universe and ultimate purpose. But in our own strength, it will become a curse and not lead us to the destination.

In these current times, as we witness the increasing departure from God's law all around us, we should not partake in the normalizing of behaviour which the law forbids. We will frequently miss the target ourselves, but we can get up again and continue towards the target if our eyes are fixed on it.

An expert in the law asked Jesus:

"'Teacher, which is the greatest commandment in the Law?'

Jesus replied:

'Love the Lord your God with all your heart and with all your soul and with all your mind.'

This is the first and greatest commandment.

And the second is like it: 'Love your neighbour as yourself.'

All the Law and the Prophets hang on these two commandments."
Matthew 22:36-40

Being strong to resist?

The whole area of sin is something I'm still trying to understand. Here's some observations that still need sorting and reworking as I understand it more.

Is resisting sin all about being strong, steadfast and willing? Not so sure about that because that doesn't necessarily lead to relationship. Like the pharisees who took great pride in keeping the law, it can all be about self. In keeping the law, it became all about comparing themselves with others.

We need a different angle on sin.

When we let Jesus cover us, it's not only about covering our bad actions but also our good actions. We don't stand before God in our own righteousness, we stand before Him in the righteousness that is by faith – that is, we trust in the covering that Jesus provides.

So, is resisting sin all about being a good person? No.

God's ultimate aim for us is that we are in a relationship of trust with Him – that means putting our precious things (good and bad) in His basket for safekeeping and concealing. He doesn't necessarily want superheroes who are strong in themselves. People say they are not sinners and are good people, but that misses the whole point when it comes to relationship with God. It's not about being 'good' and having a shiny halo. The worldly press is like a pack of wolves when it comes to pointing out people's failings – that's because they are part of that system of one-up-manship and personal merit.

Here are some factors needing attention.
1. Feed the spiritual person so that we are more able to be led by the spirit than the body.
2. Admit and be open about your weakness – own it and recognise that we are (spiritually) poor.
3. Forgive and be forgiven. This is all about letting the relationship continue. See the word NSA, meaning, 'forgive'.
4. It's all about being forgiven.

Taking the example of Adam and Eve eating the forbidden fruit… What was the real sin – eating the fruit or mistrusting God? I believe the core of it and the real issue was a mistrust of God and His word. It was a breaking of relationship. So, when we think about sin – perhaps we need to get away from the physical, visible aspect of it and get directly to the spiritual aspect – what is it doing to relationship?

It has been said that addiction is not a substance or habit disorder but a social disorder. It can't be denied that there's a physical craving, but addiction has been shown to have a very strong connection to people having a lack of trust and connection in their relationships – especially their earlier years.

Perhaps there are two angles we can look at sin from – prevention and repair.

The addiction treatment programs state that overcoming addiction is all about connection.

XY – Life, Stomach

וֹיַח

*Genesis 2:7 The LORD God formed the man from the dust of the ground and breathed into his nostrils the breath of **life**, and the man became a living being.*

What exactly is life all about? Is there more to it than just breathing?

The word XY[1] [khay], translated as 'life' first appears in the creation:

*Genesis 1:20 And God said, "Let the water teem with **living** creatures, and let birds fly above the earth across the expanse of the sky."*

*Genesis 1:30 "And to all the beasts of the earth and all the birds of the air and all the creatures that move on the ground-- everything that has the breath of **life** in it-- I give every green plant for food." And it was so.*

When God created the first man, he made the physical body first and then breathed life into him. All the creatures of the sea are described as having life, but they don't all breathe in the same manner as land creatures do. But I suppose they do have some kind of breathing.

Perhaps there is more to life than just breathing:

---

[1] XY Strong's 2416

> *Genesis 2:9 And the LORD God made all kinds of trees grow out of the ground-- trees that were pleasing to the eye and good for food. In the middle of the garden were the tree of **life XY** and the tree of the knowledge of good and evil.*

Adam and Eve were permitted to eat from any tree except the tree of the knowledge of good and evil. So, we can presume they were able to eat from the tree of life. They already had breath, so why would they need to eat from a tree of life?

> *Genesis 3:22 And the LORD God said, "The man has now become like one of us, knowing good and evil. He must not be allowed to reach out his hand and take also from the tree of life and eat, and live forever."*

By eating from the tree of life they would have eternal life.

> *Here's another angle on life: Psalm 22:26 The poor will eat and be satisfied; they who seek the LORD will praise him-- may your hearts **live** (XYH[1]) forever!*

> *Psalm 71:20 Though you have made me see troubles, many and bitter, you will restore my **life** (XYH) again; from the depths of the earth, you will again bring me up.*

The two quotes above from David's Psalms talk about a life beyond the physical body. Psalm 71:20 even seems to be prophetic of Jesus being raised from death – from under the ground.

Though the creatures of the sea and land were given life, their life isn't necessarily eternal.

The X (wall) tells how life is beyond the visible and physical – as we see in Psalm 22. The word RWX [ruakh] (spirit) also contains the letter X for that same reason. The physical meaning of RWX is wind and breath. When God breathed into Adam, it seems likely He was breathing spirit into him.

The letter Y (arm) often brings the idea of work or destining something (throwing). God breathed life or spirit into us for a reason and a destiny.

---

[1] XYH – [khayah] Strong's 2421

It seems that life is more than something you look at. A body may have all the visible parts but if it's not working it has no life. Life is also beyond the physical body we have.

The Y (arm) often talks about a destiny. Y has the value of 10 which talks about a wholeness derived from the combination of the physical and spiritual persons (5 + 5 = 10).

The idea of destiny (Y) brings us to the idea of what life is for. Is it just for the present or is the real purpose of life all about life being a means to our destiny? Life is defined by its destiny and purpose. The X talks about something which is beyond the visible – which also talks about what is beyond the visible present. Perhaps the word XY could also be translated as 'existence for a purpose'.

XYW – Beast

Y⌒⌐H

> *Daniel 7:17 'The four great **beasts** (XYW) are four kingdoms that will rise from the earth.*

The Beast or beasts are mentioned in both the prophetic books of Daniel and Revelation.

The Hebrew word translated as, 'beast' is spelt XYW[1] [khaywa] and is from the root XY.

The root has the physical meaning of 'stomach' and the abstract meaning of 'life'.

A beast is something which has been given life.

I can't see any reason why the word XYW should be translated as, 'beast' except that it's a living thing. The word, 'beast' in modern English brings a connotation of something which is huge, ominous and unfriendly. In the Biblical context, none of these features is present. And so, the translation

---

[1] XYW Strong's 2423

using the word, 'beast' is I think misleading. In the Old Testament, XYW is only used in the book of Daniel, quite likely because Daniel is the only book in the Bible to be written in Aramaic.

XYW is used in the literal context of any animal in the field and not specifically a cow, but in a symbolic sense it's used differently.

> *Daniel 7:23 He gave me this explanation: 'The fourth beast is a fourth kingdom that will appear on earth. It will be different from all the other kingdoms and will devour the whole earth, trampling it down and crushing it.'*

The beasts are four kingdoms.

> *Daniel 7:17 The first beast is like a lion with the wings of an eagle. It stood on two feet like a man and the heart of a man was given to it.*

Could this first beast be the Commonwealth? It's not actually destroying anything and is permitted to live during the millennium.

> *The second looked like a bear. It had three ribs between its teeth and was told to get up and eat its fill of flesh.*

Could this be communism, expressed in Russia and China? Russia is not part of the World Economic Forum but is a formidable force.

> *The third beast looked like a leopard. It had four wings and four heads and was given authority to rule.*

This beast didn't kill anyone. Could it be the USA – which is considered to be the most prominent power today – immediately prior to the fourth beast?

This fourth beast is the last before the Kingdom of heaven takes its place. The last beast wasn't in the likeness of any known animal. It has iron teeth and bronze claws to crush and devour its victims. It was different to all the other beasts and had ten horns. An additional horn came up among the ten and deposed three horns. 10 + 1 − 3 = 8 kingdoms. This new horn had eyes like the eyes of a man and a mouth that spoke boastfully. It spoke against the Most High and oppressed the saints. He tries to change the set times and laws. The saints will be handed over to him for a time, times and half a time. Can we presume three and a half years – the last half of the tribulation.

What could these ten kingdoms be and the three which are deposed?

I'm presuming the fourth beast to be a global government which is comprised of 10 kingdoms. Most likely the main countries of the World Economic Forum (WEF). Wikipedia states the following about the WEF,

> *"(The WEF) suggests that a globalized world should be governed by a self-selected coalition of multinational corporations, governments and civil society organisations which it expresses through initiatives like the Great Reset and the Global Redesign."* [1]

An arm of the WEF is the Young Global Leaders forum which has graduates in top government positions (including presidents and prime ministers) all around the world.[2]

I suggest to the reader that you do some of your own research in this regard. Some topics to research are the Global Redesign Initiative (GRI), Civil Society Organisations (CSO), and the Coalition for Epidemic Preparedness Innovations CEPI.

God will convene His court with a great multitude and the beast will be thrown into the blazing fire. I presume this is the start of the millennium in which Jesus will reign.

The other beasts were stripped of their authority but were allowed to live for a time (presumably during the millennium).

The book of Revelation follows on with the story of the same Beast, though we don't have the Hebrew script for it.

> *Revelation 13:5 The beast was given a mouth to utter proud words and blasphemies and to exercise his authority for forty-two months.*

---

[1] https://en.wikipedia.org/wiki/World_Economic_Forum#cite_ref-5
[2] https://en.wikipedia.org/wiki/Young_Global_Leaders

> *Revelation 13:8 All inhabitants of the earth will worship the beast-- all whose names have not been written in the book of life belonging to the Lamb that was slain from the creation of the world.*
>
> *Revelation 13:15-17 He was given power to give breath to the image of the first beast, so that it could speak and cause all who refused to worship the image to be killed.*
>
> *He also forced everyone, small and great, rich and poor, free and slave, to receive a mark on his right hand or on his forehead, so that no one could buy or sell unless he had the mark, which is the name of the beast or the number of his name.*
>
> *This calls for wisdom. If anyone has insight, let him calculate the number of the beast, for it is man's number. His number is 666.*

I understand that the Beast which requires everyone to worship itself is something which has been given life by the Serpent. It's not exactly stated, but I consider that the Beast will be something created by humanism – a physical entity such as a computer or robot. The Serpent will give it life so that it can talk. The super-computer will be built with the ruse that it represents the thoughts of all of humanity – like a super democracy. But behind the democratic ruse, it will be controlled by those who follow Humanism and the Serpent. All of humanity will be required to take the mark of the Beast which will likely be in the form of a chip implanted into the hand or on the forehead. People are already doing this in Europe and China. A likely reason given for this is that it will serve as a contact trace to track the movement of a global epidemic.

We should not shy away from conspiracy talk in our society – which is exposing hidden and harmful acts and agendas.

When conspiracy exposers are silenced and ridiculed by society and the administration, that is a dangerous society indeed – which we now have! There is currently a huge campaign in mainstream press against, 'conspiracy theories'. The campaign is to rebrand conspiracy as non-critical thinking, non-scientific, flat-earthers, anti-social, false news, harmful to the community and even worthy of a visit to the doctor!

The definition of conspiracy is a harmful plot or act which is being carried out deceitfully. It is naïve and irresponsible to say that there is no conspiracy in the modern world. Nazi Germany silenced and killed those who objected to the deceit of their administration. We should not go there again. The current world, as we well know, is full to the brim of heartless, heavy-handed, freedom-denying governments. To get away with it, they must pull the wool over people's eyes to the point where society is powerless to respond – at which point, it's no longer done in secret. We're nearing that point now. Now is not the time to stop exposing conspiracies. It is our duty to humanity!

Nazi Germany was a master in the science of propaganda. Millions of Jews were loaded onto trains. Most did not dream that those trains were leading to their death. Of course, they were not told in the mainstream press! Knowing now that those trains drove them to their death – would you rather someone state the possibility that the train ride may not be what it was advertised as - or remain silent? Those Jews never dreamt that a well-educated and 'superior' society would do such a thing – it was preposterous! Prior to going on the trains, they were, however, aware that society was being turned against them – for 'good and scientific' reasons. This is what is being done today. Nazi Germany was a master in the science of propaganda. The science of propaganda has advanced in leaps and bounds since that time.

We must learn from history. We are in very serious and dangerous times indeed. Now is not the time to be silent!

One thing which a secular person cannot grasp when trying to understand why there is a lot of conspiracy talk around nowadays – relates to Biblical prophecy. A secular person says there has to be sound physical evidence for any suggested scenario. However, a lot of non-secular people believe in Biblical prophecy, which looks beyond the immediate physical. The prophecy states that there will be an Anti-Christ who rules the world and forces everyone to take his mark in order to be able to buy and sell. God's people are commanded to come out of this system and not participate in it.

This will be a sign of the end times. This prophecy sets up a target marker which gives current events context. The dots line up. When a current event appears to be heading towards that marker, then it sounds alarm bells. There is a lot of anti-Christ talk around these days, so it's not surprising that people are watching the dots line up and connecting them.

There may well be many who don't believe in that prophesy but nevertheless are concerned for the violation of human rights and freedoms.

XLL – Pierced

∠∠H

> *Isaiah 53:5 But he was **pierced** for our transgressions, he was crushed for our iniquities; the punishment that brought us peace was upon him, and by his wounds we are healed.*

XLL[1] [khalal] is from the root XL which has the idea of leading through. Children of XL include, bore, earring, sick, disease, twist, dance, wall. It seems to include the idea that the boring may involve twisting of an awl to get through.

The X (wall) is the material, and the L (shepherd's staff) brings the idea of direction which has come through to the other side. If piercing is the physical picture, what is it telling us about the spiritual? Could it be about passing through the physical to the other side – the spiritual? It takes some twisting and struggle to get through.

The opposite spelling, LX [lakh] brings the idea of moisture, lick, filthy and tablet – perhaps with the idea that it's about a surface which isn't penetrated. Something is going to the surface and is seen on the surface.

The physical suffering (piercing) which the Messiah received for our failings, was to bring us to the other side of the physical – into the spiritual where we are accepted because of our acceptance of Him alone, not by our physical performance. We are healed in that what happens to our physical

---

[1] XLL Strong's 2490

body and mind is no longer of consequence to God. So, LX is where filth is seen on the outside – which is what happens if we don't accept the work of the Messiah to punch through to the other side.

Is it coincidence that the Arabic word for 'vinegar' is also XL? While Jesus was on the cross being pierced, the soldiers offered Jesus vinegar. This action was in direct response to Jesus' call, 'My God, my God, why have you forsaken me'. This cry was referring us to Psalm 22 which was prophetic about Jesus suffering, including being pierced.

> *Matthew 27:46-48 About the ninth hour Jesus cried out in a loud voice, "Eloi, Eloi, lama sabachthani?" - which means, "My God, my God, why have you forsaken me?"*
>
> *When some of those standing there heard this, they said, "He's calling Elijah." Immediately one of them ran and got a sponge. He filled it with wine* **vinegar**, *put it on a stick, and offered it to Jesus to drink.*

Could there be an ancient connection between 'pierce' and 'vinegar' going back to Aramaic – the common ancestor of Hebrew and Arabic?

XNN – Beauty

Psalm 41:4 I said, "O LORD, have **mercy (XNN)** *on me; heal me, for I have sinned against you."*

XNN[1] [khanan] is from the root XN. Children of this root include:
  XN[2] ᕽϟ (camp, beauty),
  XNWT[3] +Υᕽϟ (room),
  TXNH[4] Ϥᕽϟ+ (supplication),

---

[1] XNN Strong's 2603
[2] XN Strong's 2580
[3] XNWT Strong's 2588
[4] TXNH Strong's 8467

XNM[1] 〜〜H (freely),
XNN 〜〜H (compassion),
XNWN[2] 〜Y〜H [khanuun] (gracious).

The name Hannah is derived from the child XNN meaning, beauty. English doesn't have the voiceless velar fricative sound X so it was replaced with the closest equivalent H.
The X (wall) is the visible surface. The letter N (seed) brings the idea of new life and design. It's the continuation of life. Another word which is also translated as beauty (NAH) also uses the letter N.
The idea of mercy and grace is very close to the idea of forgiveness. All these ideas contain the idea of the continuation of life. The word NSA, translated as 'lift' and 'forgive' also contains the letter N and is followed by the letter S (thorn), which brings the idea of holding onto or grasping the continuation of life.

> Exodus 34:6 ..., "The LORD, the LORD God, the compassionate (RXWM[3] [rakhuwm]) and gracious (XNWN) God, slow to anger, abounding in love and faithfulness."

XSH – Refuge

屮ㅋH

> Isaiah 57:13 "When you cry out for help, let your collection of idols save you! The wind will carry all of them off, a mere breath will blow them away. But the man who makes me his **refuge** (XSH) will inherit the land and possess my holy mountain."

The word XSH[4] [khasah] is from the root XS. Other children of this root include:
XWS[5] ㅋYH [khuws] (spared – one who has been given refuge),

---

[1] XNM Strong's 2600
[2] XNWN Strong's 2587
[3] RXWM Strong's 7349 (merciful)
[4] XSA Strong's 2620
[5] XWS Strong's 2347

YXS[1] ⟨glyphs⟩ (lineage). Is lineage a kind of refuge? We turn to our tribe in times of difficulty.

The letter X (wall) likely represents the wall of the refuge – an enclosed place. The S (thorn) often speaks about holding onto something. This contrasts with being cut off and separated. A circle of thorn bushes was also used as a refuge for a camp to enclose the animals and people.

Refuge is about grasping onto God so that we don't get blown away. XSH is often translated as, 'trust' and has some of the same components as another word BThX[2] [bathakh] also often translated as, 'trust'.

XPShY – Free

⟨glyphs⟩

*Isaiah 58:6 "Is not this the kind of fasting I have chosen: to loose the chains of injustice and untie the cords of the yoke, to set the oppressed **free (XPShY)** and break every yoke?"*

The word spelt XPShY[3] [khophshi] is from the root XPSh. Other children of XPSh include:
XWPSh[4] ⟨glyphs⟩ [khuwphish] (horse),
XPShWT[5] ⟨glyphs⟩ [khaphshuut] (separate).

A horse likely expresses the idea of running free. Being separate is about not being tied to something such as a slave master or debt.

XPSh is likely derived from XP which has the meaning of cover and innocence. There is a close spiritual connection between the two. In the year of Jubilee, every debt is to be forgiven and every slave freed. God forgives us by covering over our sin – by putting it out of sight by covering it with his

---

[1] YXS Strong's 3187, 3188
[2] BThX Strong's 982
[3] XPShY Strong's 2670
[4] XWPSh Strong's 2667
[5] XPShWT Strong's 2669

hand – his Son. That is the true and ultimate freedom – to be free from debt and to be able to make our own choice.

The letter X (wall) likely brings the idea of being beyond the wall.

The letter P (mouth) brings the idea of an opening.

The letter Sh (teeth – for cutting) brings the idea of being separated.

It seems to me that in these current times when our freedoms are being challenged, we can take lessons from Adam and Eve, the Israelites escaping Egypt, and the temptation of Jesus in the desert.

In the current time, we have a choice (like Adam & Eve): to listen to God or to go the way which seems more appealing to our selfish needs. If we go along with the mainstream society and governments, we are being promised all the privileges we've come to expect. But if we reject the offers of 'security' and trust our instincts to follow God's ways, then the way ahead may seem a little uncertain – trust is involved. In the end, trust is involved both ways – to trust humanity or trust God. Only one has the better outcome.

The Israelites were slaves in Egypt. While they complied and did what they were told, they were given what they needed. But when they were released and followed God into the desert, they suddenly discovered that there was no food nor the securities they had as slaves. Everything was very uncertain. But God did come through for those who trusted. He didn't come through for those who didn't trust. They perished.

If we agree to go along with the humanist governments of today, to believe and do everything we are told, including complying with all the extensive global controls, we are being assured 'safety, normality and freedom'. But if we don't trust the government, we are told that we will not be permitted to participate in the privileges of 'normal' society. The way ahead looks very uncertain. We will be tested to trust in God instead of humanity.

Jesus was tested in the desert by the Serpent who made him a tempting offer. The Serpent said that if Jesus bowed down and submitted to the

Serpent, the Serpent would give him the rule of the earth. Jesus replied, "It is written, Worship the Lord your God and serve Him only".

So, where's the freedom? Is it with the Serpent who promises that we will be able to do anything we like on the earth? Or is it with God whom we will serve? The Serpent is making a false promise. God is not giving us any false ideas of an easy path.

We, too, are currently being offered free reign of the earth (which is really a lie) if we comply and submit to the New World Order. But we must remember what is decreed in writing – that we must serve and worship only the Lord our God.

Adam and Eve received a proposal from the Serpent that if they turned away from God's command, they would not die but would receive many pleasures. If they had trusted God's word, they would have continued to have all their needs met in abundance.

TWXRT – Beyond the Immediate

*Psalm 39:7 "But now, Lord, what do I look for? My **hope** is in you."*

TWXRT[1] [towkheret] is also written with an L instead of R – as TWXLT [tokhelet].

It's from the root XR which brings the idea of something beyond the immediately visible.

Children of the root XR include:
MXR[2] [makhar] (later),
MXRT [makharat] (tomorrow),
XRR[3] [kharah] (burn),

---

[1] TWXRT Strong's 8431
[2] MXR Strong's 4279
[3] XRR Strong's 2734

AXR 𐤏𐤇𐤀 [aakhar] (delay, after, other),
AXRYT +𐤉𐤏𐤇𐤀 [aakhariit] (end),
AXWR 𐤏𐤉𐤇𐤀 [aakhuur] (behind, back),
XWR[1] 𐤏𐤉𐤇 [khur] (white),
TWXRT +𐤏𐤇𐤉+ [tukharat] (hope).

The letter X (wall) talks about what's beyond the visible wall. The letter R (head) talks about something important.

Hope is something important beyond the immediately visible.

Another word translated as hope is TQWA[2] [tiqwa] from the root QW. But this word has a very different meaning.

> Proverbs 10:28 The **prospect** *(TWXRT) of the righteous is joy, but the* **hopes** *(TQWA) of the wicked come to nothing.*

TQWA means 'waiting' and 'cord'. It has the idea of being held back. There is a hope for something, but it comes to nothing because it's being held back – it can't go any further than the cord will let it.

---

[1] XWR Strong's 2353
[2] TQWA Strong's 8615

Th – Teth – Basket

The letter Th is the 9th letter of the alphabet. Its name Teth doesn't have any meaning, but the word spelt ThTh [theth] means, 'mud' so it could well relate to a container made with clay. Or could it be a basket used for carrying mud? Even today in Bedouin communities, a goat skin bag is first filled with a clay solution so that the clay particles fill the pores to prevent the rapid escape of liquid. Subsequently it's filled with water, which may seep gently out to be evaporated and therefore cool the liquid inside.

Another word which means, 'basket', is spelt ThNA[1] [thenaa].

The word ThA[2] [thaa] means, 'sweep' and 'broom' which likely points to the broom being made from fibre similar to what a basket was made from.

The basket is commonly used to store precious things away from children or animals. It's often tied or hooked up on a high place such as the central pole of the tent or house. The word BThX[3] [bathakh] means, cling and trust – to entrust your precious things to someone.

The word AB means, tent pole and father. Just as we place our precious things in the basket which clings to the tent pole, so also, we place our trust (for our precious things) in our Heavenly Father.

In what I call the alphabetical Psalms (Psalm 119), a section (verses 65-72) has each line starting with the sound Th. This whole portion very much expresses trust in God.

---

[1] ThN Strong's 2935
[2] ThA Strong's 2894
[3] BThX Strong's 982

ThWB – Good

ט Y ב

*Psalm 119:68 You are **good**, and what you do is good; teach me your decrees.*

ThWB[1] [thowb] is from the root ThB.

I understand good to be all about relationship. In contrast, evil is about separation.

Trust is a central building block of relationship. In the root ThB, trust and safekeeping (Th) is going to the relationship (B). Trust is the glue of relationship. What better picture to illustrate the concept of 'good'? In contrast, deceit is the tool of separation and evil.

A good idea is something which brings a good outcome. Relationship and God's family is certainly the best outcome possible. This is God's central purpose for humanity.

There's an interesting link to the Arabic word 'thowb' which is a full length (usually white) gown worn by men. The white covering over a person brings a strong connotation of a covering of purity and goodness over a person. The person appears good. Perhaps there is a connection between the Arabic word 'thowb' and the proto-semitic word of the same spelling – with the original meaning of 'good'.

Jesus is our 'thowb' – our covering of righteousness – for those who choose to wear it. The catch is that it covers everything – our bad and our good deeds. We don't come before God in our own merit but on the merit of the purity which Jesus, our thowb, brings.

---

[1] ThWB Strong's 2896

ThHR – Cleanse

𐤈𐤅𐤇

*Psalms 51:2 Wash away all my iniquity and **cleanse** (ThHR) me from my sin (XThA)*

The word ThHR[1] [thaher] meaning 'cleanse' is from the root ThR. Other children of ThR include:

MThRA[2] [math-raa] (target, prison),
ThRY[3] [tarii] (fresh),
AThR[4] [aathar] (shut),
ThWR[5] [thowr] (range, row),
ThYR [thiir] (village).

It's hard to see a common theme in the children. A common theme shared between ThHR (cleanse) and XThA (sin) is the idea of a **target**. XThA talks about missing a target – the target being relationship and family with the Father.

The children of ThR seem to talk about entrusting (Th) items to an area of containment (Th) for an important purpose (R). To keep things within a parameter. A target is a parameter to aim for.

What does a target or parameter have to do with cleansing? Or is cleansing a correct translation of ThHR? To get a better idea of the meaning of ThHR, let's look at some more context of use.

> *Leviticus 13:17 The priest is to examine him, and if the sores have turned white, the priest shall pronounce the infected person clean; then he will be **clean**.*

---

[1] ThHR Strong's 2891
[2] MThRA Strong's 4307
[3] ThRY Strong's ???
[4] AThR Strong's 6113
[5] ThWR Strong's 2905

*Leviticus 13:58 The clothing, or the woven or knitted material, or any leather article that has been washed and is rid of the mildew, must be washed again, and it will be **clean**.*

*Leviticus 14:14 The priest is to take some of the blood of the guilt offering and put it on the lobe of the right ear of the one to be **cleansed**.*

The contexts seem to talk about being within an acceptable parameter – such as complying with the law. It's often used in the context of removing an impurity.

The religious people of Jesus time were obsessed with physical cleanliness. But David in Psalm 51:2 was talking more about a spiritual cleanliness – which can be attained, as David stated, by asking God to cleanse. He does this by covering over our failings with His life blood. He effectively paid the bride price to bring us into His Father's house. We enter into His family not on our own merits but because we accept the marriage proposal of the Son.

So ThHR (being within the parameter) is very much the opposite to sin – which is missing the mark – being way off the parameter.

ThWT – Fasting

*Daniel 6:18 Then the king returned to his palace and spent the night **without eating** (ThWT) and without any entertainment being brought to him. And he could not sleep.*

Fasting ThWT[1] [thawt] was and is used to put aside the physical in order to engage with the spiritual.

The letter Th talks about keeping something precious. We keep our physical vulnerability to ourselves. But we're moving away from that towards the destination (T) which is our ultimate spiritual destiny. We leave

---

[1] ThWT Strong's 2908

our focus of holding onto our precious physical vulnerability and self, and instead, set our focus on our ultimate destination – which is being in relationship with God in His family.

This word is only used once in the Bible, largely because it's Aramaic which is used only in the book of Daniel – because Daniel was living in Assyria where Aramaic was spoken.

Elsewhere, the word translated as, 'fasting' is from the word spelt TsWM[1] [tsowm] from the root TsM.

> *Isaiah 58:5 Is this the kind of **fast** (TsWM) I have chosen, only a day for a man to humble himself? Is it only for bowing one's head like a reed and for lying on sackcloth and ashes? Is that what you call a **fast**, a day acceptable to the LORD?*

Other children of TSM include:
TsMH[2] ᛋ [tsamah] (veil),
TsMA[3] ᛋ [Tsamaa] (thirst),
TsYMAWN[4] ᛋ [tsimmawn] (dry land).

The letter Ts was written with a symbol of a man lying down. Perhaps this refers to the humility and vulnerability of fasting.

The letter M (water), has the numerical value of 40 which talks about a testing which fasting is very much about. Jesus fasted in the desert for 40 days.

The important thing to be aware of when fasting, is that it serves to help us put aside the physical so that we can enter into the spiritual. In many cases, when fasting, we don't cross over and it remains a physical feat of achievement.

Isaiah 58:6-11 continues on to say:

---

[1] TsWM Strong's 6684
[2] TsMH Strong's 6777
[3] TsMA Strong's 6770
[4] TsMAWN Strong's 6774

*"Is not this the **kind** of fasting I have chosen: to loose the chains of injustice and untie the cords of the yoke, to set the oppressed free and break every yoke?*

Is it not to share your food with the hungry and to provide the poor wanderer with shelter-- when you see the naked, to clothe him, and not to turn away from your own flesh and blood?

Then your light will break forth like the dawn, and your healing will quickly appear; then your righteousness will go before you, and the glory of the LORD will be your rear guard.

Then you will call, and the LORD will answer; you will cry for help, and he will say: Here am I. "If you do away with the yoke of oppression, with the pointing finger and malicious talk, and if you spend yourselves in behalf of the hungry and satisfy the needs of the oppressed, then your light will rise in the darkness, and your night will become like the noonday.

The LORD will guide you always; he will satisfy your needs in a sun-scorched land and will strengthen your frame. You will be like a well-watered garden, like a spring whose waters never fail.

Y – Yud – Throwing Hand

The word spelt YD[1] [yud] means 'hand' (noun), 'throw' (verb) and 'destiny' (abstract). It's meaning appears to relate to the whole arm. The letter K is similar, meaning 'palm' and 'press' – relating more to the hand.

The letter Y is the 10th letter in the alphabet which is recognized as signifying the completion of God. The letter 10 often represents the joining together of the physical and the spiritual – the divine Father joining with the physical Son. The Ten commandments[2] are comprised of two sets of five. The first four relate directly to our relationship with Father God and the fifth with our human father and mother – though it could ultimately also relate to the relationship with our Heavenly Father.

The second 5 relate to our relationship with humanity.

In the Tabernacle, there are 5 curtains on one side and 5 on the other[3]. When they are joined together in the middle with pegs, they are one in purpose. It's significant that the word AXD, translated as 'one', means to join two together. The value of 1 has a close relationship with the value of 10. The number ten tells us about a joining (one) with divinity (ten) acting on it.

The letter Y is the first letter of God's name YHWH so is thought to represent God.

The letter Y is used as a prefix on verbs to express the idea of 'he will' (the intentional act of a third person singular). The letter Y brings the idea of destining something – setting it on course as an intention. How does Y bring the idea of a third person singular? Perhaps because it talks about someone who is not necessarily immediately visible in the same room. It's

---

[1] YD Strong's 3027
[2] Bible, Exodus 20
[3] Bible, Exodus 26

strongly associated with the name of God. We recognise his existence, but he's not necessarily associated with being visibly present in front of us.

YDA – Praise, Thanks

*Daniel 6:10 Now when Daniel learned that the decree had been published, he went home to his upstairs room where the windows opened toward Jerusalem. Three times a day he got down on his knees and prayed, giving **thanks** (**YDA**) to his God, just as he had done before.*

This word YDA[1] [yidaa] is Aramaic so is found only in Daniel. The physical meaning is 'throw'. It's from the root YD, meaning 'hand'.

It seems that in the context of YD, the Y (hand) is either receiving something – and therefore giving thanks in response, or it is offering something – giving thanks.

Another possibility is that Y talks about destining something. Could the act of giving thanks actually be an act of keeping us on track towards our ultimate destiny. It's affirming God's guiding hand in our lives.

The letter D brings the idea of humility – which comes from the idea of the tent door hanging passively to be moved by whoever passes through. A child of YD – TWDH[2] [tawdah] - means 'thanks' and 'confession' which very much involves humility – to reveal and put aside the vulnerable physical self-pride. Daniel's act of praying on his knees is a physical expression of this word. It's an expression of worship.

---

[1] YDA Strong's 3029
[2] TWDH Strong's 8426

Y – YUD – THROWING HAND

YHWH - Yahweh

ﬡﭏﬡי

*Genesis 15:2 But Abram said, "Lord (ADNY) **GOD (YHWH)**, what can you give me since I remain childless and the one who will inherit my estate is Eliezer of Damascus?"*

The first time YHWH[1] (Yahweh) is used by a human in the Bible is in Genesis 15:2, although in Genesis 2:4, it is the LORD God (Yahweh Elohiim) who creates the heavens and the earth. YHWH is often translated as GOD (4x) or LORD (6510x). But these English words don't tell us much about its meaning. The origin of the meaning of the English word 'God' is murky.

YHWH can be read as a word; The core word being HWH – which means, 'to exist' or otherwise translated 'I am' – the name by which God made himself known to Moses. A simple reading of any Semitic language has the letter Y at the front meaning, 'he is doing' – so Y-HWH would mean 'He exists'. The Y in this function also brings the idea of the verb being continuous in time – past, present and future.

The Y (arm) is commonly associated with the idea of throwing – which relates to the spiritual idea of destiny. Throwing is destining something to a target. Teaching is about destining a person – helping them to reach a learning outcome or destination.

The word YHWH paints a picture of two persons connected together – one divine and one human. The letter H was written with the symbol of a person. The first H (person) is paired with the letter Y – YH. This talks about the divine person. The second H is paired with the letter W – which has the value of 6 – representing humanity – created on the 6th day – the completion of God's creation. WH talks about the human person.

Also, in YHWH, the W sits between the two H letters – joining the two together. The letter W was written with the symbol of a tent peg and has the meaning of connecting.

---

[1] YHWH Strong's 3069

We can combine the two key meanings of Y (to exist and destine) together to say that YHWH (God) is sovereign – He exists on His own merit and makes and determines His own identity. This is in keeping with the word AL also translated as, 'God' which means, 'to guide'. Sovereignty has the idea of having control of destiny – to guide one's destiny and existence.

How does the idea of sovereignty apply to humans? It is important that each person can choose their own destiny. Without the ability to choose our own destiny and identity, we lose our humanity. But we don't have complete power to determine what happens to us.

If we put our destiny in God's hands then our destiny is assured, no matter what happens to us on this earth.

Other people and governments frequently barge in on our sovereignty and try to control us, but our ultimate destiny for eternity is assured when we put our trust in God.

The Serpent wants to remove us from our designed destiny through deceit (debt) – spelt NShA [1] [nashaa]. The letter N (seed) represents the design for our destiny. The letter Sh (teeth) talks about cutting off that destiny.

In contrast, God does everything to allow us to choose our own destiny. He set in place a way by which we can be set free of our debt. Let's look at debt from a different angle. It's not only about owing something to someone. Debt takes away our freedom to do whatever we like with our lives. It removes our sovereignty. This is the opposite to what the Serpent promised us. He told Adam and Eve that if they ate from the forbidden tree that they would become like God[2] – to not be bound by the rules of anyone – including the rule to not eat from the tree.

Humanism, which is now prevalent in our society, education and government system, aims to claim humanity's autonomy from God – to not be accountable to any rule beyond self. We can be what we choose to be including changing our God-given gender.

---

[1] NShA Strong's 5377
[2] Bible, Genesis 3:5

Y – YUD – THROWING HAND

Actually, God never said anything about becoming like God[1].

What many think of as freedom is, in fact, separation from God and a denial of what gives us meaning – relationship.

In a physical sense, God put in place the year of Jubilee where every fifty years every slave should be set free, and every debt forgiven. In a spiritual sense, He put in place the means by which our destiny could be assured when we trust in Him. Our destiny in Him is to be part of His eternal family – which requires us to enter His family by putting our trust in the Father.

The gold standard in the Bible is God's family – not individual independence. But certainly, we are not to be controlled as slaves in debt.

There doesn't appear to be any real adequate English translation of YHWH, so we can either use a term like Sovereign Lord, God – or we could use the name which He instructed us to call Him by, YHWH (Yahweh).

YWNH – Jonah

*Luke 11:29 As the crowds increased, Jesus said, "This is a wicked generation. It asks for a miraculous sign, but none will be given it except the sign of **Jonah**."*

The story of Jonah (YWNH[2] [yownah]) has some similarities to the story of Jesus. Jonah was thrown off the ship so that the whole ship could be saved – like Jesus was crucified to save many. After being thrown off the ship, Jonah was put into the belly of the large fish for 3 days and nights. This is a similarity which Jesus brought our attention to regarding His own time in the grave – the sign of Jonah.

The name Jonah is spelt in Hebrew as YWNH. It means 'dove'. It's from the root YN.

---

[1] Bible, Genesis 2:17
[2] YWNH Strong's 3124

The letters Y and N certainly appear prophetic of the life of Jonah.

The letter Y talks about destining something.

The letter N talks about the continuation of life and forgiveness.

Jonah was destined to bring forgiveness to the city of Nineveh. He initially fought that destiny, but God turned him around and gave him a second opportunity.

It's interesting that Jonah had experienced the trial by sea and water just as Noah had.

> *Genesis 8:8 Then he (Noah) sent out a **dove (YWNH)** to see if the water had receded from the surface of the ground.*

How does the idea of 'dove' connect with the letters YN? The first mention of a dove in the Bible is in relation to the dove which Noah sent out (Y – throw, destine) to see if there was any land. When the dove returned with a branch in its beak, that was indeed a clear sign that life was returning to the earth (N – continuation of life).

While I was living in Jordan, I was flatting with some Iraqi Christians who were refugees from the Gulf War across the border in Iraq. One of them, an elderly woman, named Ukh (sister) Shmoony was from the city of Nineveh where there is now a very strong community of Christians. Their faith, devotion and quality of character made me look like a baby. The word 'Shmoony' in Hebrew means, 'eight'[1]. I understand this number to be talking about leaving the physical and crossing over into the spiritual. This woman and many from her country had certainly done that. The root of her name Sh M N even talks about her pilgrimage:

The letter Sh (teeth) talks about being cut off. She had been cut off and separated from her physical homeland.

The letter M (ocean) talks about then going into an unknown land where they needed to trust God.

---

[1] Strong's 8083 [shem-o-neh]

The letter N (sprouting seed) talks about how they then found continuation of life in their new land, but this time in a more spiritual sense.

The name Noah is spelt NX[1] [no-akh] and is from the word NWX meaning, 'rest'.

> *Genesis 5:29 He (Noah's father) named him **Noah** (NX) and said, "He will **comfort (NXM)** us in the labour and painful toil of our hands caused by the ground the LORD has cursed."*

How did Noah comfort the people in their labour and painful toil on the ground? Most people were insulting Noah while he was building a huge boat. I guess when the floods came that certainly gave the people and land a rest.

The Hebrew word translated as; 'comfort' is NXM[2] [nakham]. This same word can also be translated as, 'regret', grieved or sorrow. In relation to humanity at that time, we read:

> *Genesis 6:6 The LORD was **grieved (NXM)** that he had made man on the earth, and his heart was filled with pain.*

The word translated as, 'grieved' is also from the same word NXM.

Perhaps the 'rest' spoken about refers to God giving humanity a rest from its evil – by removing the evil for a time and bringing a fresh start. Surely Noah grieved (NXM) for the people in their painful toil and evil. Certainly nothing he did appeared to comfort the people! But the flood was a comfort or rest for humanity from the evil.

---

[1] NX Strong's 146
[2] NXM Strong's 5162

YM – Day

> *Genesis 4:3 In the course of **time (YWM)** Cain brought some of the fruits of the soil as an offering to the LORD.*

The word YWM[1] [yawm] is from the root YM. Children of YM include:
YM[2] (sea),
YMM [3] (spring),
AYM[4] [ay-maw] (terror),
YWM [yom] (day).

It's not so easy seeing the underlying meaning shared between these children. Perhaps it's the progression, flowing forth (Y – destine, throw) of an unknown (M unknown).

The word, YWM can also mean a period of time – obviously longer than the time the sun shines on the earth during one turn of the earth.

> *Genesis 5:4 And the **days** of Adam after he had begotten Seth, were eight hundred years.*

One way to view YWM is as a period of testing or teaching. As we see in the word YR, the Y talks about destining something (throwing an object or teaching someone). The letter M talks about a time of testing. It seems to me that time is of particular value to humanity. Our life on earth is certainly our time of testing to make us ready for eternity – to be in God's family or not. Perhaps this is the central purpose of time.

---

[1] YWM Strong's 3117
[2] YM Strong's 3220
[3] YMM Strong's 3222
[4] AYM Strong's 367

Y – YUD – THROWING HAND

TWRH – Teach, Torah

*Psalm 1:2 But his delight is in the **law (TWRH)** of the LORD, and on his law he meditates day and night.*

The word TWRH[1] [torah] is from the root YR. Children of YR include:
YAR[2] [yaar] (river),
YRA[3] [yiraa] (fear),
YRH[4] [yirah] (throw, rain, teach),
YWRH[5] [yowreh] (first rain),
TWRH (teaching – Torah).

The Y (arm) brings the idea of throwing something. The R (head) talks about something important. So combined, it's about throwing towards something important – the target – destining. Both throwing and teaching have the underlying idea of destining something. When you throw something, you hold an object for a time moving towards a target and then release that object to continue alone towards that target. Teaching is similar – we walk with someone guiding them towards a target and then at some point we release them to move alone towards that target.

A significant child of the root YR is YRWShLM – Jerusalem [yerushalom].

---

[1] TWRH Strong's 8451
[2] YAR Strong's 2975
[3] YRA Strong's 3374
[4] YRH Strong's 3384
[5] YWRH Strong's 3138

YRWShLM – Jerusalem

> *Isaiah 2:3 Many peoples will come and say, "Come, let us go up to the mountain of the LORD, to the house of the God of Jacob. He will **teach (YRH)** us his ways, so that we may walk in his paths." The law will go out from Zion, the word of the LORD from **Jerusalem (YRWShLM)***

The word Jerusalem [yerushalom] is two words – spelt YRW and ShLM. Together this means, 'betrothed'. Most people will not have heard of this interpretation. Judaism gives Jerusalem the meaning of 'City of Peace' and from my experience in talking to Jewish people, they do not welcome the interpretation of 'betrothed' – most likely because they don't recognize the importance of Jesus the groom. Here's how I arrive at that meaning:

The word YRW is from the root YR meaning, 'to destine'.

The word ShLM means, 'completion'. So together we get the meaning of destined for completion.

The word meaning, 'bride' is spelt KLLH which is from the root KL which also means completion. In the book of Revelation, Jerusalem is shown to come down as a bride. Which is not in the writings of Judaism.

> *Revelation 21:2 I saw the Holy City, the new **Jerusalem**, coming down out of heaven from God, prepared as a bride beautifully dressed for her husband.*

The wedding feast and the final entry of the bride into the house of the groom is not yet. But until then, God's people are betrothed. If the bride is one who has been made complete, then the one who is betrothed is one who is destined for completion.

Who is the bride – God's people – the city of God?

> *Revelation 21:12-14 It (the city Jerusalem) had a great, high wall with twelve gates, and with twelve angels at the gates. On the gates were written the names of **the twelve tribes of Israel**. There*

were three gates on the east, three on the north, three on the south and three on the west. The wall of the city had twelve foundations, and on them were the names of **the twelve apostles of the Lamb.**

God's physical family, the twelve tribes of Israel have their names written on the gates. God's spiritual family represented by the 12 close friends of Jesus, are the spiritual family who have their names written on the twelve foundations. We should note that when building a city wall, the foundations are built first and the gates are the last to be added. Does this reverse the idea that the physical family of Israel came first? Not really, because the spiritual aspect of God's people has always been there. There are plenty of people in the biological family of Israel who have turned away from God. Only those who accept the groom, Jesus, will be His bride. As Jesus said:

John 14:6 "I am the way and the truth and the life. No one comes to the Father except through me."

Perhaps the fact that Israel is the gates of the city refers to many from Israel recognising Jesus as the Messiah at a late stage in history – in the end times. God's bride (Jerusalem/God's people) will be complete when the people of Israel accept the groom (Messiah).

K – Kaph – Palm of Hand

The letter K is named Kaph, spelt KP which has the meaning of the palm of a hand and the palm leaf. By far the most common translation is as 'hand'.

The letter K has the numerical value of 20 and is the 11th letter in the alphabet. K and L are at each side of the centre line of the alphabet.

Other translations are an extension of the hand concept:

Something which holds, such as the socket of Jacob's hip (Genesis 22:35).

An implement which has a cup-like design such as a spoon or bowl. (Exodus 25:29).

Children of the root KP include:
KP[1] [kaf] (hand),
KPP[2] [kafaf] (to bow),
AKP[3] [ekef] (press, pressure),
KPH[4] [kafah] (tame).

We can expect to see one of these concepts present in words using the letter K.

We can imagine how the letters K and P bring the idea of holding or encircling an object. The K (hand) has to do with holding. The letter P (mouth) is an encircling and enclosing part of the body.

The letter K is used as a preposition bringing the meaning of 'as' and 'like'. Could this connect to the K being at the centre of the alphabet, to one side of the centre line which functions as a line of reflection. The K side of the line is like (a reflection of) the L side of the line. Mankind was built in the

---

[1] KP Strong's 3709
[2] KPP Strong's 3721
[3] AKP Strong's 404, 405
[4] KPH Strong's 3711

likeness of God, and we see mankind in the far end of the K side – as Adam. On the L side of the line is the source of the likeness – God.

Could it be that at one time, two hands were put up side by side as a reflection to communicate that something is the same.

An example of this meaning can also be seen in Arabic, for example the word 'kitha', meaning, 'like this'.

The letter K is used at the end of a noun to express 'your' (second person, singular, masculine possessive). Could this be indicating to us that the letter K (hand) is about an outstretched hand, reaching out to another – in a way similar to the palm front stretched out beyond the main trunk?

KL – Completion

Children of the root KL include:
KLH[1] 𐤊𐤋𐤄 [kalah] (completion),
KLY[2] 𐤊𐤋𐤉 [kal-ii] (vessel),
KLYH[3] 𐤊𐤋𐤉𐤄 [kaliyah] (kidney),
TKLT[4] 𐤕𐤊𐤋𐤕 [takalit] (blue or violet),
TKLYT[5] 𐤕𐤊𐤋𐤉𐤕 [takaliit] (boundary),
KLYWN[6] 𐤊𐤋𐤉𐤅𐤍 [kil-law-yone] (failure),
KLLH[7] 𐤊𐤋𐤋𐤄 [kal-lah] (bride),
AKL[8] 𐤀𐤊𐤋 [aw-kal] (eat),

---

[1] KLH Strong's 3617
[2] KLY Strong's 3627
[3] KLYH Strong's 3629
[4] TKLT Strong's 8504
[5] TKLYT Strong's ??
[6] KLYWN Strong's 3631
[7] KLLH Strong's 3618
[8] AKL Strong's 398

AKLH¹ 𐤔𐤋𐤊𐤀 [aaklah] (food),
KLA² 𐤀𐤋𐤊 [ka-laa] (restrain, prison),
MKLAH³ 𐤄𐤀𐤋𐤊𐤌 [mukalaah] (fold),
HKL⁴ 𐤋𐤊𐤄 [hakal] (house, temple),
KHL⁵ 𐤋𐤄𐤊 [kahal] (able),
KWL⁶ 𐤋𐤅𐤊 [kool] (sustain, all),
YKL⁷ 𐤋𐤊𐤉 [ya-kal] (able),
KYL⁸ 𐤋𐤉𐤊 [Kiil] (villain).

KL appears to bring the idea of a containing boundary which marks the full extent of something. The K (palm of hand) likely brings the idea of a containment as in a cupped hand. The constraint is like a boundary which marks the completion of what it contains.

The letter L (shepherd's staff) brings the idea of leading, direction and purpose. A boundary is a kind of leading tool – the fold for the sheep.

So together, perhaps K and L are talking about the completion of a purpose. Certainly, the word KLLH (bride) is the completion and full extent of a purpose.

KL represents the joining together (completion) of the human and divine because it's at the exact centre of the alphabet where they join in the middle. The human is at the start of the alphabet with the letter A, and the divine is at the end with the letter T. The two are complete when they join together in the middle.

The letter values K (20) and L (30) join together to make 50 – which is the product of 10 (divinity) acting on a person (5).

Could the year 2030 also be a point of completion – when the groom comes to take his bride? When the New Jerusalem is placed on earth?

---

¹ AKLH Strong's 402
² KLW Strong's 3607
³ MKLAH Strong's 4356
⁴ HKL Strong's 1964, 1965
⁵ KHL Strong's 2428
⁶ KWL Strong's 3557
⁷ YKL Strong's 3201
⁸ ??

The letters K and L straddle the exact centre of the alphabet – the centre line is between the two letters. The root KL means, 'completion'.

The letters K and L are also the 11th and 12th letters of the alphabet. This rings of the 11th and 12th sons of Israel – who became the completion of his physical family'.

We're still awaiting the completion of God's spiritual family.

Romans 11:25… Israel has experienced a hardening in part until the **full number of the Gentiles** *has come in.*

TKLT – Blue, Violet

Exodus 26:31 "Make a curtain of **blue (TKLT)***, purple and scarlet yarn and finely twisted linen, with cherubim worked into it by a skilled craftsman."*

The word TKLT[1] [tekeleth] is derived from the root KL and I understand it to mean 'violet', though many will be adamant it means 'blue' – the national colour of Israel.

Rabbis have recently done research to identify the true colour of TKLT. They found DNA evidence from ancient garments which indicate that the dye used to produce the colour came from a sea snail known as Murex. It was found that used fresh, the colour would be violet, but if faded in the sun, it would become a lighter shade closer to sky blue. So, it seems to me the study has some grey area, so to speak. The dye was used throughout the Mediterranean and took so many snails to produce a small amount, that it was more valuable than gold. It was reserved for royalty.

The colour violet is at the far extent of the colour spectrum – at its completion. This relates to the last letter of the alphabet - T, which marks the completion. The letter T talks about the completion of the human story.

---

[1] TKLT Strong's 8504

Note the use and position of the letter T in the word TKLT. T is at both extremities.

Note also that the most common way for people to see the colour spectrum is in the rainbow. The rainbow has the colour violet on the inside of the arch. So, no matter what side you read the colours, you will always arrive at the violet last.

The letters KL mark the centre of the alphabet. So, when we look at the rainbow from the centre, the first colour we come to is violet on either side. So too the word TKLT has the letter T on both sides of it.

Judaism usually interprets the word TKLT as blue – like the colour of the sky – as shown on their national flag. But I believe it must relate to violet because this colour agrees with the root of the word KL – which talks about being at the boundary of completion.

Another word SPYR (sapphire) is closer to the blue of the sky and is associated with the throne of God which is made of sapphire, clear as the sky.

But then it all depends on how many divisions you divide the colour spectrum into. In theory, there are limitless divisions you can make. We commonly divide the rainbow into 7 colours. But you could just as easily justify dividing it into three, such as the primary colours of light – red, green and blue. Or the primary colours of art – red, yellow and blue. In which case, the colour blue would be part of the same division as violet.

I see that there are three equal divisions in the alphabet with 7 letters in each. These three mark the three eras of the human story – 4000 years of physical law, 2000 years led by the spirit and 1000 years of direct rule by Jesus on the throne. That gives us a total of 21 letters. The 22nd letter T marks the start of a new journey of humanity beyond the earth that we know, into eternity. In our current physical body, we can't see beyond the colour violet, but we know theoretically, that there is an infinite range of colour beyond violet, just as there is a life beyond what we can physically see on this earth.

AKN – Sure

*Psalm 66:19 but God has **surely (AKN)** listened and heard my voice in prayer.*

*Isaiah 53:4 **Surely** he took up our infirmities and carried our sorrows, yet we considered him stricken by God, smitten by him, and afflicted.*

The word spelt AKN[1] [aken] means to be sure of something. It's from the root KN.

The letter K seems to bring the idea of a firm, sure and taming hand.

The letter N (sprouting seed) brings the idea of knowledge. The seed contains the genetic design of the plant.

So combined we have the idea of knowing something for sure – a truth to build our lives on.

The root KN includes the children:
MKWNH[2] [mekonah] (base),
AKN (surely),
KHN[3] [kohen] (adorn, priest),
KNH[4] [kanah] (flatter),
KWN[5] [koon] (firm),
MKWN[6] [makon] (foundation, dwelling)

AKN brings the idea of something which we can rely on and know to be truth. The uses of AKN in the Bible relate to the author stating something

---

[1] AKN Strong's 403
[2] MKWNH Strong's 4350
[3] KHN Strong's 3548
[4] KNH Strong's 3655
[5] KWN Strong's 3559
[6] MKWN Strong's 4349

which he considers must be a truth. It's not like someone seeing a loaf of bread in his hands and saying, 'Surely this is a loaf of bread!' He would have no need to affirm what he is holding.

How do we **know** with certainty who's telling the truth? For example, one of our children was talking about the gods of Māori culture and the conversation came around to the question of which god or gods do we believe. Gods (those whom we follow and give our lives to) are all around us. Is our god science or the government? In the current times, there's a lot of mud-slinging about misinformation and fake news. What is true in today's world? Who do we believe? Who do we place at the helm of our lives?

Here's some elements to consider in our choice of where to put the controls and sure foundations of our life.

1. What is the character of the person or organisation? What direction are they heading in? Personally, I believe that truth is something which leads to our ultimate destination – to build God's eternal family. If it doesn't, then it's not a solid foundation for our lives.
2. Does it have cohesion, consistency and integrity? This is where an ultimate destination is useful.
3. Do you take your direction from the crowd, social media or mainstream media, or do you take the time to examine things for yourself? Truth isn't defined by the majority. The majority can be easily swayed by charismatic leaders. We should not worship the god of democratic government.
Many scientists will claim peer review as a test of truth and reliability. But peers can be chosen according to your leaning and institution. A university which promotes the theory of evolution will naturally be full of peers with the same view.
4. Do they claim to have science on their side? Those who claim to oppose fake news say that the other side is not scientific and is not based on logical thinking. Any side can make this claim, but I think that those who think that science is impartial are naive. Actually, those that do claim scientific and factual backing are often using it

to whitewash their story. They will claim that science is not compatible with religion and that science is the measure of truth. They can easily, deliberately omit or manipulate facts to suit their story. To claim that others don't think logically is arrogant. There was a time when scientific study was done by those who had time on their hands because they had family money. But now scientific study is done mainly by those who are paid to do so. And those who give the funds get to choose the direction of the research. Those corporations who have the money, can choose how they present the scientific findings to the public – which to reveal and which to retain.

5. Do they claim to be the *only* source of truth? This is an arrogant claim and is what cult leaders do and those who want to take control. A good test is to ask: Do I feel afraid to speak out or that I will be cancelled? This in itself is not a test of truth because you could be afraid to talk about cannibalism, for example, in public. Though many evils are now being normalised in public domains. Truth is becoming increasingly considered to be anti-social.

6. Do they have the mass media at their disposal? Now, just because someone controls the mass media doesn't automatically make them false, but control of the mass media does suggest a monopoly and a one-sided presentation of a story to the bulk of the population. People tend to follow the crowd, and so the one who controls mass media, has the power to influence the majority. As we've seen in history, it's very dangerous for leaders to have control of the mass media. There's a lot of truth in the saying, "Power corrupts, and absolute power corrupts absolutely."

7. Do they present a one-sided story by censoring anything which doesn't support their view? This in itself isn't an indicator of truth because people on both sides will favour their own view, but when a media source, which claims to be impartial, practices censoring, then that's a strong indicator that it's not allowing the audience to decide for themselves – which is deliberate control. They may claim that censoring is to protect the public from harm, but that excuse is

an age-old one and is really all about control. It's about the few making decisions for the masses.
8. Will telling their story bring them significant wealth and power, or will it cost them? Financial and power gain is a significant bender of truth. People naturally have a tendency towards self-gain and others are second in their mind. In contrast, those who stand up for what they believe, for the purpose of informing others, will do so without personal gain. There is a greater chance of them telling the truth if they have nothing to gain. Having said that, there are plenty of people on both sides of the story who will gain financially just by getting internet popularity, but not to the scale of large corporations and governments. Exploitation is alive and well in global trade and global trade is the major influencer of political leaders.
9. Look at history. Has anything like this happened before? Probably not exactly, but there are lessons to be learnt from similar patterns.
10. Do your homework and look at both sides. There's a lot of deception and fake news out there, but the more widely you look, the better the picture you will get. It's like picking blackberries, the more angles you look at the bush from, the more berries you will find.
11. Don't stay in the comfort zone for the sake of staying in the comfort zone. Don't take the easy path just because it appears easy. Just because something is easy doesn't mean that it will lead you to a good place.
12. Don't think that because other people have more experience than you that they are right. This is a trap especially for younger persons who naturally have less experience of the world. They will have a greater tendency to follow those they perceive to have more experience than themselves.
13. Are you too trusting? Trust can be a good thing if you have a good relationship with the person. Trust is the building block of good relationships. But we need to be careful of who we trust.
14. Try to follow where the story will eventually take you. Will the story, as a whole, take you to a good destination? Is the tail wagging the

dog? The tail may be taking the limelight, but what is the rest of the dog doing?

15. Is there a wolf in sheep's clothing? Are there some seemingly noble causes which may be concealing something else? It only takes a gram of poison in a cup of sugar to kill someone.
16. Is fear a deciding factor in our decision? Fear is a major tool of control. People should take great care of their freedom and so should always avoid control for any reason. There is, however, an important place for cooperation and working together.
17. Follow your heart or instincts. Instinct is formed by the sum total of your experiences. I also believe that we are born with some natural instinct which has been handed down from our ancestors. We can see that many creatures have innate or instinctive knowledge for survival which is not all learnt. I think God has also created humans with instinctive knowledge in their genes which aid in their journey towards God's ultimate purpose for them.

KHN – Priest

*Genesis 14: 18. And Melchizedek king of Salem brought forth bread and wine: and he was the **priest (KHN)** of the most high God. And he blessed him, and said, Blessed be Abram of the most high God, possessor of heaven and earth: And blessed be the most high God, which hath delivered thine enemies into thy hand. And he gave him tithes of all.*

The word spelt KHN[1] [kohen] is from the root KN. We often hear KHN pronounced as the Jewish family name 'Cohen' – Leonard Cohen for example.

What do the letters KN tell us about what a priest is and how does a priest link to the idea of a foundation or something which is true? The root KN

---
[1] KHN Strong's 3548

talks about a firm place. Does the priest provide a firm place in society or is he leading people to a firm place?

I always had the idea that a priest represented the people to God, and a king represented God to the people. Both king (MLK) [melek] and priest (KHN) use the letter K. Could it be that the king is bringing a firm taming hand to the people? And the priest is bringing surety and knowledge of God to the people?

In the Old Testament, the priest was someone who stood before God on behalf of the people. The people couldn't enter into the inner sanctuary. Now Jesus fulfils the role of standing before God on behalf of the people. At His death on the cross, the inner curtain separating the people from the sanctuary was torn in two.

> *Matthew 27:50,51 And when Jesus had cried out again in a loud voice, he gave up his spirit. At that moment the curtain of the temple was torn in two from top to bottom. The earth shook and the rocks split.*

Could it be that KN talks about the priest covering (K) the people and bringing them to forgiveness (N) – prophetic of Jesus?

KBR – Multiply

*Job 35:16 So Job opens his mouth with empty talk; without knowledge he **multiplies** (KBR) words.*

The word KBR[1] [kabar] appears only once in the Bible, but I include this word to illustrate how number values are sometimes used in the meaning of a word.

---

[1] KBR Strong's 3527

There's a mathematical pattern in the letters K (20), B (2) and R (200). What they share in common is the value of 2. K (20) has a multiplication by 10. B is the common denominator. R (200) has a multiplication of 100.

In Arabic, KBR means 'large' or to make larger.

This is one indication that the letters of the alphabet were put in order simultaneously to the words being formed, because the order of the letters in the alphabet bring meaning to the word.

It appears that when number values are used, a relationship of one acting on another involves a multiplication.

On the other hand, when there is a joining together, there is addition. The letter W (tent peg) is sometimes used to indicate joining.

KPR – Atone, Cover

*Exodus 30:10 And Aaron shall make an **atonement (KPR)** upon the horns of it once in a year with the blood of the sin offering of **atonements**: once in the year shall he make **atonement** upon it throughout your generations: it is most holy unto the Lord.*

Children of KPR include:
KPR[1] [kippur] (cover),
KPYR[2] [kef-eer] (village, young lion),
KPWRT[3] [kapooret] (lid),
KYPWR[4] [kippur] (atonement).

The holiest day of the Hebrew calendar is Yom Kippur (KPR), known in English as the Day of Atonement. The root meaning behind atonement is the provision of a cover.

---

[1] KPR Strong's 3722
[2] KPYR Strong's 3715
[3] KPWRT Strong's 3727 (used only as the cover/lid of the sacred Ark)
[4] KPYR Strong's 3725

The letter K (hand) talks about a covering. Physically, that was done by God in the garden of Eden when God provided a skin to cover the nakedness of Adam and Eve. This involved the first killing of an animal to provide the skin.

Spiritually, Jesus later provided a covering of humanity by His own death on the cross. Jesus became the cover by which humanity could come to God.

The letter P (mouth) may represent an opening or speech. Could the K (hand) before P (mouth) be the hand covering the mouth?

The letter R (head) indicates an important purpose which is the end result of KPR.

Is there any significance of the Hamas attack on Israel on the Day of Atonement (Yom Kippur) on 12th October 2023? Hard to say, but a lot of people lost their lives. Yom Kippur was originally instituted so that people would be saved by the cover of an animal sacrifice. On this day in 2023, the opposite happened – the opposite to God's plan. Instead of a covering of the sins of humanity, the worst of the sin and depravity of humanity was uncovered.

The close relative or perhaps the parent of KPR is XP meaning, cover and innocent. K and X have similar pronunciation - The letter K has the same point of articulation as X with the difference being that X has friction. The opposite spelling of XP is PX which brings the meaning of to blow and bellows – fanning a fire. Far from being covered, the fire of destruction is made to be hotter and more noticeable – blown up from a spark to a raging fire. Instead of mercy and atonement, there is judgement from both sides. Instead of relationship there is separation. And that separation is sending waves of separation across the globe as people and nations take passionate sides. Faced with the depravity of humanity, people are wanting to point the finger away from themselves to others.

KTB – Write

口✝(((

Psalm 102:15-18 The nations will fear the name of the LORD, all the kings of the earth will revere your glory. For the LORD will rebuild Zion and appear in his glory. He will respond to the prayer of the destitute; he will not despise their plea. Let this be **written (KTB)** *for a future generation, that a people not yet created may praise the LORD.*

There's something awesome about writing (KTB[1]) [katab] I can't quite put my finger on. As we see throughout the Bible and in Psalm 102:18, writing is a means of putting something in place to span time. It may be akin to the speaking of God such as God speaking creation into being, for example, "Let there be light."

The letter K brings the idea of using the hand for writing. But it may also extend to the idea of the firm hand taming and bringing direction.

The letter T brings the idea of a sign put in place as a marker. It expresses a purpose and target.

The letter B talks about relationship. Writing is a means of relationship.

The hand brings direction to the scribing tool to create signs which communicate a message which brings relationship between the scribe and reader.

*Exodus 17:14 Then the LORD said to Moses, "***Write** *this on a scroll as something to be remembered and make sure that Joshua hears it, ..."*

---

[1] KTB Strong's 3789

L – Lamed – Shepherd's staff

The word spelt LMD [lamed] is the modern name for the letter L and means, goad and learn. It's likely that the older name was LM [lam] – which Arabic still uses. LM includes the meanings of furrow, towards. These two meanings share the common idea of indicating a direction. In the context of Hebrew and Arabic use, L generally brings the idea of direction and leading.

Used as a word in its own right, it means, 'to', 'towards' or 'for what?'

The letter L has the numerical value of 30 and is the 12th letter in the alphabet. The number 12 speaks of God's family. His family are those who accept God's leading and direction.

The shape of the letter is more like a hooked shepherd's staff. The hook in a wooden staff is usually formed by cutting a branch just below a fork, then leaving one side of the fork long to form the staff and one side short to form the hook. The hook was useful for catching goats and sheep especially in the pen. It is also useful to keep balance when walking on rocky ground. You can certainly see it's resemblance to the modern English letter L.

LB – Heart

*Genesis 8:21 The LORD smelled the pleasing aroma and said in his **heart (LB)**: "Never again will I curse the ground because of man, even though every inclination of his **heart** is evil from childhood. And never again will I destroy all living creatures, as I have done."*

Deuteronomy 29:4 But to this day the LORD has not given you a **mind** *(LB) that* **understands** *(YDʕ) or eyes that see or ears that hear.*

What is the heart? In modern English it refers to the organ inside our body which pumps blood. The Hebrew word spelt LB[1] [lab] is translated as 'heart' in English translations, but there is absolutely no indication in the Biblical context that LB refers to the pumping organ. Some Bibles translate LB as 'mind'. Consistently LB refers to the core part of our being which has to do with directing our life.

It's very much part of our spiritual being. Perhaps there's no word in English which fully expresses the meaning of LB. The English word which comes to mind for me is, 'will' – as an abstract noun. I understand that there are two aspects of a human which give us direction – the physical body and the spiritual will. There are many parts of our body which affect our behaviour. It's been shown that even our gut bacteria have a lot of influence on our mood. Bacteria, of course, are not a human organism but dwell within us. Apparently, the human body is comprised of more bacterial cells than human cells! Now we start to cross the line where our exterior environment is allowed to direct our path – which is the case for much of our lives. But our spiritual will (LB) can choose our direction independent of exterior or interior physical forces.

The letter L refers to leading. The letter B denotes relationship and what is within. So put together, LB appears to be indicating something which leads us in relationship. And it should ideally lead us to relationship. But if our heart is hardened, then it will lead us away from relationship.

The function of the LB as described in an English translation of Deuteronomy 29:4 is to understand or perceive. The original Hebrew word used is YDʕ which comes from the root Dʕ, meaning knowledge.

---

[1] LB Strong's 3820

LBN – White

*Isaiah 1:18 "Come now, let us reason together," says the LORD. "Though your sins are like scarlet, they shall be as **white (LBN)** as snow; though they are red as crimson, they shall be like wool."*

LBN[1] [laban] (white) is used to describe a state of purity. Is it related to the root BN meaning 'son' and to build? Could it signify leading (L) to the Son (BN)? The letter L is very commonly used to point and lead to something, so it could very easily be pointing to the Son (BN) as the place of purity.

Other children of the root LBN include:
LBN[2] [leban] (brick – baked white),
LBNH[3] [lebanah] (moon),
LBWNH[4] [lebownah] (frankincense),
LYBNH[5] [libneh] (poplar – tree with white bark).

Laban in Arabic means a fermented milk – presumably referring to its white colour. As an everyday object, milk (haliib in Arabic) would have been the best illustration of white.

White is the combination of all colours in the spectrum. Some consider white to be at the centre of the colour spectrum because all other colours refract either side from white light. Note that the letter L is at the centre of the alphabet.

The son of God is the physical and visible manifestation of God, so the colour white which represents the full spectrum of light may be a good symbol of the Son.

---

[1] LBN Strong's 3835
[2] LBN Strong's 3843
[3] LBNH Strong's 3842
[4] LBWNH Strong's 3828
[5] LYBNH Strong's 3839

The Son of God is also the cover for our sins, so it's appropriate to say that though our sins are as scarlet, they shall be as white as snow.

MLQWSh – Latter Rain

ܫܩܘܠܡ

*Deuteronomy 11:14 then I will send rain on your land in its season, both autumn and **spring rains (MLQWSh)**, so that you may gather in your grain, new wine and oil.*

In Israel, the latter rain comes in Spring and is the last rain for a crop. After this final rain, the crop will begin to ripen off in the warmer summer months, ready for harvest.

Prophetically and spiritually, we are perhaps in the time of the latter rain.

MLQWSh[1] [malqowsh] comes from the root LQSh[2] [leqesh] meaning to gather and later growth.

The letter L in this context could indicate what is leading. In this context, leading up to the final harvest.

The letter Q (sun on the horizon) talks about the concentrating of something – gathering together. The sun going down may also talk about nearing the end of something.

The letter Sh (teeth) could be talking about separating something out – perhaps taking the harvest from the field then separating out the weeds from the wheat.

> *Matthew 13 38 The field is the world, and the good seed stands for the sons of the kingdom. The weeds are the sons of the evil one, and the enemy who sows them is the devil. The harvest is the end of the age, and the harvesters are angels. As the weeds are pulled up and burned in the fire, so it will be at the end of the age.*

---

[1] MLQWSh Strong's 4456
[2] LQSh Strong's 3954

We can expect to see a spiritual rain (time of spiritual outpouring and nourishing) in the later times before the final gathering in of those who accept the groom.

M – Mem – Ocean

The Hebrew letter M has the name Mem which has its origins in the word Mayiim, meaning waters. It essentially refers to the ocean.

There's a curious picture in the account of creation. Before creation, there is said to be an ocean:

> *Genesis 1:2 Now the earth was formless and empty, darkness was over the surface of the deep, and the Spirit of God was hovering over the* **waters** *(MYM).*

Is this ocean (M) symbolic of a great unknown which existed before the creation of the known (N – sprouting seed)? Since the great unknown existed before the creation, it could be that the ocean took its name from the great unknown. Perhaps Genesis 1:2 should instead translate the Hebrew word MYM as 'a great unknown'! Surely water was created along with the rest of creation. The building block of light was created on the first day.

The letter M also has the numerical value of 40 which is used in the Bible in relation to a time of testing, for example the 40 days and nights that it rained while Noah was in the ark, 40 years the Israelites wandered in the desert, and Jesus fasting for 40 days in the desert. These testing times are a time of unknown where we learn to trust in God.

The letter M is used in most of the question words – to which it brings the idea of an unknown. For example,

MY[1] ᒥᴍ [mi] (who, whose, whom),
MDWS[2] ⴲᴍ [maddowah] (why, how),
MH[3] ᴍ [mah] (what)
MTY[4] ᒥ†ᴍ [matay] (when),

---

[1] MY Strong's 4310
[2] MDW3 Strong's 4069
[3] MH Strong's 4100
[4] MTY Strong's 4970

MN ܀ [min] (what, who, where).

The letter M is at the start of the question word because a question starts with an unknown then provides some information about the nature of the unknown.

Physical objects in Hebrew frequently serve as pictures of spiritual truths, so we can expect to see a connection between the physical object and a spiritual truth.

The ocean and testing both have in common the idea of a great unknown. We are put through a time of unknown for the purpose of leading us to move beyond our own pride and ability towards trust in God.

Let's take a moment to try and appreciate how the ocean gives us the idea of almighty and a fathomless unknown. Imagine being in a fishing boat 6000 years ago. As we push offshore, we first experience the waves, sometimes even huge ones, which persistently and forever wash ashore. Then soon, we lose sight of the ground underneath us. What was known and solid is now unknown. We have no idea what lies beneath us. There could be rocks, reefs, sea monsters or huge fish beneath us. It's an environment which is alien to us. If we drop anything overboard it's lost forever.

We are tossed about like a stick on the huge waves, powerless to do anything.

After an hour or so of sailing, we completely lose sight of the land. There are no markers on the ocean to show us where we are, though experienced voyagers know how to read the stars in the infinite awesome sky overhead.

Even today, the ocean depths are largely unexplored – especially in places like the Mariana Trench which is about 11 kilometres at its deepest. The tallest mountain (Mt Everest) is almost 9 kilometres high.

The letter M is used as a preposition, bringing the meaning of 'from', 'of' and 'out of'. Could it be that out of the great unknown comes new beginnings. The letter N (sprouting seed) comes directly after the letter M in the alphabet. The letter N also speaks about knowledge. A great unknown and time of testing births the known and certainty.

The letter M is also used as a derivational prefix on nouns to derive a new noun with the meaning of a place or doer. For example, if English had this prefix it would add onto the word bake to make baker (answering the question, who does it?). It would also form the word bakery (answering the question, where is it done?).

The M in AL-HYM – Elohiim

The letter M is found in God's name Elohiim. This name is made up of two parts – El, meaning God, and the suffix, '-hiim'. Hiim has both a physical meaning and a spiritual meaning. The physical meaning is plurality – talking about two or more. There is a dual suffix but that is only used for identical pairs of something. Its spiritual meaning implies something or someone being almighty. So Elohiim should be translated as something like, 'Almighty God'. The letter H in hiim was written with the symbol of a person with arms raised ⼭. It brings the meaning of the existence of a person and exclamation of something amazing – a wow! So, the combination of wow and unfathomable could be translated loosely but not completely as something like, 'almighty'.

Before we start thinking about what the ocean shows us about our relationship with God, let's look some more at His name Elohiim.

The EL is often translated as, 'God', but it actually means 'guide'. This is clearly seen in the letters. A is the ox which is led. The L is the shepherd's staff or yoke which is used to guide and direct the ox. The ox is a physical picture of humanity, who is being led by God.

The AL is followed by the suffix '-HYM' which has two meanings. It can mean plural (two or more) and it can bring the meaning of almighty and unfathomable. Both meanings are applicable to God's name.

When we consider God's fathomless and awesome nature, we must also include in that, an engagement of trust – much like being in a small vulnerable boat, trusting the direction of our lives to His unfathomable awesomeness.

MLH – Word, Speak

2 Samuel 23:2 *"The Spirit of the LORD spoke through me; his **word** (MLH) was on my tongue."*

Daniel 3:22 *The Kings **command** (MLH) was so urgent...*

The word MLH[1] [milah] comes from the root ML. Other children of ML include:

MLL[2] [malal] (speak),
AMYL[3] [amiyl] (branch),
MLA[4] [malaa] (fill),
MLAH[5] [melaah] (firstfruits),
MLYA[6] [meliya] (fatling),
MLWA[7] [melwaa] (filling),
MYLWAH[8] [millwaah] (setting – to be filled with a precious stone),
HMWLH[9] [Hamuwlah] (speech),
MHL[10] [mahal] (mix, weaken),

---

[1] MLH Strong's 4405
[2] MLL Strong's 4448
[3] AMYL Strong's 534
[4] MLA Strong's 4390
[5] MLAH Strong's 4395
[6] MLYA Strong's 4806
[7] MLWA Strong's 4393
[8] MYLWAH Strong's 4396
[9] HMWLH Strong's 1999
[10] MHL Strong's 4107

MWL¹ ⟨Y⟩ [mool](front, circumcise),
TMWL² ⟨Y⟩+ [temool] (before, formerly).

The children of ML appear to have a theme of bringing substance and filling. It appears in front of us. Perhaps the theme is to be manifest before us in all its fullness.

The letter M denotes an unknown or a vast quantity and L denotes leading.

ML appears to be talking about a fulness or manifestation which leads.

Could ML be the origin of the English word 'million'? Million is from the Latin 'mille' which had the idea of a great number or quantity. The Hebrew ML also has the similar idea of a fullness.

The Arabic word, 'milyaan' (from the root ML) means to be full.

MLH is used extensively in the book of Job but rarely anywhere else.

Another word used to mean word is DBR, which is used more extensively.

MLK – Kingdom

*Psalm 22:28 - for **dominion (MLWKH)** belongs to the LORD and he rules over the nations.*

The root of MLWKH³ [meluwkah] is MLK⁴ The other children of MLK include:

MLK⁵ [melek] (reign, king, counsel),

---

¹ MWL Strong's 4236
² TMWL Strong's 8543
³ MLWKH Strong's 4410
⁴ MLK Strong's 4427
⁵ MLK Strong's 4428

MLKH¹ 𐤌𐤋𐤊𐤄 [malkah] (queen),
MLKWT² 𐤌𐤋𐤊𐤅𐤕 [malkoot] (kingdom).

Jesus often spoke about the Kingdom of Heaven. It could be that He also has in mind the counsel of heaven – which is from the King.

The letter M may refer to a large quantity or domain, The L (shepherd's staff L) refers to leading. The letter K (firm taming hand) likely refers to the ruler holding and having responsibility for his domain.

> *Isaiah 9:7 Of the increase of his government and peace there will be no end. He will reign on David's throne and over his kingdom (MMLKH³), establishing and upholding it with justice and righteousness from that time on and forever. The zeal of the LORD Almighty will accomplish this.*

> *Matthew 7:21 "Not everyone who says to me, 'Lord, Lord,' will enter the **kingdom** of heaven, but only he who does the will of my Father who is in heaven."*

Another word which is similar and also connects to the Kingdom is MLAK (angel). This is from a different root LK which carries the idea of a messenger rather than a ruler.

AMN – Amen

> *Psalm 41:13 Praise be to the LORD, the God of Israel, from everlasting to everlasting. Amen and Amen.*

AMN⁴ [amen] is from the root MN.

---

¹ MLKH Strong's 4436
² MLKWT Strong's 4438
³ MMLKH Strong's 4467 [mamlakah]
⁴ AMN Strong's 543

The root MN[1] seems to be talking about moving from an unknown to something surer. The letter M denotes the unknown. The letter N (sprouting seed, genetic information) refers to the known. So, we're moving from the unknown to the known and continuing life – more certain.

MN [min] as a word means, 'from' – which is part of a question or answer about origin.

The letter M presents a state of unknown.

The letter N then brings information to make something known.

The children of the root MN are many:
MN[2] [man](what?),
MNT[3] [menat] (portion),
MYNYN[4] [miyn-yan] (number),
AMN[5] [amen] (firm, amen),
AMNT[6] [ament] (truth),
AMWN[7] [amown] (craftsmen – one who is firm in talent),
AWMNH [amuneh] (pillar),
AMNH[8] [amnah] (nourished),
MAN[9] [ma-an] (refuse - *verb*),
MNH[10] [maneh] (number, time, Maneh – a unit of measure),
TMWNH[11] [temownah] (likeness),
YMN[12] [ye-me-n] (right side),

---

[2] MN Strong's 4478
[3] MNT Strong's 4521
[4] MNYN Strong's 4510
[5] AMN Strong's 542, 543
[6] AMNT Strong's 571 - It appears in my dictionary with the alternative spelling of AMT - with is apparently a variant from the Masoretic text. The original was AMNT - which certainly reflects the meaning brought from the root MN.
[7] AMWN Strong's 525
[8] AMNH Strong's 545, 546, 548
[9] MAN Strong's 3985
[10] MNH Strong's 4488
[11] TMWNH Strong's 8544
[12] YMN Strong's 3233

TYMN[1] ⟨hebrew⟩ [tay-men] (south),
MYN[2] ⟨hebrew⟩ [min] (from).

AMN [aamen] tells us that something is sure – In the context of Psalm 41:13 it agrees with the everlasting to everlasting – God is sure in that he does not change

'Amen' occurs 30 times in the Old Testament and 29 times in the New Testament. Perhaps I'm making too much of this, but it seems there should be 30 in the New Testament also. However, the New Testament story is not yet finished. I'm sure there will be another almighty 'amen!' at the finish of the story when we go to dwell with Jesus – when God's family is completed!

Is there any significance to the number 30? The letter L has the value of 30 and this letter talks about God leading His family. The letters M and N have the values of 40 and 50. There's an obvious sequence and story. God leads his people (30) and his people respond with affirmation (40 and 50).

The most frequent use (12 times) of the word is in Deuteronomy where the people agree with the laws (God's leading) presented to them, e.g.

> *Deuteronomy 27:26 "Cursed is the man who does not uphold the words of this law by carrying them out." Then all the people shall say,* **"Amen!"**

It's noteworthy that the word is used 12 times by God's family, the 12 tribes of Israel. Note also that 'amen' is a word which is used only by God's children – not by God and not by those who are not His children. It's a word dedicated for the use of God's children to affirm their relationship with God.

---

[1] TYMN Strong's 8486
[2] MYN Strong's 4480

AMNT – Truth

*Psalm 25:5 guide me in your **truth** (AMNT) and teach me, for you are God my Savior, and my hope is in you all day long.*

AMNT[1] [ament] is from the root MN and adds an affix T to the word AMN. The letter T (completion and destination) shows us that truth leads us to where we need to go. That really is the best definition of truth.

The root MN shows that truth is about moving from something unknown like the ocean and moving towards information – like the genetic information in the seed.

What is the definition of truth?

What is the purpose of truth?

Truth needs to lead us in a direction that is good for us and leads us to a good destination.

There may be two different angles on truth. One is around facts and physical evidence. The other is around relationship and trust. There is a lot of overlap.

Our Western secular culture says that truth is found only in hard physical evidence. However, there are fathoms more to reality and truth than what we can humanly measure or describe. Sometimes, people will say that truth is whatever is good for them. 'Science' does stretch the boundaries when it comes to physical evidence, when it puts out theories which connect the dots of physical evidence. Two significant examples are:

1. The theory of evolution which tries to explain how life forms came to be.
2. The theory of what causes global warming.

---

[1] AMNT Strong's 571

There may be hard evidence that there is global warming and climate change, but how that came to be can only be postulated. It could be a natural phenomenon such as has been seen in history or it could be man-made or a combination of both.

Both theories of climate and evolution have and are being used to push a humanist agenda. Evolution says that there is no God. Climate change says that humans must take control, or the world as we know it will end. The trouble is, in the hands of power-greedy people, that control will result in the control over human lives, which is abuse. But like the ancient Greek god Zeus, they will say that the control and destruction of humanity is necessary to save the planet earth. I wonder if many high-level anti-Christ influencers today take their cues from ancient Greek mythology – as if it were some kind of Bible. Greek mythology has certainly been prominent in humanist educational institutions for millennia, including the present time.

People can use 'scientific evidence and studies' to support their own agendas. It's possible to manipulate physical evidence to support a variety of agendas. If your truth is from 'facts', you may say that truth is relative. Perhaps relative to your culture, or the physical evidence at hand at that time.

The Hebrew word translated as truth talks about something which is firm and doesn't change over time. It's like a foundation – something you can build your house on. It's something you can trust the valuable things in your life to for safekeeping.

Truth can be a principle which you hold to be important. Such as freedom of choice for all – provided it doesn't affect the freedom of choice for others.

It's possible to choose a way of truth – to have a life which upholds truth. In contrast, some see that their own agendas are more important than presenting truth to others. They will deliberately present an untruth to others to preserve their own interests or ideologies. They may even think that telling an untruth, hiding the truth or being deceptive will, in the long run, bring wider humanity to a better place – according to their own ideology. Their ideology is seen as more important than the rights of individuals.

Putting respect for persons, family, and relationship first, is a good truth foundation. Spiritual foundation is the most important because it's all about eternal relationship – we act as a family supporting one another.

Who would you trust more – the person who will get personal gain at your expense, or the person who is giving something of themselves to give voice to a truth.

I think truth has to do with whether it's pointing us to our destination. If it's not pointing us to our destination of present and eternal family with God, then it's not true.

If the destination of eternal family is not connected to your measure of truth, then it seems that your truth can be derived from anywhere and changed at any time.

Perhaps truth is also about relationship – in contrast to knowledge. There is a prevalent idea in modern society that truth is only found in science – such as can be found in university studies and research. God says to us that unless we become like little children, we cannot enter the kingdom of heaven. This is saying that trust in our relationship with God must come before personal knowledge. The attainment of knowledge can be all about ourselves and our own abilities. This is heading in the opposite direction of relationship – which is all about moving beyond ourselves and our own resources – to place our precious things with our Father.

A child learns from and imitates those whom they have a significant relationship with – those whom they look up to. That relationship is key to the direction they take. They will follow that person whom they respect or admire. That person is their source of truth.

MYN ~ Man

The English word, 'man' likely has its origins in the Hebrew word MYN[1] [meen]. In the Proto-Germanic origins of English, 'man' referred to mankind. Germanic has its origins in Indo-European which is located in the Northern Iraq area – which is essentially also the origin of Proto-Semitic.

The word MN means, 'from where?' When asking about the origin of mankind, the answer is, 'From God' because Adam was created in the image of God. The word MYN means, 'a kind' and 'from'. Both words talk about an origin, for example a Border Collie dog is a kind of dog. It shares the same origin as a wolf.

Likewise, all members of mankind share the same origin. Also, humanity is the same kind of being as God because we share a common image. I understand that image to be a tri-nature – a will, spirit and body (physical manifestation). Within the one being of God, there are also two elements which direct – the person of the Father and the person of Jesus. So too, in a human person there are two elements which direct us – our will and our body. As with God, the two directing elements share the same spirit which connects them.

YMN – Right Hand

YMN[2] [yaman] comes from the root MN. YMN means 'right side'. This contrasts with the left hand. There are two words in Arabic which both mean, 'left hand' – YSAR and ShMAL. The latter is also used in Hebrew.

The letter Y (hand) is a prefix on each root Y-MN and Y-SAR.

---

[1] MYN Strong's 4327, 4480, 4481
[2] YMN Strong's 3231

In Arabic, YSAR is from the word SAR, which means to steal. In contrast, the right hand is firm and honest, while the left hand is much less reliable. In Semitic culture the right hand is used for honourable things such as greeting, eating and writing. The left hand is used for toileting and dirty tasks. It would be an insult to greet someone with your left hand.

The country named Yemen derives its name from the same word YMN which brings the meaning of an honourable country.

While I was studying Field Linguistics, I asked God about which country I should work in. I read the account of when Jesus asked the fishermen to cast their net on the right side of the boat. Later in the day, after I read that, I spoke with someone who had been working in Yemen. He told me that the name Yemen meant, 'on the right side'. This was a strong confirmation to me that I should go to Yemen. An additional pointer was that I had been studying Amharic which is in the same South Semitic family of languages.

I was also encouraged by the story of the fishermen in that when they obeyed Jesus by casting their net on the right side of the boat - something that didn't make sense - they were rewarded with a huge catch. I believe this is God's purpose for Yemen.

MRYM – Bitter

*Exodus 15:20 Then **Miriam** the prophetess, Aaron's sister, took a tambourine in her hand, and all the women followed her, with tambourines and dancing.*

The mother of Jesus also had the name Miriam, spelt MRYM[1] [mir-yawm]. But as with many names in the Bible, when the New Testament was translated into Greek, the Greek speaking translators departed from the original Hebrew names. Her name would have been the same as the sister of Moses – Miriam. Could there be some prophetic similarity between Mary

---

[1] MRYM Strong's 4813

the mother of Jesus and Miriam? While Miriam wasn't the mother of Moses, she was instrumental in connecting Moses with the people. In a different way, Mary was instrumental in bringing forth Jesus to the people.

MRYM is from the root MR whose other children include:
MR[1] 𐤌𐤓 [mar] (bitter, trickle),
MRY[2] 𐤌𐤓𐤉 [meri] (rebellion),
MRRH[3] 𐤌𐤓𐤓𐤄 [mererah] (gall, bile – acid from stomach),
MRWRH[4] 𐤌𐤓𐤅𐤓𐤄 [merorah] (venom),
AMR[5] 𐤀𐤌𐤓 [amer] (weak),
MAR[6] 𐤌𐤀𐤓 [maar] (irritate),
MHR[7] 𐤌𐤄𐤓 [mahar] (quickly, hurry, purchase),
MWHR[8] 𐤌𐤅𐤄𐤓 [mou-har] (dowry),
MWRH[9] 𐤌𐤅𐤓𐤄 [mowrah] (razor, archer),
MWR[10] 𐤌𐤅𐤓 [moor] (Myrrh. In the Biblical contexts it seems this was a pleasant-smelling spice/gum),
YMR[11] 𐤉𐤌𐤓 [yemur] (exchange).

It's easy to see how the letters MR bring the basic meaning of bitter.

The letter M likely talks about a time of testing – which may be bitter. It moves on from there to the letter R which talks about a high place or something important.

So why was MRYM a good name to give a girl? And in particular, the sister of Moses (Miriam) and the human mother of Jesus (Mary)? It turns out, that the life of Mary the mother of Jesus may not have been a bed of roses. I suspect there were some very challenging moments in her life,

---

[1] MR Strong's 4751
[2] MRY Strong's 4805
[3] MRRH Strong's 4845
[4] MRWRH Strong's 4846
[5] AMR Strong's 535
[6] MAR is not found in the Bible, but it is a word in the vocabulary!
[7] MHR Strong's 4116, 4117, 4118
[8] MWHR Strong's 4119
[9] MWRH Strong's 4177
[10] MWR Strong's 4753
[11] YMR Strong's 4171

beginning with having a child out of wedlock in a society which stoned adulterers – though she was betrothed to Joseph. It was also a bitter pill for her to lose her son in her older years.

It's interesting to note that Miriam's father had a name with the same main consonants AMRM[1] 𐤌𐤓𐤌𐤀 [Amram] (high people).

MShH – Moses

*Exodus 2:10 When the child grew older, she took him to Pharaoh's daughter and he became her son. She named him **Moses (MShH)**, saying, "I **drew** (MShH) him out of the water."*

Note how the name Moses MShH[2] [mo-sheh] is spelt very similar to the name Messiah MShYX 𐤇𐤉𐤔𐤌 [mashiach] (anointed one). The letter X in MShYX talks about moving past the physical into the spiritual. Moses wasn't able to cross over into the promised land because he represented the physical law – an attainment of man (H). In contrast, the Messiah is able to take us across into the Promised land of being in God's family.

What is shared in common between the two words, is the root MSh, which has the meaning of grasping hold or touching something – perhaps with the idea of something being physically tangible.

Is there a link between MShY[3] [meshi] (silk) and the idea of being anointed with oil (MShYX)– which also has a soft silky sensation?

The tasks of both Moses and the Messiah of saving God's people is very similar but there is one important difference regarding entering into the Promised land. Joshua and Jesus (who share the same Hebrew name YShϟ) the Messiah were able to lead their people across by Trust in God – not self-attainment of the Law.

---

[1] AMRM Strong's 6019; Exodus 6:20
[2] MShH Strong's 4872
[3] MShY Strong's 4897

See the story of Joshua later in this book.

The name MShH is from the root MSh, which has the children:
MShY ⟩⟨⟩⟨⟩⟨ [meshi] (silk – possibly a thread which is made by being pulled out – soft to the touch),
MShSh[1] ⟨⟩⟨⟩⟨⟩⟨ [mashash] (grope/grabbing),
AMSh [2] ⟨⟩⟨⟩⟨⟩ [amesh] (Yesterday, time past, an experienced reality),
MShH[3] ⟨⟩⟨⟩⟨⟩ [mawshah](draw out, pull out),
MWSh[4] ⟨⟩⟨⟩⟨⟩ [moosh](touch, remove).

The letters MSh certainly do tell the story of Moses.

The letter M is the sea or water. The letter Sh (teeth) talks about cutting or dividing. God enabled Moses to lead the Israelites through the sea by dividing the sea so that they could walk through on dry ground.

But Moses initially received his name from the princess who named him because she drew him out of the water. This suggests a different spelling of MSH, because the letter S (thorn) talks about grasping. However, the letter Sh (teeth) could bring the idea of separating Moses from the water – drawing him out. There's a curious relationship between the two letters Sh and S in the Semitic languages, for example Hebrew will spell the word meaning 'peace' as Shalom, but Arabic will spell it Salaam.

MShYX – Messiah

*Daniel 9:25 "Know and understand this: From the issuing of the decree to restore and rebuild Jerusalem until the **Anointed One** (MShYX), the ruler, comes, there will be seven 'sevens,' and sixty-*

---

[1] MShSh Strong's 4959
[2] AMSh Strong's 570
[3] MShH Strong's 4900
[4] MWSh Strong's 4185

two 'sevens.' It will be rebuilt with streets and a trench, but in times of trouble."

The Anglicized word 'Messiah' doesn't appear in most translations of the Bible. 'Messiah' is from the Hebrew word spelt MShYX[1] [maw-shee-ach] which is used 39 times throughout the Old Testament. It's translated in the King James version of the Book of Daniel as 'Messiah' only twice. Other versions such as the New International version never translate as 'Messiah' but where KJV translates as 'Messiah', the NIV uses 'Anointed One'- which reflects the actual meaning of the word.

MShYX is from the root MShX whose children include:
MShX[2] Hᴄᴏᴍ [meshakh] (smear, oil),
MShXH[3] ᵠHᴄᴏᴍ [mishkhah] (ointment),
MShYX Hᴜᴄᴏᴍ (smeared – Messiah).

The meanings of the letters could be:

M represents a liquid and an unknown.

The Sh (teeth) could refer to being separated apart for something.

The X (wall) talks about something beyond the physically visible.

We know that anointing was an act of marking someone as being set apart for a special task – as prophet, priest or king. It was a spiritual task as indicated by the letter X.

Why choose the act of anointing someone with oil to commission them to a task? It was and is normal practice in the hot countries of the Middle East to greet and farewell a visitor by putting a fragrance on them – to refresh them from the smell and sweat of the journey. Often the oil was the medium for the fragrance and was a good way of applying the fragrance so that it remained on the person. Other means used, include wafting fragrant smoke into the clothes. But applying an oil from a bottle is certainly easier, more

---

[1] MShYX Strong's 4899
[2] MShX Strong's 4886, 4889
[3] MshXH Strong's 4888

pleasant and perhaps remains on the skin better especially if you want to remove layers to cool down.

It's a simple way of blessing someone. So perhaps the anointing is a way of sending someone on a journey – in a spiritual sense as well. The letter X is often used in the context of going beyond the walls of the house – on a journey.

The first use of the word MShX (as Messiah in KJV) is in Daniel with regard to the End Times:

> *Daniel 9:26 After the sixty-two 'sevens,' the* **Anointed One** *(MShX) will be cut off and will have nothing. The people of the ruler who will come will destroy the city and the sanctuary. The end will come like a flood: War will continue until the end, and desolations have been decreed.*

It's another whole subject to work out End Times timing, but perhaps now is the time to start keeping an eye on events.

Note also that the number 7 is represented by the letter Z, which comes before the letter X (8). Could the seven sevens be talking about what comes before crossing over into the spiritual?

MWT – Mortality, Death

> *Genesis 2:17 "…but you must not eat from the tree of the knowledge of good and evil, for when you eat of it you will surely* **die** *(MWT)."*

In the above scripture, the Hebrew language expresses the idea of 'surely die' by a repetition of the word, saying MWT [mowt] MWT [mowt]. It doesn't use the word meaning 'surely'. Doubling the verb could be a Hebrew way of expressing intensity, but c ould this possibly be also pointing to a double death – both physical and spiritual – which is the case if we reject a relationship with God. However, if we welcome a relationship with God, death will lead us to our ultimate destination – to dwell with the Father as his family for eternity.

The word MWT[1] comes from the root MT whose children include:
MT ✝ 〰 (mortality, man),
MWT ✝ Y 〰 (death),
MTY[2] ᴗJ ✝ 〰 [mattay] (when).

The word 'when' answers a question or unknown (M) with a destination or completion point (T).

MWT is a likely origin of the English word Mortality – it shares the same root consonants MT. The English suffix -ality is not part of the root word.

The letter M talks about a time of testing or unknown, and then moves on from there to a destination. The testing is likely our life on earth – which is a time of many unknowns. It could also relate to what we think of death – a great unknown. But when we do die, we will see things much more clearly – we will have moved on from our earthly life where we couldn't see God and there were many unknowns – to a place where we are face to face with God and we will know for sure what our destiny is.

The letter T talks about a destination. Death has brought us to our destination.

It's interesting that MT also has the meaning of 'man'[3]. Another more commonly used word meaning, 'mankind' is spelt ADM.

The spelling of MT as used to refer to men appears to be in the context where the people are shown to be truly mere mortal in their behaviour – people who have rejected the spiritual and eternal:

> *Deuteronomy 28:62 You who were as numerous as the stars in the sky will be left but **few** (MT) in number, because you did not obey the LORD your God.*

---

[1] MWT and MMWT Strong's 4191
[2] MTY Strong's 4970
[3] MT Strong's 4962

> *Psalm 17:14 O LORD, by your hand save me from such **men (MT)**, from **men (MT)** of this world whose reward is in this life*

God's word to Adam in the garden saying that he would surely die if he rejected the spiritual was true. If Adam wanted to be focused on the physical, then he would certainly become nothing more than that – a MT!

While we are in the human body, we are certainly not in a stable state in contrast to God. But by joining ourselves to God's family, we enter eternal life – what we were created for. In fact, the whole physical universe was put into place for this purpose. And when that purpose is completed, the whole physical universe will be rolled up.

> *Isaiah 34:4 All the stars of the heavens will be dissolved, and the sky rolled up like a scroll; all the starry host will fall like withered leaves from the vine, like shrivelled figs from the fig tree.*

The physical universe and life are but a temporary stage for humanity to come to God.

N – Nun – Sprouting Seed

The letter N was drawn with the symbol of a sprouting seed. It brings the idea of the continuation of life. The seed is also a store of a huge amount of genetic information. Its physical size is deceptive in regard to its significance. Inversely, the vast size of the universe is deceptive in regard to its significance. The seed also brings the idea of information and design.

The sprouting seed is a picture of resurrection after death.

It has the numerical value of 50, which relates Biblically to the Year of Jubilee when all debts were to be forgiven, slaves freed, and land returned to original owners. Forgiveness is all about allowing the continuation of life..

The continuation of life is a strong thread and theme in the Bible, and we see it in several key words. It relates to our ultimate destination which is family. Nun is about the continuation of the ultimate plan and design – like the pathway or cord which leads us to our destination. Relationship with God and others will ultimately lead us to our destination of being part of the family dwelling with Jesus the groom in the house of our Heavenly Father.

The name Nun, spelt NWN[1] [noon], means 'to continue'. Its root is NN. The two Ns together tell the story of a sprouting seed continuing to grow until it matures to produce a seed of its own, which in turn will also sprout.

Other children of this root include NYN[2]  [niin] (heir – one who continues the family line).

---

[1] NWN Strong's 5125
[2] NYN Strong's 5209

NAH – Pasture

*Psalm 23:2 He makes me lie down in **green pastures**, he leads me beside quiet waters, ...*

Verse 6: Surely goodness and love will follow me all the days of my life, and I will dwell in the house of the LORD forever.

Psalm 23 is a description of life into eternity. It comes after Psalm 22 which talks about the completion of the earthly era which ends with Jesus ruling the nations. Jesus pointed us to Psalm 22 by quoting the first line of it when his physical body was about to die on the cross:

"My God, my God, why have you forsaken me?"

The word NAH is from the root NA.

The letter N as we've seen, talks about a place where life can continue.

The letter A (Aleph) represents the ox being led and guided – spiritually it represents humanity being guided to our destination. God is not about leading us to just lie in the grass of the pasture, nor leading us beside a relaxing water. It's essentially about leading us to a place where we can be at rest and find sustenance.

A reversal of spelling (AN) seems to bring about an opposite meaning including: island, ship, complain, vanity, without. Perhaps it's talking about the leading (A) continuing (N) but without arriving anywhere. Many do live a life of AN, but we were designed for NA.

NDB – Offer Willingly

> *Exodus 35:21 and everyone who was **willing** (NDB) and whose heart moved him came and brought an offering to the LORD for the work on the Tent of Meeting, for all its service, and for the sacred garments.*

The word NDB[1] [nadab] is also a root – whose children include:
NDB (offer willingly),
NDBH[2] ⌐⌐⌐ [nedabah] (freewill offering),
NDYB[3] ⌐⌐⌐ [nadiib] (willing, noble),
NDYBH[4] ⌐⌐⌐ [nediibah] (honour/dignity).

To offer to God willingly is a key quality to aim for and worth understanding more. A heart that is not willing won't make it to the destination.

> *Chronicles 29:17 I know, my God, that you test the heart and are pleased with integrity. All these things have I given **willingly** (NDB) and with honest intent. And now I have seen with joy how **willingly** (NDB) your people who are here have given to you.*

The N talks about continuation. To be willing is very much about wanting to stay with something for the long run.

The letter D (door) may indicate humility – from the hanging nature of the tent door. Perhaps NDB involves humility in making our offering – as an act of respect to the other.

The letter B talks about the destination of relationship and family which results from being willing to continue.

---

[1] NDB Strong's 5068
[2] NDBH Strong's 5071
[3] NDYB Strong's 5081
[4] NDYBH Strong's 5082

NXSh – Serpent

> *Genesis 3:1 Now the **serpent** was craftier than any of the wild animals the LORD God had made. He said to the woman, "Did God really say, 'You must not eat from any tree in the garden'?"*

The first mention of the Serpent (NXSh[1]) [nakhash] is in the Garden of Eden.

The first thing the Serpent does is bring humanity to question the truth and reliability of what God is saying. Nothing has changed today, and this is entrenched in our culture, governments, and education.

Other children of the root NXSh include:
NXSh[2] [nakhash] (divination) and
NXShT[3] [nakhashet] (bronze)

What's the connection between bronze and serpent?

Many snakes in the Middle East area are bronze coloured (sandy brown). The colour provides good camouflage in the dry rock and sand regions. But there are other connections.

> *Numbers 21:9 So Moses made a bronze (NXShT) snake (NXSh) and put it up on a pole. Then when anyone was bitten by a snake and looked at the bronze snake, he lived.*

Why was Moses commanded to do this? The Serpent has had its success by being hidden and deceptive. But now it's being held up high for all to see. Could it be that God had in mind that by bringing the Serpent out into the open for all to see that we would see the evil for what it is, turn from it and have the opportunity to live?

---

[1] NXSh Strong's 5175
[2] NXSh Strong's 5172
[3] NXShT Strong's 5178

N – NUN – SPROUTING SEED

The letter N talks about the continuation of life – which is God's original and ultimate intention. This is the starting point, but things move on from here.

The letter X (wall) talks about what is out of sight – hidden in the spiritual realm.

The letter Sh (teeth) talks about being cut off - the final result.

The Serpent cuts the continuation of life. And many don't believe he exists because we can't see him physically. But his work covers the earth and every aspect of life.

It's worth noting that the early manufacture of bronze contained the poison arsenic. You couldn't see the poison but, of course, you became ill. People, at the time, also likely didn't know that the bronze was causing their illness. So it is with the Serpent – he remains unknown to many and brings spiritual and physical sickness to many.

Arsenic naturally occurred in many ore sources, and it was at some point found that ore containing arsenic produced a stronger bronze, so arsenic was added. The process of smelting brought the greatest risk of poisoning as the smith inhaled the fumes – leading to peripheral neuropathy – causing weakness in legs and feet. Interestingly, one of the curses which God put on the Serpent was that the Serpent would lose his legs and be forced to crawl on his belly.

NSA – Forgive

Psalm 25:18 Look upon my affliction and my distress and **take away** *(NSA) all my sins.*

The word spelt NSA[1] [nasaa] actually means 'to lift'. It's from the root NS whose children include:

---

[1] NSA Strong's 5375

NS¹ 𐤎𐤍 [nes] (standard – a pole lifted up for communication),
MNSH² 𐤔𐤎𐤍𐤌 [menaseh?] (trial, temptation),
ANS³ 𐤎𐤍𐤏 [aanas] (compel),
NSA (lift, forgive),
NSAT⁴ 𐤕𐤀𐤎𐤍 [nisaat] (gift),
MNSA⁵ 𐤀𐤎𐤍𐤌 [manasaa] (burden, cloud),
NSYA⁶ 𐤀𐤉𐤎𐤍 [nasiyaa] (chief – one who's been lifted up as a standard or someone important in the community),
NSWAH 𐤄𐤅𐤎𐤍 (wagon – for carrying a load/burden),
NWS 𐤎𐤅𐤍 (to flee),
MNWS 𐤎𐤅𐤍𐤌 (refuge – the place to flee to).

The idea of lifting or raising possibly comes from the idea of the seed sprouting (N)– moving upward. The letter S (thorn) brings the idea of grasping hold of something. So lifting is to hold something and move it up. It could be that the meaning of the letters is not so much related to the physical sense of the word, but more to the spiritual sense – to forgive.

The word NSA could be understood in the spiritual sense as the continuation of life (N) being held onto (S). This contrasts with the opposite of forgiveness, which is spelt NShA, meaning to deceive and put into debt – which is placing a burden on someone. The letter Sh is the teeth – which cuts off the continuation of life. See more about NShA in its section.

God commanded Israel to keep a Jubilee year every 50 years – which was when all debts were to be forgiven, slaves released, and land returned to original owners. This was the lifting of a burden. Being 50 years apart would mean that it would happen in the lifetime of every person who had lived a normal life.

---

[1] NS Strong's 5251
[2] MNSH Strong's 4531
[3] ANS Strong's 597
[4] NSAT Strong's 5379
[5] MNSA Strong's 4853
[6] NSYA Strong's 5387

*Psalm 25:1 To you, O LORD, I **lift up** (NSA) my soul.*

*Psalm 28:9 Save your people and bless your inheritance; be their shepherd and **carry** (NSA) them forever.*

*Psalm 32:1 Blessed is he whose transgressions are **forgiven** (NSA), whose sins are covered.*

*Psalm 143:8 Let the morning bring me word of your unfailing love, for I have put my trust in you. Show me the way I should go, for to you I **lift up** (NSA) my soul.*

Forgiveness is the antidote to deception because deceit is putting a load on someone, whereas forgiveness is lifting the burden. Forgiveness is all about the continuation of life which is about certainty. Deceit in contrast is all about placing people into an unknown or more specifically a place where they think they know yet they are on false ground – worse than being in a place of unknown. Being in a place of unknown is not God's best plan for us, but since Adam rejected a relationship with God, humanity has been wandering in the unknown desert. However, God uses the place of unknown so that we can build our trust in Him. But the place of deceit leads us to think that we have everything under control so that we don't trust in God. We take life into our own hands and don't follow God's guiding.

Compare the two words, forgive NSA and deceit NShA. Both begin with the letter N (continuation of life). Forgiveness proceeds to the letter S (thorn) which brings the meaning of grasping. So, the continuation of life is grasped or clung onto. The idea of grasping hold of is akin to the idea of clinging. This same idea is found in the word translated as, 'trust' – which literally means to cling onto.

In contrast, the letter Sh in NShA is the teeth, which cuts off the continuation of life. NShA means 'debt', so it diverts the life from our own soul to another master. It puts a load on us.

It occurred to me that when my daughter is going through a period of defiant behaviour and acting out, that instead of giving consequences such as losing out on something or expressing anger, I should offer her a way out of her darkness and isolation. Instead of walking away from her, as an expression of rejecting the bad behaviour, I should help to lift her out by offering quality time and relationship. Having said that, I do think consequences for actions do have their place in learning personal responsibility.

NR – Light

*Psalm 119:105 Your word is a **lamp** (NR) to my feet and a light (AWR) for my path.*

The word NR[1] [nir] is from the root NR whose other children include:

NAR[2] [naar] (reject. In Arabic NAR means, 'fire'),
NHR[3] [nehar] (flow, bright, river),
NHRH[4] [neharah] (light),
NHYR[5] [nehiyr] (insight),
NWR[6] [noor] (fire),
NYR [niir] (plough, break up).

There is another word AWR which also means, 'light'. It must have a different shade of meaning. We see AWR as the first element of creation:

*Genesis 1:3 And God said, "Let there be **light** (AWR)," and there was light.*

Both words use the letter R. It seems as though the R (head) is bringing the idea that light reveals something important – something that we need to know.

---

[1] NYR Strong's 5216
[2] NAR Strong's 5010
[3] NHR Strong's 5103, 5104
[4] NHRH Strong's 5105
[5] NHYR Strong's 5094
[6] NWR Strong's 5135

The letter N is likely bringing the idea of a continuation – a flow. This applies to both a flow of light and water.

So together, NR may be revealing important or useful information.

The idea of NYR (plough) may come from the N meaning continuation. There's the picture of the ox pulling the plough, being led towards the destination to keep a straight line. This represents humanity being led towards our final destination. Our continuation on the plough line is about continuing towards what's most important (R).

NHR – River

*Genesis 2:10 A **river** watering the garden flowed from Eden; from there it was separated into four headwaters.*

NHR is from the root NR which seems to bring the idea of a continuation or flow to a source.

The concept of the river NHR[1] [nahar] is one that we would benefit from understanding in more depth as we'll see from the following scriptures.

The idea of a flow and continuation is critically central to Biblical themes. The river is found in both the Garden of Eden at the start of the human story, and at the end in the eternal garden, flowing from the throne of God. Perhaps it infers the continuation of God's rule and the continuation of life.

> *Revelation 22:1,2 Then the angel showed me the **river** of the water of life, as clear as crystal, flowing from the throne of God and of the Lamb down the middle of the great street of the city. On each side of the river stood the tree of life, bearing twelve crops of fruit, yielding its fruit every month. And the leaves of the tree are for the healing of the nations.*

---

[1] NHR Strong's 5104

How is river associated with its siblings, fire (NWR) and light (NHRH)? Could it be the idea of a flowing?

The letter N (sprouting seed) is about the continuation of life. The idea of continuation is akin to a flowing.

The letter R (head) points to what is most important and perhaps fundamental.

So, it's appropriate that the river in Revelation 22 is the flowing of the water of life.

Light is also a fundamental flow of life. Light was created first as the fundamental building block of life. Light is the first and simplest ordering of energy.

The opposite ordering of the letters to form the root RN brings the meaning of 'shout', specifically to shout for joy. This is a flowing out of life from the head.

NShA – Debt

> Genesis 3:13 Then the LORD God said to the woman, "What is this you have done?" The woman said, "The serpent **deceived** (NShA) me, and I ate."

NShA is from the root NSh whose children include:
NShA[1] ܕܘܫܐ [nashaa] (debt, deception),
MNShA[2] ܕܘܫܐܡ [manshaa] (interest on a loan, usury),
NShH[3] ܗܘܫܐ [nashah] (forget),
NShH[4] ܗܘܫܐ [nasheh] (tendon),

---

[1] NShA Strong's 5377
[2] MNSHA Strong's 4855
[3] NShH Strong's 5382
[4] NShH Strong's 5384

NWSh[1] ܢܘܫ [nuwsh] (despair).

The letter N (sprouting seed) speaks about the continuation of life. The letter Sh (teeth) talks about cutting something. So NSh is about cutting off the continuation of life.

Note that NShA is the opposite meaning to NSA: holding onto the continuation of life, to forgive and lift a burden.

The first time the word NShA appears, is when the serpent deceived Eve:

Notice how the word 'Serpent' (NXSh) uses the same letters plus the X (beyond the visible).

How did the Serpent deceive Adam and Eve? He led Eve to believe that the physical was more important than the spiritual. That the taste and sight of the fruit and the knowledge it would bring was more important than the trust relationship with God. We see the same deception today.

How is deception a debt and a burden? The burden is death and separation from God. There's no greater burden on humanity.

Many are led to believe that they have no burden and that they live a perfectly good life. That may be true in the present, but the end result will not be so pleasant.

The serpent convinced Eve to think that God wasn't to be believed – which is the great lie that is prevalent today. Then he convinced her to think that she wouldn't really die. But that was a lie on two accounts: The truth is, she would die - spiritually first – then physically.

The serpent (NXSh) is the agent of deception and burdens (NShA). Breaking the relationship.

Jesus the Son (BN) is the agent of forgiveness and lifting the burden (NSA). Repairing and continuing the relationship with Father God.

Notice the letter N threading and flowing through the whole story.

---

[1] NWSh Strong's 5136

When the disciples of Jesus asked Him what the signs of the end times will be, the first thing Jesus said was:

> *Luke 21:8,9 "Watch out that you are not **deceived**. For many will come in my name, claiming, 'I am he,' and 'The time is near.' Do not follow them. When you hear of wars and revolutions, do not be frightened. These things must happen first, but the end will not come right away."*

The first comment by humanity about the Serpent is in relation to his act of deception, and the last mention of the Serpent also identifies him as being the one who deceived humanity:

> *Genesis 3:13 The woman said, "The serpent **deceived** me, and I ate."*

> *Revelation 20:10 And the devil, who **deceived** them, was thrown into the lake of burning sulphur, where the beast and the false prophet had been thrown. They will be tormented day and night for ever and ever.*

We should not be overly confident in our ability to spot the deceptions of the Serpent. He is the world's greatest master of deception, and the art of deception is all about making people think that there's nothing out of the ordinary about what's happening. Perhaps the greatest tool we have is to follow God's word in our everyday lives as close as we can. We need to be aware of just sounding humanist arguments which claim to have the physical needs of humanity at heart.

If God say's not to eat the fruit off the tree in the middle of the garden – don't – even if it may sound at odds with what the majority says!

S – Samech – Thorn

It seems that the original name for the letter Samech was Sin[1] – meaning thorn. Samech is the *modern* name for the letter.

It appears that there's been some interchange or mixing up of the letter S and Sh in Hebrew history. In the modern alphabet and in the Hebrew Bible, the letter Sh can be pronounced as both [s] and [sh] or spelt with S or Shin in the same phonemic position, without any apparent reason.

The Hebrew word, 'Shalom' is pronounced and written as Salaam in Arabic. This leads me to explore the possibility of the original spelling being SLM.

The word spelt SMX (Samech, the modern name for the letter S), brings the meaning of rejoice and joy.

The word spelt SN (Sin, the older name) means, 'thorn'. I'm not aware of any connection between the Hebrew word Sin and the English word 'sin', apart from the obvious identical spelling.

Ultimately, we should be able to get a better idea of which meaning applies by looking at how it's used in different contexts. It does seem to work better with the meaning of thorn – which often includes the meaning of grabbing or holding fast. This is illustrated in the account of Abraham finding a ram stuck in a thorn bush.

Cut thorn bushes were also used to make a coral to fence the sheep in and help protect them from attack.

S has the numerical value of 60.

From the time of Moses, sixty is the age where someone appears to be considered elderly. People lived much longer earlier on. The value of a

---

[1] Not necessarily related to the English word 'sin'.

dedication vow[1] of a man aged between twenty and sixty was fifty shekels of silver. But over sixty it reduced to fifteen shekels. Curiously, the letter S is the 15th letter in the alphabet.

Fifteen cubits (approximately 7.5m²) is a significant measurement in the design of the temple.

In the New Testament, a widow was not to receive assistance unless she was over 60.

SBB – Surround

*Psalm 32:10 Many are the woes of the wicked, but the LORD's unfailing love **surrounds** (SBB) the man who trusts in him.*

SBB[2] [sabab] means 'surround' and is from the root SB.

The letter S here, likely depicts the coral made of cut thorn bushes which surrounds the house (B) to contain and protect the flock.

It could also be that the house (B) or God's family is what surrounds the man who trusts in Him.

Other children of the root SB include:
SYBH[3] ⟨symbols⟩ [siibah] (turn of events),
MSB[4] ⟨symbols⟩ [mesab] (around),
SBA[5] ⟨symbols⟩ [sabaa] (drunkard – one who turns around),
SYB[6] ⟨symbols⟩ [siyb] (elder).

---

[1] Leviticus 27:2-7
[2] SBB Strong's 5437
[3] SYBH Strong's 5438
[4] MSB Strong's 4524
[5] SBA Strong's 5433
[6] SYB Strong's 7867, 7868

SR ~ YShRAL – Israel

*Genesis 32:28 Then the man said, "Your name will no longer be Jacob, but **Israel (YShRAL)**, because you have struggled(ShRYT) with God and with men and have overcome."*

The word 'Israel' is spelt YShRAL[1] [ysra-el] and is made of two words YShR and AL. The AL is normally translated as, 'God' but means, 'to guide'.

The origin of YShR is said to be SRH, meaning to turn in another direction – also translated as revolt, rebellion, turn away. This is another example of seemingly free exchange between S and Sh.

If we look at the actual spelling of YShR, that brings a meaning of, 'straight, remnant, bow cord, which doesn't seem to relate to the meaning given in Genesis 32:28, which has to do with struggling and overcoming.

Children of the root SR include:
SR[2] [sar] (noble, stubborn, turn in revolt. Perhaps the ancestor of the English word sir)
SRN[3] [seren] (Lord, axle),
MSWR[4] [masowr] (saw for cutting – perhaps the ancestor of the English, 'saw'),
MSRH[5] [misrah] (government),
ASR[6] [aaser] (bind, decree),
ASYR[7] [asayr] (prison),

---

[1] YShRAL Strong's 3478
[2] SR Strong's 5620, 8269
[3] SRN Strong's 5633
[4] MSWR Strong's 4833
[5] MSRH Strong's 4951
[6] ASR Strong's 633
[7] ASYR Strong's 615, 616

SAWR[1] 𐤎𐤅𐤏𐤓 [seor] (knead bread – with a twisting and wrestling action. Could this be the origin of the English word 'sour' – from sour dough?),
SHR[2] RHS [sahar] (round),
SRH[3] HRS [sarah] (struggle, turn), SWR[4] [suwr] (remove, turn aside, rule),
YSR[5] RSY [yasar] (to correct, instruction). The Arabic meanings of SR include YSAR [yisaar] (to the left) and SR [sir] (steal).

In the children of SR, we can see a common theme which S (thorn) brings relating to grasping and binding.

There's a combined action of grasping with the determination that requires not letting go, even when the object is turning around.

Also, the letter R (head) relates to the top which talks about coming out on top – to rule.

It's not difficult to see how these ideas connect to God's naming of Israel with the idea that Israel would wrestle and come out on top to rule. It's a description of how Jacob wrestled with the angel, but it's also prophetic of the history of Israel – who would wrestle with God but could overcome in the end – not in the sense of overcoming God but in the sense of persevering and winning.

We should note that it was Israel who has been wrestling with God, and it was one of her sons, Jesus who was the champion to finally win the fight and rule. The Serpent has been trying to destroy Israel for ages past so that he could ultimately prevent God's plan through Jesus.

John, in the New Testament, tells us about overcoming to the end:

> *1 John 5:5 Who is it that overcomes the world? Only he who believes that Jesus is the Son of God.*

---

[1] SAWR Strong's 7603
[2] SHR Strong's 5469
[3] SRH Strong's 8280
[4] SWR Strong's 5493
[5] YSR Strong's 3256

This defines what overcoming the world is – to finally believe that Jesus is the Son of God.

Revelation talks about overcoming at least 8 times, all in association with an eternal reward.

> *Revelation 21:7 He who overcomes will inherit all this, and I will be his God and he will be my son.*

Jesus asks us to persevere:

> *Matthew 7:7 "Ask and it will be given to you; seek and you will find; knock and the door will be opened to you."*

We need to know that overcoming is not all about our own abilities and strengths. Jesus tells us:

> *John 16:33 "I have told you these things, so that in me you may have peace. In this world you will have trouble. But take heart! I have **overcome** the world."*

Our perseverance is very much about trusting in the One who has overcome.

SLTh – Pardon

> *Exodus 34:9 "Although this is a stiff-necked people, **forgive** (SLTh) our wickedness and our sin, and take us as your inheritance."*

> *Isaiah 55:7 Let the wicked forsake his way and the evil man his thoughts. Let him turn to the LORD, and he will have mercy on him, and to our God, for he will freely **pardon** (SLTh).*

There is another word NSA which is also translated as 'forgive'. What's the difference? The thing which they have in common is the letter S (thorn) bringing the idea of grabbing hold of. But it could be that the S is used with a different meaning in SLTh[1] [salath]. Another thing they have in common is that SLTh is from the root SL, which, like NSA also has the meaning of lifting out of debt.

In the word SLTh, it could be that the S brings the idea that debt is holding the person in bondage. The letter L then talks about leading out of the bondage to a place of safe keeping Th (basket).

SLTh is used exclusively for God forgiving humanity.

NSA on the other hand is often used for human action – to bear up something, or to exalt. Only a handful of times is it used in relation to God's forgiving.

Forgiving certainly needs to be part of our everyday lives because without it we will not grow and move towards our destination. As Jesus says:

> *Matthew 6:14 For if you forgive men when they sin against you, your heavenly Father will also forgive you.*

We can't necessarily forget a wrong that someone has done to us, and we may need to do something to try and prevent the harm from happening again. But we must not allow the harm from another person to stop our lives in its tracks – both for the harmer and the harmed. To be able to forgive, we will benefit greatly from seeing a greater end result which is working towards everyone being in God's family. Let's allow life to continue.

SMX – Rejoice

> *Leviticus 23:40 On the first day you are to take choice fruit from the trees, and palm fronds, leafy branches and poplars, and* **rejoice** *SMX before the LORD your God for seven days.*

---

[1] SLTh Strong's 5545 (although Strong's says it's pronounced salach, the Hebrew letters are indeed the Th)

Rejoicing is a concept we've perhaps shelved and forgotten about in our daily lives. But God has instructed us to rejoice for good reason. We will do well to try and understand this concept better and to make it part of our lives and our relationship with God. It's a key element in our trust relationship with God and one another. Without it, negativity may clog our wheels.

We are actually commanded or invited to rejoice always, in both the Old Testament and the New Testament. In the New Testament, Paul is adamant:

Rejoice in the Lord always. I will say it again: Rejoice!
Philippians 4:4

The Greek word used in Philippians 4:4 for rejoice is 'chairo' and has the meaning of rejoice, be glad, be well, thrive, hail (in a salutation or greeting). I wonder if this word is related to the Spanish word 'chao' used to wish a person good health and safety when saying goodbye.

There are several Hebrew words with a similar meaning of rejoicing. They all start with different letters, but I've grouped them together here so that by comparing them we may get a get a better idea of the unique nature of each. They include SMX/ShMX (rejoice), ʕLTs (be triumphant), GYL, RNN (sing for joy), SWS, AShR (happy). There is an overlap in meanings between these words, and a lot which is unique to each. We should also be aware that an English understanding of a word such as rejoice doesn't necessarily equate entirely with the Hebrew word from which it's translated. So, we do well to dig further to understand what the Hebrew word is telling us and how to make it a reality in our lives.

Back to the Hebrew word SMX[1] Note this word is often spelt ShMX in the Hebrew Bible but pronounced [samakh]. It's often also spelt SMX in dictionaries. So where do we take our meaning from – the Sh or the S? We should get some ideas as we look at the meanings and use of the word.

What does the context of SMX tell us?

It's used 152 times in the Old Testament. Many times in Deuteronomy, God commands all to SMX.

---

[1] SMX Strong's 8055

There are 51 uses of SMX in the Psalms.

It's well worth reading through some of the uses in the Bible to see just how significant this concept is for life:

> *Deuteronomy 26:11 And you and the Levites and the aliens among you shall **rejoice** in all the good things the LORD your God has given to you and your household.*
>
> *Deuteronomy 27:7 Sacrifice fellowship offerings there, eating them and **rejoicing** in the presence of the LORD your God.*
>
> *Psalm 9:2 I will be **glad** (SMX) and rejoice (SLTs) in you; I will sing praise to your name, O Most High.*
>
> *Psalm 33:21 In him our hearts **rejoice** (SMX), for we trust in his holy name.*
>
> *Isaiah 9:3 You have enlarged the nation and increased their joy; they **rejoice** (SMX) before you as people rejoice at the harvest, as men rejoice (GYL) when dividing the plunder.*
>
> *Proverbs 10:1 A wise son brings **joy** (SMX) to his father, but a foolish son grief to his mother.*
>
> *Proverbs 12:25 An anxious heart weighs a man down, but a kind word **cheers** (SMX) him up.*
>
> *Proverbs 13:9 The light of the righteous **shines brightly** (SMX), but the lamp of the wicked is snuffed out.*
>
> *Zechariah 10:7 The Ephraimites will become like mighty men, and their hearts will be **glad** (SMX) as with wine. Their children will see it and be joyful (SMX); their hearts will rejoice (GYL) in the LORD.*
>
> *Hosea 7:3 They **delight** (SMX) the king with their wickedness, the princes with their lies.*
>
> *Jonah 4:6 Then the LORD God provided a vine and made it grow up over Jonah to give shade for his head to ease his discomfort, and Jonah was very **happy** (SMX) about the vine.*

The context of the above verses appears to indicate that SMX has a lot to do with being thankful and grateful. SMX is also the main word used in the context of a command.

SMX is likely related to the simpler root SM which talks about a place to put stuff.

If we go with the use of Sh and the root ShM, we get the children with meanings of breath, aroma, desolate, guilt, garlic (a food with intense smell). ShM doesn't appear to fit the meaning of rejoicing!

What do the letters of SMX tell us?

We need to put the letters in context of the usage of the word, but at first glance they indicate as follows:

The S (thorn) tells us about holding onto something – such as grasping hold of God in trust.

The M (ocean) moves on from the grasping to a great unknown. This takes us into the spiritual.

The X (wall) talks about going beyond the physical into the spiritual.

So put all together perhaps there's the picture of letting go of the physical circumstances which may surround us and entering into the awesomeness of God.

If Paul tells us that we should rejoice always, then that would indicate that our rejoicing shouldn't be conditional on what's around us. SMX is not limited to waving palm branches, dancing or singing, but it does appear to involve trusting in God and looking beyond our immediate circumstances. It may help us to have a deliberate outward expression of that trust and thankfulness, but it must start with our heart.

ʕLZ – Triumph

*Psalm 28:7 The LORD is my strength and my shield; my heart trusts in him, and I am helped. My heart leaps for **joy** (ʕLZ) and I will give thanks to him in song.*

ʕLZ[1] [ʕalaz] is frequently translated as exult, triumph and rejoice.

*Psalm 60:6 God has spoken from his sanctuary: "In **triumph** I will parcel out Shechem and measure off the Valley of Succoth."*

*Habakkuk 3:17-19 Though the fig tree does not bud and there are no grapes on the vines, though the olive crop fails and the fields produce no food, though there are no sheep in the pen and no cattle in the stalls, yet I will **rejoice** in the LORD, I will be joyful in God my Savior. The Sovereign LORD is my strength; he makes my feet like the feet of a deer, he enables me to go on the heights.*

Habakkuk tells about rejoicing despite the physical circumstances around him. The letters ʕLZ appear to support this idea. The letter ʕ (eye) does talk about the visible. Habakkuk recognises the visible troubles of his environment but moves on from there.

The letter L (shepherd's staff) talks about leading or pointing. Perhaps that refers to the phrase "Yet I will" – an important part of triumphing.

The word finishes with the letter Z (plough) which frequently talks about a sacrifice which invites us to leave behind the physical so that we can gain spiritually.

---

[1] ʕLZ Strong's 5937

S – SAMECH – THORN

ʕLTs – Be lifted

*1 Samuel 2:1 Then Hannah prayed and said: "My heart **rejoices** in the LORD; in the LORD my horn is lifted high. My mouth boasts over my enemies, for I delight in your deliverance."*

ʕLTs[1] [ʕaLaTs] has the dictionary meaning of 'triumph'. It's likely from the root ʕL which has the meaning of being above or upon.

ʕLZ [ʕalaz] has a similar meaning and likely shares the root ʕL. It could well be a variant of the same word. The sounds Ts (pronounced as Dh) and Z are very similar in sound.

The letter Ts (man on side) doesn't seem to bring anything to the meaning of triumph unless it's talking about being on or above (ʕL) the person on the ground who's been conquered.

*Psalm 5:11 But let all who take refuge in you be glad (SMX); let them ever sing for joy (RNN). Spread your protection over them, that those who love your name may **rejoice** (ʕLTs) in you.*

*Psalm 25:2 in you I trust, O my God. Do not let me be put to shame, nor let my enemies **triumph** over me.*

*Psalm 68:3 But may the righteous be glad (SMX) and **rejoice** (ʕLTs) before God; may they be happy and joyful (SWS).*

GYL – Rejoice

*Isaiah 9:3 You have enlarged the nation and increased their joy (ShMXH); they rejoice SMX before you as people rejoice at the harvest, as men **rejoice** GYL when dividing the plunder.*

---

[1] ʕLTs Strong's 5970

This word is widespread in the Bible with 44 occurrences including 19 in Psalms and 11 in Isaiah.

GYL[1] is from GL meaning a round thing or to go around like spinning.

Another child of GL is GAL[2] ∠👁‍🗨↖ [gaal] which means 'to redeem' – to bring back around.

The G (foot) is often used to bring the idea of turning. The L (shepherd's staff) talks about a direction. So combined there's the idea of going around. The shepherd's staff (∠) was also used for halting a fleeing animal – to turn it around.

Spiritually, the G (foot) could talk about humility.

The L could be about being led. So together it could say that from humility we can be led – and it's this that brings us joy. This also relates to redemption. Many uses refer to having joy in God's salvation. Isaiah 9:3 doesn't necessarily talk about salvation though it could talk about coming out of a place of humility to a richer place.

*Psalm 2:11 Serve the LORD with fear and **rejoice** with trembling.*

GYL is very often paired with SMX:

*Isaiah 25:9 This is the LORD, we trusted in him; let us **rejoice** (GYL) and be **glad** (SMX) in his salvation.*

RNN – Sing for Joy

*Psalm 5:11 But let all who take refuge in you be glad (SMX); let them ever **sing for joy** (RNN). Spread your protection over them, that those who love your name may rejoice (ʕLTs) in you.*

---

[1] GYL Strong's 1523
[2] GAL Strong's 1350

*1 Chronicles 16:33 Then the trees of the forest will sing, they will **sing for joy** before the LORD, for he comes to judge the earth.*

*Job 38:7 while the morning stars **sang** together and all the angels shouted for joy?*

RNN[1] [ranan] (ringing sound) is from the root RN whose other children include:

AWRN[2] [awren] (perhaps a pine tree which possibly grew rattle like cones or seed pods),

RNH[3] [ranah] (rattle),

RWN[4] [rawn] (shout, murmur).

It's not clear how the letters RN would bring the meaning of shouting or a loud sound. The letter R (head) does bring the idea of something up high which may support the idea of a loud sound. The letter N (sprouting seed) brings the idea of a continuation. So, a continuous high could well bring the idea of a loud sound.

Could R (head, top, high) and N (sprouting seed, plant) be talking about a high tree which sings in the wind?

Loud singing is certainly an expression of joy!

SWS - Joyful

*Psalm 68:3 But may the righteous be glad (SMX) and rejoice (ʕLTs) before God; may they be happy (ShMXH) and **joyful** (SWS).*

---

[1] RNN Strong's 7442
[2] AWRN Strong's 766
[3] RNH Strong's 7439
[4] RWN Strong's 3885

*Zephaniah 3:17 The LORD your God is with you, he is mighty to save. He will take great **delight** (SWS) in you, he will quiet you with his love, he will rejoice (GYL) over you with singing."*

SWS¹ [soos] (swallow bird, rejoice, horse) is from the root SS whose other children include:

SS² ╪╪ [sas] (moth),

MSWS³ ╪Y╪〰 [masows] (joy).

The creatures of moth, swallow, horse all seem to be a metaphor for a dancing motion.

Some Hebrew scripts write this word with an Sh instead of the S. But it appears that S is the original spelling.

The letter S (thorn) frequently brings the meaning of a twisting motion – which is the typical response of an animal which is stuck on a thorn.

We get something of the swoosh sound when a swallow passes close by. Perhaps even a moth will make that sound against the silence of the night.

SPR – Sapphire

*Exodus 24:10 And they saw the God of Israel. Under his feet was something like a pavement made of **sapphire**, clear as the sky itself.*

The colour sapphire is seen at the two thirds position on the colour spectrum, reading the spectrum from the red end. It's normally a light sky blue especially when pure with light shining through – as with the sky.

The letter S is also two thirds through the alphabet.

---

[1] ShWSh Strong's 7797
[2] ShSh Strong's 5580
[3] MSWS Strong's 4885

The word meaning sapphire is spelt SPYR[1] 𐤎𐤐𐤉𐤓 [safiir] and is from the root SPR. Its children include: SPR[2] [saphar] (record, scroll, census, scribe – Could this be the origin of the English word 'cypher'?), SPWRH[3] 𐤎𐤐𐤅𐤓𐤄 [sephorah] (number).

What is the underlying meaning which the root SPR brings? The root SP has the idea of a bringing together e.g., gather, whirlwind, edge, consume, add. So perhaps SPR has the idea of a summation of what is important.

The letter S (thorn) brings the idea of grasping something. The letter P (mouth) has the idea of enclosing something. Together they bring the idea of encapsulating something – such as a summation, gathering or framing.

Sapphires are certainly an important (R) stone with an important spiritual significance, and they do seem to act as the edge or frame of something important such as the throne surrounds the king sitting on it. They are on both the ground, foundation and overhead as we see in the scriptures below.

Sapphires appear to have an important spiritual role and appear in a few prophetic scenes.

> *Exodus 28:18 in the second row (of the ephod) a turquoise, a sapphire and an emerald.*
>
> *Isaiah 54:11 "O afflicted city, lashed by storms and not comforted, I will build you with stones of turquoise, your foundations with **sapphires**."*
>
> *Ezekiel 1:26 Above the expanse over their heads was what looked like a throne of **sapphire**, and high above on the throne was a figure like that of a man.*

I understand the two thirds position of the colour in the spectrum relates to the two thirds position in human history. It signals the start of the final third era where Jesus rules the earth from his sapphire throne for 1000 years.

---

[1] SPYR Strong's 5601
[2] SPR Strong's 5608
[3] SPWRH Strong's 5615

It's not a chronological two thirds but relates to the end of two parts of history, with the last third part yet to come.

The letter S is the 15th letter of the alphabet. In a similar way that the 22nd letter (T) relates to Psalm 22 and Revelation 22, could the 15th letter also relate to Psalm 15 which talks about who may dwell in the sanctuary and on the holy hill? These two locations act as a kind of seating or encapsulating something important – such as a throne does for a king.

Revelation 15 includes a description of a sea of glass which could likely be the same colour and appearance as sapphire. This chapter also talks about what will happen immediately prior to the ending of the second era of history.

> *Revelation 15:1-2 I saw in heaven another great and marvellous sign: seven angels with the seven last plagues-- last, because with them God's wrath is completed. And I saw what looked like a sea of glass mixed with fire and, standing beside the sea, those who had been victorious over the beast and his image and over the number of his name. They held harps given them by God.*

ע – Ayin – Eye

The sound ע is not found in the English language. In modern Hebrew it's silent but in most other Semitic languages, it's a voiced pharyngeal fricative. It sounds a little like a mooing camel. It's like a voiced letter H – formed in the back of the throat.

The letter ע was written with the symbol of an eye. The name for the letter is spelt עYN [ein], meaning, 'eye'. It's from the root עN meaning 'watch', 'eye' and 'affliction'.

The word עYN[1] is also used to mean 'a spring' in the sense of an opening in the ground. The letter N likely refers to a continuous flow. In other uses, the letter ע appears to be used to bring the idea of an opening, e.g. Lע[2] means 'throat'. It's the 16th letter of the alphabet and has the numerical value of 70. What is the Biblical significance of 70? There appear to be two elements acting together: 7 multiplied by 10 equals 70. I understand the number seven to be the completion of the physical. This contrasts with the number 10 which I understand to be talking about divine completion. A multiplication relationship is all about one acting on another, rather than joining as in addition. So, divinity (10) acting on the physical (7) results in 70.

How do we see this concept showing itself in the Bible? We see it most notably in groups of God's people who become the founders of a new beginning:

After the flood, 70 descendants of Noah formed 70 nations. (Genesis 10)

The nation of Israel began with 70 Hebrews when they first went to Egypt. (Exodus 1).

---

[1] עYN Strong's 5869
[2] Lע Strong's 3930

Moses appointed 70 elders to be the governing body of Israel after leaving Egypt. (Numbers 11).

Jesus sent out seventy-two pioneers to heal and proclaim the coming of the Kingdom of God in Luke 10.

ʕBRY – Hebrew

> *Jonah 1:9 He answered, "I am a **Hebrew** and I worship the LORD, the God of heaven, who made the sea and the land."*

The name, 'Hebrew' is spelt ʕBRY[1] [ʕabriy] and is from the root ʕBR. It was first used by the Canaanites to describe Abram – then came to be used of his descendants by God's promise – the Israelites. The word means to cross over – from beyond.

Other children of ʕBR include:

ʕBR[2] 𓂝𐤁𐤓 [ʕabar] (to cross, beyond, wrath),

MʕBR[3] 𓂝𐤁𐤓𐤌 [maʕabar] (a crossing, ford),

ʕBWR[4] 𓂝𐤁𐤅𐤓 [ʕabuwr] (produce, purpose, reason).

What do the letters ʕBR tell us about the meaning?

The letter ʕ (eye) may talk about what's visible in the present and current location. Or could it be like Moses looking across the valley to the promised land? He couldn't cross over because he didn't trust God at the waters of Meribah[5]. He didn't follow God's instruction but instead did what he had done previously as if to follow a law. He brought the law to the people and

---

[1] ʕBRY Strong's 5680
[2] ʕBR Strong's 5674
[3] MʕBR Strong's 4569
[4] ʕBWR Strong's 5668, 5669
[5] Bible, Numbers 20:12

ʕ – AYIN – EYE

was under law himself. Relationship (B) and trust is what allowed Joshua to lead God's people over.

The letter B (house) may talk about a relationship or a family.

The letter R (head) may talk about an important purpose which is beyond the present.

Put together, we get the story which starts in the visible current location and time. We then move into God's family which is the door to the other side and our ultimate purpose.

After Abram left his homeland and was arriving at the new land:

> Genesis 12:6 Abram **travelled through (ʕBR)** the land as far as the site of the great tree of Moreh at Shechem. At that time the Canaanites were in the land.

ʕBRY may well have been a term equivalent to, 'foreigner'. Abram had come from outside the land of Canaan, from beyond the great desert of Iraq. However, the name could also be prophetic because God has a plan for the Hebrews which is beyond the physical.

ʕD – Witness

> Joshua 22:34 And the Reubenites and the Gadites gave the altar this name: **ʕD** – A Witness Between Us that the LORD is God.

When the Israelites came to the Promised Land, the descendants of Reuben and Gad decided not to live in Canaan but to remain across the Jordan. They built a pile of stones to be a lasting reminder between Israel and themselves that they were part of the children of Israel and worshipped the same God. They named the memorial pile of stones ʕD[1] [ʕad], meaning, 'a witness between us'.

---

[1] ʕD Strong's 5707

The letter Ꞩ (eye) brings the idea of seeing or witnessing something.

The letter D (door) brings the idea of reciprocation – there is an agreed witness (Ꞩ) or testimony between (D) two or more people.

A child of ꞨD is ꞨDH[1] [Ꞩedah] which talks about a gathering of people with a common purpose or witness. It was used of the assembly of Israel, but also for any gathering including troublemakers.

The word ꞨD is used 69 times in the Bible.

> *Proverbs 14:5 A truthful **witness** does not deceive, but a false **witness** pours out lies.*
>
> *Isaiah 43:10 "You are my **witnesses**," declares the LORD, "and my servant whom I have chosen, so that you may know and believe me and understand that I am he. Before me no god was formed, nor will there be one after me."*
>
> *Isaiah 43:12 "I have revealed and saved and proclaimed-- I, and not some foreign god among you. You are my **witnesses**," declares the LORD, "that I am God."*

It appears that being a witness to God's working is a task given to us in the present time.

> *Acts 1:8 "But you will receive power when the Holy Spirit comes on you; and you will be my **witnesses** in Jerusalem, and in all Judea and Samaria, and to the ends of the earth."*
>
> *Acts 5:32 We are **witnesses** of these things, and so is the Holy Spirit, whom God has given to those who obey him.*

---

[1] ꞨDH Strong's 5712, 5713

ʕZR – Help

*Psalm 33:20 We wait in hope for the LORD; he is our **help** and our shield.*

In Psalms, the word ʕZR[1] [ʕezer] is frequently used in association with the shield. In Genesis 2:18, it's in the context of answering the problem of Adam being alone. It seems to be an important word which is well worth understanding better because it relates to the purpose for Eve being created. I understand that Eve was created so that ultimately Jesus could be born to be our ultimate helper to enable humanity to not be separated from God.[2]

The letter ʕ (eye) may relate to seeing a need.

The letter Z relates to physical work.

The letter R (head) talks about something important or perhaps coming out on top.

*Genesis 2:18 The LORD God said, "It is not good for the man to be alone. I will make a **helper** suitable for him."*

*Psalms 121:2 My **help** comes from the LORD, the Maker of heaven and earth.*

ʕDN – Eden

*Genesis 2:8 Now the LORD God had planted a garden (GN) in the east, in **Eden** (ʕDN); and there he put the man he had formed.*

---

[1] ʕZR Strong's 5828
[2] See the section ANSh – Man and Woman

The word spelt Eden is from the Hebrew word spelt ʕDN[1] [ʕeden], which means, delight and pleasure. Children of ʕDN include:

ʕDNH[2] 𐤘𐤍𐤃𐤏 [ʕadenah] (yet, remaining, continuing),
MʕDN[3] 𐤍𐤃𐤏𐤌 [maʕadan] (delicacy),
MʕDNH[4] 𐤘𐤍𐤃𐤏𐤌 [maʕadanah] (chain),
ʕYDN[5] 𐤍𐤃𐤉𐤏 [ʕiydan] (time).

We should note that Eden wasn't the garden, but a garden was planted in Eden – a place in the East. So, our study of Eden may be talking about a place larger than the garden.

> *Genesis 2:10 A river watering the garden flowed from Eden; from there it was separated into four headwaters (Pishon, Gihon, Tigris and Euphrates.*

The river watering the garden came from the area of Eden. And upsteam from there are the convergences of four rivers. Today the lowest convergence is the Tigris and Euphrates at a place called AlQurnah which is about 70 kilometers upstream of Basrah in Iraq. If the location of these two rivers is the same as in ancient times. Then it would appear that the area of Basrah is about where the garden was located. Today it still has gardens irrigated from the river which is about 400m wide at that point. It's about 100km inland from the Arabian Gulf Sea.

The letter ʕ (eye) surely relates to a visual delight.

The letter D (door) may talk about something reciprocal. Could that relate to the reciprocal relationship God had with humanity in the garden? He walked and talked with Adam and Eve in the garden. A garden has a distinct purpose which sets it apart from the rest of nature. It was a place deliberately made for the purpose of God and humanity to be together.

The letter N (sprouting seed) likely relates to the plants growing in the garden. It could also be a place of continuation.

---

[1] ʕDN Strong's 5731
[2] ʕDNH Strong's 5728
[3] MʕDN Strong's 4574
[4] MʕDNH Strong's 4575
[5] ʕYDN Strong's 5732

؏ – AYIN – EYE

Perhaps there's also a spiritual story in the letters.

The ؏ may relate to the knowledge and things of physical pleasure which Adam and Eve chose over their relationship with God.

The D (door) may relate to the door which was then closed on them. On the other side of the door was the humility of mortality.

The letter N may relate to the promised forgiveness which God offers to us so that life and relationship may continue. This is of far greater significance to God than a physical garden and its meaning. See the section on N to get a fuller picture of this very important letter.

؏SR – Tenth

The word ؏SR[1] [؏asar] means tithe and ten. ؏SR appears in the Bible text as ؏ShR but in the dictionary as ؏SR. Another case of variation between Sh and S. In Arabic the number 10 is spelt ؏ShR.

Note how the word ؏SR includes the meaning of 'tithe' which means to give a tenth. The word ؏ShR starts with the value of 70 (؏) then moves to the value of 60 (S). That shows that 10 has been given – a tithing of 10. The letter R had the value of 200 and is the 20th letter in the alphabet. There's a multiplication of 10 between 20 and 200. The number 20 tells me about divinity (10) acting on relationship (2). A numerical relationship of acting on something talks about multiplication, and a relationship of joining something is an addition. Could the word be telling us that when we give (subtract 10) we will then see a return (multiplied by 10)?

> Mark 10: 29.30 "I tell you the truth," Jesus replied, "no one who has left home or brothers or sisters or mother or father or children or fields for me and the gospel will fail to receive a hundred times as much in this present age (homes, brothers, sisters, mothers,

---

[1] ؏SR Strong's 6237

children and fields-- and with them, persecutions) and in the age to come, eternal life.

Tithing is an act of trust in God, and we can expect a mutual reciprocation where God will act on our relationship.

Ten is a significant number. It appears to represent divinity – the joining together of two persons. The letter H represents a person and has the numerical value of five. Two sets of 5 makes 10. The two persons are the divine Father and the human Son.

A tenth is also the amount each person is to tithe to the temple under the law. What's the significance of a tenth?

A tenth is the result of dividing by ten – the reverse of multiplying by ten which is God acting on something. Could the tenth signify man allowing or inviting God to act on something?

The whole ten parts is what God has given – God acting on man, and the return of the tenth is a recognition of that gift. It seems that the tenth is a metaphor for what we give back to God. We actually give Him our full trust and everything we have. We trust Him to lead our whole life.

During the period of law, we were required to give a tenth to the temple. But now that we are not directed by the law but by the Spirit, we give ourselves to the family of God. We no longer need to pay the priests and the cost of running the temple. God's family can function perfectly fine in any gathering of people without the infrastructure that was required during the period of law.

When the disciples of Jesus were admiring the temple, he said to them:

John 2:19 "Destroy this temple, and I will raise it again in three days."

The disciples were baffled about this, but Jesus was talking about replacing the temple with his own body and family. His rising from the dead was the raising of the temple.

ϒ – AYIN – EYE

ϒT – Time

*Ecclesiastes 3:11 He has made everything beautiful in its **time** (ϒT). He has also set **eternity** (ϒWLM) in the hearts of men; yet they cannot fathom what God has done from beginning to end.*

Children of the root ϒT include:
ϒT[1] [ϒat] (time, season – a moment in time for a particular purpose),
ϒTY[2] [ϒitiy] (ready, appointed),
ϒTH[3] [ϒatah] (now),
ϒWT[4] [ϒuwt] (speak in season).

How does ϒT relate to a moment in time? ϒ relates to something seen and knowledge. The letter T relates to the completion and end point of God's purpose for the physical earth – and time as we know it. So, a time or season is something known (seen) along the path which is measured in relation to the completion point. In a way, there's two completion points by which we measure time against. We have a man-made measure of time relative to the birth of Jesus – B.C. and A.D. But I think God measures time relative to when this visible (ϒ) physical world will come to an end and we will arrive at our ultimate destination (T), which will be the start of eternal life as God's family. Perhaps when we pass that marker and come out the other side, time will look very different – especially as we enter into an eternal existence. Perhaps we'll cease to have any measure of time.

The word translated as 'eternity' is spelt ϒWLM[5] [ϒowlam]. Note how it also starts with the letter ϒ, so talks about starting with the visible physical but then leading (L) onto the unmeasurable (M) eternity.

---

[1] ϒT Strong's 6256
[2] ϒTY Strong's 6261
[3] ϒTH Strong's 6258
[4] ϒWT Strong's 5790
[5] ϒWLM Strong's 5769

P – Pe – Open Mouth

The letter P was drawn with the symbol of a mouth. The root PA means, 'mouth' and 'edge.' The mouth often brings the idea of speaking or an enclosure/perimeter.

Another word PH [peh] also means 'mouth' and 'blow'.

The Arabic word for mouth is PM [fum].

The Aramaic PWM [fawm] is very similar.

There is no sound [p] in other Semitic languages. The most likely original sound could be an [f] sound either produced with the upper teeth on the lower lip, or with both lips together to produce a bilabial fricative – which sounds much like an [f] sound.

To get a better idea of its range of meaning, we'll look at some roots to see how it's used.

PDH – Redeem

> *Psalm 34:22 The LORD **redeems** (PDH) his servants; no one will be condemned who takes refuge in him.*

PDH[1] [fadah] (redeem) is from the root PD whose other children include, PDWT[2] ✝️𐤉𐤃𐤋 [fedawt] (ransom, division, distinction), APD[3] 𐤃𐤋𐤀 [afad] (gird - for securing the ephod, part of the equipment worn by the high priest),

---

[1] PDH Strong's 6299
[2] PDWT Strong's 6304
[3] APD Strong's 640

P – PE – OPEN MOUTH

APWD[1] 𐤃𐤅𐤐𐤀 [efowd] (ephod – outer garment of the high priest).

There are a variety of Hebrew words which bring a similar idea of God reaching out to help and save us:

GAL 𐤋𐤀𐤂 [gaal] (redeem),
XSH 𐤇𐤎𐤇 [khasah] (refuge),
ThHR 𐤓𐤄𐤈 [thaher] (cleanse),
KPR 𐤓𐤐𐤊 [kafar] (atone, cover),
NSA 𐤀𐤎𐤍 [nasaa] (forgive),
SBB 𐤁𐤁𐤎 [sabab] (surround),
SLX 𐤇𐤋𐤎 [salakh] (forgive),
ʕZR 𐤓𐤆𐤏 [ʕezer] (help).

(These have all been discussed under their root letters.) Many think that they don't need help or rescue, but they are unaware of the deep water they are in. The Serpent is the master of deception and will happily keep us in the dark about what is around the corner. Also, allowing another to reach out to us to assist is a sign of trust and humility, which is key to relationship. Without relationship we lose meaning. Relationship is key to being part of God's family into eternity.

What is the connection between redemption and the ephod? I would expect that the ephod is prophetic in a visual way of the spiritual concept of redemption.

> *Exodus 28:4-8 These are the garments they are to make: a breast piece, an ephod, a robe, a woven tunic, a turban and a sash. They are to make these sacred garments for your brother Aaron and his sons, so that they may serve me as priests. Make them using gold, and blue, purple and scarlet yarn, and fine linen.*
>
> *Make the ephod of gold, and of blue, purple and scarlet yarn, and of finely twisted linen--the work of a skilled craftsman. It is to have two shoulder pieces attached to two of its corners, so that it can be fastened. Its skilfully woven waistband is to be like it – of*

---

[1] APWD Strong's 646

one piece with the ephod and made with gold, and with blue, purple and scarlet yarn, and with finely twisted linen.

There is the Biblical idea that God will cover us with a garment so that our sin is covered. God made clothing for Adam and Eve in the garden after they disobeyed Him. In a spiritual sense, when we accept Jesus as our leader and husband, Jesus becomes our cover – like the ephod garment. The colours of the ephod tell a redemption story – told in order in which the colours are listed:

Gold, spelt ZHB ⌂ℽ⌐ [zahab], starts with the letter Z which is the seventh letter of the alphabet – a third way through the alphabet. The colour gold (yellow) is also a third the way through the colour spectrum. The first of the three eras of human history is the era where God leads His people by the law. This is where humanity discovers that they can't reach God by means of fulfilling laws – which is all about their own strength and resources.

Blue, spelt TKLT +∠⍩+ [tekelet], should be translated as violet – which some would say is in the blue range of colours. The word TKLT is from the root KL which means, completion. From KL we get the word KLLH ℽ∠∠⍩ [kallah] (bride – the one who has been made complete through marriage). The bride needs to be purchased (redeemed) by the groom. Jesus, the groom, paid the bride price by His death on the cross – which is in the shape of the letter T – which also means completion – of a contract. When Jesus paid the bride-price, the bride was legally His, though they would wait till the groom had prepared a room in his father's house before the bride would go to dwell with Him. But at Jesus' death the contract was completed, as shown in the letters KL.

Purple, spelt ARGMN ⌐ᴍ∧ꝅꙋ [argaman], is not a colour in the colour spectrum but is made up from the combination of the two colours violet (blue) and red (scarlet). Violet represents divinity and red represents humanity. Jesus was both divine and human. At His crucifixion, the soldiers dressed Him in purple cloth, which was a sign of royalty. Although the soldiers meant this as a mockery, it was symbolic of the humanity and divinity of Jesus. Jesus had to be human so that He could pay a human price for the redemption of His bride. But He's also divine because He's the physical expression of God - the Father, in whose house we will dwell forever – as has been His intention for humanity from day one.

Scarlett is spelt ShNY[1] ⌇ [shani], which is from the root ShN meaning teeth. Could this be the origin of the English word 'shiny'? Scarlett is the colour of the gums – red. But the root ShN tells a prophetic story of redemption. The letter Sh (which has the name ShN) talks about being cut off. We were cut off from God when we chose personal gain over relationship. However, the letter N (sprouting seed) talks about new life. The letter N has the numerical value of 50 which talks about the year of Jubilee when, every fifty years, all slaves were to be released and all debts forgiven. They had been redeemed.

So scarlet talks about being cut off but then brought back into relationship through being forgiven our debt.

A scarlet cord was hung out of the window of the prostitute Rahab's window, so that when the Israelite soldiers came to attack Jericho, she and her family with her would be saved. In fact, she became one of Jesus ancestors, joining the line of the continuation of life.

The word SNY is usually accompanied by the word TWLS[2] which is translated as 'worm' but can also refer to the insect coccus ilicis which is the source of the scarlett dye. Curiously the pairing of these two words is used interchangeably:

Exodus 26:31 "Make a curtain of blue, purple and scarlet SNY TWLS yarn and finely twisted linen, with cherubim worked into it by a skilled craftsman. 33 The **curtain** will separate the Holy Place from the Most Holy Place.

Exodus 26:36 "For the entrance to the tent make a curtain of blue, purple and scarlet TWLS SNY yarn and finely twisted linen-- the work of an embroiderer.

---

[1] ShNY Strong's 8144
[2] TWLS Strong's 8438

It appears that the only difference is that TWLƻ SNY is used for the main, first entrance of the tabernacle, and SNY TWLƻ is used for the inner separation between the Holy Place and the Most Holy Place.

SNY TWLƻ or TWLƻ SNY are seemingly used in the same context by the same author. TWLƻ is from the root Lƻ which brings the meanings of throat and crimson. The throat is a crimson colour. Other children of this root include the meanings of swallow and devour. The letter L (staff) talks about something going to the opening ƻ (eye).

Fine linen is white. The bride is dressed in fine linen when her husband takes her to his house to be his wife forever. White speaks of purity. She has been covered by the white garment provided by her husband.

So, what do the letters PD have to do with redemption and covering? The letter P (mouth) often brings the idea of encircling or enclosing. Could it be talking about the original state before being redeemed, of being closed in?

The D (door) may bring the idea of an opening so that we are no longer closed in – we are redeemed.

PLL – Pray

*Psalm 5:2 Listen to my cry for help, my King and my God, for to you I **pray (PLL)**.*

There are a few words which are translated as, 'pray' –
PLL[1] [palal] (plead, intervene, mediate),
NA[2] [na] (beseech),
ƻTR[3] [ƻatar] (entreat),
QRA[4] [qara] (cry out, proclaim),

---

[1] PLL Strong's 6419
[2] NA Strong's 4994
[3] ƻTR Strong's 6279
[4] QRA Strong's 7121

TXNH[1] ⌇ [tekhinnah] (supplication), and
TsLA[2] ⌇ [tsela] (Aramaic pray).

PLL [falal] comes from the parent root PL which seems to have the underlying meaning of proclaiming/speaking a directive, so that its other children include:

PLYL[3] ⌇ [feliyli] (judgement).

Other children are less clear:

APL[4] ⌇ [afel] (dark),

PLH[5] ⌇ [falah] (distinct),

PWL[6] ⌇ [fuul] (bean) Could the bean be something you eat (P mouth) and is bent (L curve on staff)?

APYL[7] ⌇ [afiyl] (late).

The P (mouth) brings the idea of speaking out something.

The L (shepherds' staff) brings the idea of a directive.

---

[1] TXNH Strong's 8467
[2] TsLA Strong's 6739
[3] PLYL Strong's 6416
[4] APL Strong's 652
[5] PLH Strong's 6395
[6] PWL Strong's 6321
[7] APYL Strong's 648

Ts – Tsad – Man on Side

The word Tsad, means, 'side'. The symbol for this letter resembles a person lying on their side with their knees pulled up. The word spelt TsDH[1] [tsadah] means to lay down. It's also translated to mean, wait, hunt, destroy. It can also be used as the question, 'Is it true?' It's used in the word meaning 'earth' (ARTs) [arets] [ardh in Arabic].

The original pronunciation of this letter is perhaps a little vague. It was apparently pronounced as Ts in both ancient and modern Hebrew, but in at least two other Semitic languages it's pronounced as a backed d (with the root of the tongue pulled back).

Strictly speaking, the sound [ts] is not a single sound, but an affricate – the combination of the two sounds t and s. There are no other affricates in the Hebrew language nor any other Semitic languages that I'm aware of, so the pronunciation of ts does seem out of place. I suspect that ts may be an influence from a European language such as Yiddish (influenced by German).

The letter Ts has the numerical value of 90 and is the 18th letter of the alphabet. The letter Ts representing a person on their side, could possibly represent a time of judgement. It comes towards the end of the alphabet story being the 18th letter. In the 18th chapter of Revelation (the last book), we read about a time of judgement on the earth. In Psalm 18, we also get a good dose of God's judgement on the earth:

> *Psalm 18:7-9 The earth trembled and quaked, and the foundations of the mountains shook; they trembled because he was angry. Smoke rose from his nostrils; consuming fire came from his mouth, burning coals blazed out of it. He parted the heavens and came down; dark clouds were under his feet.*

---

[1] TsDH Strong's 6658a

Why am I selecting out the Psalms for following this prophetic sequence? The proclamation of Jesus on the cross, quoting the first line of Psalm 22 is what gave me the first clue that there's a prophetic sequence in Psalms. There seems to be a sequence from at least Psalm 18 (Ts) through to Psalm 22 (T) which align with the last 5 letters of the alphabet in theme. Psalm 23 goes beyond the alphabet and the story of humanity on earth and introduces us to eternity beyond.

The letter following after Ts in the alphabet is Q (sun on the horizon) which is a picture of God's glory and holiness (QDSh). Read more about that in the section on Q.

Psalm 119 which has sections representing each of the letters of the alphabet, starts off the section for Ts with:

Psalm 119:137 Righteous are you, O LORD, and your laws are right.

Read from Psalm 119:137-152 for the Tsad section.

The first word is TsDYQ (righteous). It also refers to the judgement of God (your laws are right).

TsDYQ – Righteous

*Genesis 7:1 The LORD then said to Noah, "Go into the ark, you and your whole family, because I have found you **righteous** in this generation."*

TsDYQ[1] [tsadiq] is the source of the name of the priest Melkizedek which is spelt MLKYTsDQ [melkiy-tsedeq]. This is made up of two words, MLK [melek], meaning king, and TsDQ [tsadiq] meaning righteous. Note that he has the name king, but he is also a priest – like Jesus.

---

[1] TsDYQ Strong's 6662

TsDQ has the physical meaning of straight and the spiritual meaning of righteous. What's the link between straight and righteousness? It ties in with the picture of the plough line[1] where we need to keep our eye on the plough marker at the end of the field so that we can plough a straight line. The plough marker at the end of the field, represents our final aim and destination which is to dwell with the Son and Father for eternity as His family. A straight line is important, not so that we can have a good ego, but so that we don't waste time and effort going off in the wrong direction. The most efficient way to get to our destination is in a straight line. A straight plough line produces evenly spaced lines which makes economical use of the farmland and seed.

Luke wrote of John the Baptist referring to a prophecy in Isaiah 43:3 -6

> *Luke 3:4-6 As is written in the book of the words of Isaiah the prophet: "A voice of one calling in the desert, 'Prepare the way for the Lord, make* **straight (YShR)** *paths for him. Every valley shall be filled in, every mountain and hill made low. The crooked roads shall become* **straight***, the rough ways smooth. And all mankind will see God's salvation.'"*

In Isaiah 43, a different Hebrew word YShR [2] [yashar] is translated as straight, though Isaiah does use the word TsDYQ as well:

> *Isaiah 26:7 The path of the* **righteous** *(TsDYQ) is level (MYShR); O upright (YShR) One, you make the way of the* **righteous** *(TsDYQ) smooth.*

All the children of the root TsDQ, have the meaning of straight.

How do the letters Ts D Q bring the idea of straight? The letter Ts likely brings the idea of laying something down flat. It may also bring the idea of a judgement or proclamation of the righteous state. The letter D may talk about reciprocal – a movement in both directions – like making something straight by pulling in both directions. The letter Q (sun on horizon) is the resulting picture of a straight or flat horizon. Of course, we know that the

---

[1] See the section on the word AWT
[2] YShR Strong's 3477

horizon is not perfectly flat, but it would have been the straightest thing known to the ancients who didn't have the privilege of flying a plane to see the curvature of the earth.

TsWM – Fasting

*Ezra 8:23 So we **fasted** and petitioned our God about this, and he answered our prayer.*

TsWM [1] [tsowm] (to fast) is from the root TsM whose other children include:

TsMH[2] [tsamah] (veil),
TsMA[3] [tsamaa] (thirsty),
TsYMAWN[4] [tsimaown] (dry land).

The letter Ts (person on ground) appears to bring the idea of vulnerability and humility. The letter M (water) at first seems to be out of place as the last letter in the word because TsM is about being without water. But perhaps the letter M brings the idea of an unknown and a time of testing and fasting, such as Jesus did in the desert for 40 days. The letter M has the numerical value of 40. It's a time of putting aside our own abilities and resources and waiting on God in trust.

Fasting was also practiced by the early Christians:

*Acts 13:2 While they were worshiping the Lord and **fasting**, the Holy Spirit said, "Set apart for me Barnabas and Saul for the work to which I have called them."*

---

[1] TsWM Strong's 6684
[2] TsMH Strong's 6777
[3] TsMYM Strong's 6771
[4] TsMAWM Strong's 6774

Fasting can be a tool to leave behind the physical to enter into the spiritual, but many fast without crossing over – it remains a physical exercise and a show of piety.

> *Isaiah 58:5-11 "Is this the kind of **fast** I have chosen, only a day for a man to humble himself? Is it only for bowing one's head like a reed and for lying on sackcloth and ashes? Is that what you call a **fast**, a day acceptable to the LORD? Is not this the kind of fasting I have chosen: to loose the chains of injustice and untie the cords of the yoke, to set the oppressed free and break every yoke?*
>
> *"Is it not to share your food with the hungry and to provide the poor wanderer with shelter – when you see the naked, to clothe him, and not to turn away from your own flesh and blood?*
>
> *"Then your light will break forth like the dawn, and your healing will quickly appear; then your righteousness will go before you, and the glory of the LORD will be your rear guard.*
>
> *"Then you will call, and the LORD will answer; you will cry for help, and he will say: 'Here am I.'*
>
> *"If you do away with the yoke of oppression, with the pointing finger and malicious talk, and if you spend yourselves in behalf of the hungry and satisfy the needs of the oppressed, then your light will rise in the darkness, and your night will become like the noonday.*
>
> *"The LORD will guide you always; he will satisfy your needs in a sun-scorched land and will strengthen your frame. You will be like a well-watered garden, like a spring whose waters never fail."*

Q – Qoph – Sun on Horizon

In most Semitic languages, the letter Q is pronounced similar to a K but with the tongue root pulled back. Note that some dictionaries write the pronunciations of q as k. While this is the best an English speaker can pronounce, it is technically an incorrect pronunciation. With some knowledge on the correct pronunciation, the sound can be pulled back to produce the q.

The name Qoph is spelt QP and is the root of the words,
QPA[1] [qafaa] (curdle – possibly with the idea of condensing),
QWP[2] [qoop] (sun),
TQWPA[3] [taqoopa] (circle).

This letter was likely originally drawn with a circle with a horizontal line through it, representing the sun on the horizon. It later evolved to have a vertical line and then it finally took the modern shape of Q in the English alphabet. Meanings it can bring include: concentration, gathering, time. It also talks in a figurative way of the glory of God. Picture the intense sun on the horizon with all the glorious colours as it lights up the sky.

Q has the value of 100 and is the 19th letter of the alphabet.

Multiple Psalms have a correlation in their numbering with the numerical value of letters. Psalm 19 makes mention of the sun and the glory of God:

> *Psalm 19:1-6 The heavens declare the glory of God; the skies proclaim the work of his hands. Day after day they pour forth speech; night after night they display knowledge. There is no speech or language where their voice is not heard. Their voice goes*

---

[1] QPA Strong's 7087
[2] QWP Strong's
[3] TQWPA Strong's

*out into all the earth, their words to the ends of the world. In the heavens he has pitched a tent for the **sun**, which is like a bridegroom coming forth from his pavilion, like a champion rejoicing to run his course. It rises at one end of the heavens and makes its circuit to the other; nothing is hidden from its heat.*

Psalm 119, which is the longest Psalm, is divided into sections by means of the first word (only in the Hebrew text) of each section starting with a sequential letter of the alphabet. So, for example, the section relating to the letter Qoph (Psalm 119:145-152) starts with the word QRA (to call). In fact, the first four verses of this section start with the letter Q:

QRA[1] 𐤀𐤓𐤒 [qaraa] (call; Verse 145 and 146),
QDM[2] 𐤌𐤃𐤒 [qadam] (stand, rise, precede; Verse 147, 148),
QWL[3] 𐤋𐤅𐤒 [qawl] (voice, call aloud; Verse 149; could this be the origin of the English word 'call'?),
QRB[4] 𐤁𐤓𐤒 [qarab] (come near. Verse 150).

*Psalm 119:145 I **call** (QRA) with all my heart; answer me, O LORD, and I will obey your decrees.*

This section also makes brief mention of the sun on the horizon:

*147 I rise before **dawn** and cry for help; I have put my hope in your word.*

Could the last letters of the alphabet, including Q, be prophetic of end times? Here's a possible interpretation:

P ⌐ (Mouth): The proclamation of the gospel to the whole world.
Ts ↳ (person on side): Talks about God's righteous judgement during a time of great troubles on the earth
Q ⊗ (sun on horizon): The gathering of the nations in a great battle. It also talks about the proclamation of the glory of God.
R 𐤓 (head): The rule of the Messiah for 1000 years.

---

[1] QRA Strong's 7121
[2] QDM Strong's 6923
[3] QWL Strong's 6963
[4] QRWB Strong's 7126

Sh ～ (teeth): The final eternal separation of those that follow the Messiah from those that don't.

T ✝ (Plough marker): Arrival at the final destination, with the completion of the marriage where the bride dwells with the groom for eternity.

QDSh – Holy

ⵚ◊ϙ

*Exodus 15:13 "In your unfailing love you will lead the people you have redeemed. In your strength you will guide them to your **holy** dwelling."*

The word QDSh[1] [kodesh] which is translated as, 'holy' actually means 'set apart for a special purpose'. Children of this root include:

QDSh[2] ⵚ◊ϙ [kadesh] (prostitute – set apart for a special purpose. A female prostitute is QDShH[3] [kedeshah],

QDYSh[4] ⵚ◊◡ϙ [qadiysh] (Aramaic. Holy, special),

MQDSh[5] ⵚ◊ϙ〜 [miqdash] (sanctuary – a place set apart for a special purpose).

The letter Q (sun on the horizon) brings the idea of something special and glorious. Also set apart and gathered to one place as the sun is set apart in the evening sky.

The letter D (door) may be akin to the curtain which separated the Inner Sanctuary in the temple. We can note that the separation wasn't a wall but a curtain which could be passed through by those whom God gave an invitation to – notably those who were commissioned and covered by the priestly garment.

---

[1] QDSh Strong's 6944
[2] QDSh Strong's 6945
[3] QDShH Strong's 6948
[4] QDYSh Strong's 6922
[5] MQDSh Strong's 4720

The letter Sh (teeth) talks about something being separated out.

*Exodus 25:8 And let them make me a **sanctuary**; that I may dwell among them.*

So why is the Spirit of God called, 'holy'? The Spirit is all about relationship which seems to be opposite to being set apart. Perhaps the two are brought together to show that there is the balance and symmetry there... The Spirit is what connects the physical Jesus with the Divine God. The Spirit brings relationship and 'set apart' together.

The exact phrase, 'Holy Spirit' is used only 3 times in the Old Testament. If you include the phrase, 'Spirit of the holy Gods' as used in the Book of Daniel by the Assyrian Gentiles, then we have another 4 occurrences making a total of seven.

*Psalm 51:11 Do not cast me from your presence or take your **Holy Spirit** from me.*

*Isaiah 63:10 Yet they rebelled and grieved his **Holy Spirit**. So, he turned and became their enemy and he himself fought against them.*

*Isaiah 63:11 Then his people recalled the days of old, the days of Moses and his people – where is he who brought them through the sea, with the shepherd of his flock? Where is he who set his **Holy Spirit** among them?*

It appears to me that in the three examples above, that the word 'Spirit' is used in relation to God's connection with humanity. The word 'spirit' could almost be replaced with the word 'connection' or 'presence'. The context of these three verses all talk about God's presence either being among us or being removed. Like the inner sanctuary (MQDSh), we can remain separated outside, or we can enter in to dwell with God. God is holy but when we are covered by the Son of God, we are able to enter in.

None of these references implies that the Holy Spirit is a separate person as the Nicene Creeds implies. They do all imply that the Spirit belongs to

God. A natural assumption would be that the Spirit is part of God's person just as a human person has a spirit.

QShR – Conspiracy

> *Isaiah 8 :10-13. 10 Devise your strategy, but it will be thwarted; propose your plan, but it will not stand, for God is with us.*
> *The LORD spoke to me with his strong hand upon me, warning me not to follow the way of this people. He said: "Do not call* **conspiracy (QShR)** *everything that these people call conspiracy; do not fear what they fear, and do not dread it. The LORD Almighty is the one you are to regard as holy, he is the one you are to fear, he is the one you are to dread."*

I can't help but notice that this speaks to our current times. Conspiracy is one of the most frequently used concepts today. The word is used in two different ways depending on which side of history you stand. One side is saying that the global players are conspiring to deceive the people of the nations to come under their control. On the other side, are those who trust the global players and who use the term 'conspiracy theorists' to describe someone who is misinformed or who follows crazy (or illogical) ideas such as the flat earth theory. But this definition ignores the reality of the meaning of the word.

The classical English definition of the word conspiracy, is an agreement and actions done in secret for the purpose of misleading or harming others who are not privy to the hidden plan. To redefine this concept is to say that the meaning no longer applies, and that conspiracy doesn't exist.

Isaiah reminds us to "Not call conspiracy everything that these people call conspiracy." In other words, take care to use the correct definition. Don't redefine it and so deny the reality of it. 'These people" refers to those who are themselves conspiring, who are, in verse 10, devising a strategy and making plans against God. These people have a view on conspiracy which is not spoken of in the same way as God's people speak of it. Their use of the word conspiracy is not true to the meaning of the word and is trying to deny the existence of any deceit because they have something to hide.

Let's look at the use and meaning of the Hebrew word spelt QShR[1] [qesher]. My initial understanding of the word comes from the Arabic meaning of the same word where it means, 'skin' – such as a fruit peel. It relates to the concept of conspiracy in that both are covering and hiding something. The outward appearance looks attractive and needed, but what's behind the skin is something harmful.

The dictionary meanings of QShR are 'to tie' and 'to conspire'. In all instances in the Bible, the word is translated as either conspiracy or treason. Ezekiel 22:25-26 speaks to our times:

> There is a **conspiracy** of her princes within her like a roaring lion tearing its prey; they devour people, take treasures and precious things and make many widows within her.
>
> Her priests do violence to my law and profane my holy things; they do not distinguish between the holy and the common; they teach that there is no difference between the unclean and the clean; and they shut their eyes to the keeping of my Sabbaths, so that I am profaned among them.

We see today that the teachers are not distinguishing between the clean and unclean and between right and wrong. They shut their eyes to God's laws. You could say this is nothing new, but it's certainly increasingly blatant and prominent in our time. As Ezekiel says, it's the princes and leaders who are conspiring against their people.

Let's look at how the letters Q Sh R bring meaning to the word.

Firstly, we'll look at the previous word in the dictionary: QShTh, meaning 'truth'. This tells me that the first two letters Q and Sh likely relate

---

[1] QShR Strong's 7195

to truth, and it's the last letter which moves on from that meaning in QShR (conspiracy) and QShTh (archer, deception).

The letter Q (sun on horizon) usually brings the meaning of condensing or gathering something. Perhaps this relates to truth in that truth involves a distilling and bringing together of ideas.

Q could also relate to our initial state of being gathered together – at least that's what the conspiracy maker would have us believe.

The letter Sh (teeth) talks about cutting and dividing – which relates to making decisions and separating out ideas. This seems to be directly opposite to Q which talks about bringing ideas together. The process of finding truth does seem to involve both.

The letter Th (basket) used in QShTh, meaning 'truth', talks about laying up something for safe keeping. This is certainly what we need to do with truth – to place it high up and value it. The basket containing valuable things was hung up high on the central pole of the house to be out of the way from harm and interference.

But in the word QShR (conspiracy), what meaning does the letter R (head) bring, and how does it change the meaning of truth to something opposite? Let's remember that QShR also means to tie. Another child of the root is QShWR, meaning 'sash', a garment tied around to cover.

In the Bible QShR is normally used in relation to a leader. The letter R (head) speaks about a leader. Treason and conspiracy normally involve an attempt at ruling or controlling or to place oneself above the truth or at the head of one's own agenda.

As I look in the Hebrew dictionary for the word QShR, I can't help noticing the word immediately after it. QShT [1] [qashat] which means 'archer'. This reminds me of the horse rider in Revelation who is holding a bow which represents deception. His purpose is to conquer and control the nations. I presume the letter T is used here because it talks about the target which the archer shoots at. The bow is thought to represent deception

---

[1] QShT Strong's 7199

because a bad bow will not shoot straight. An arrow also can strike a person without them seeing it coming.

R – Resh – Head

The name of the letter R is spelt RSh, which brings the meaning of head, first, principle, top, ruler, chief, beginning. The letter was written with the symbol of a head. For a period, it was written as a left facing P. The Romans faced it right, likely because they started to write from left to right. They also added a tail (R) to distinguish it from P.

The first five letters making up the first two words in the Bible are B R Sh Y T. It's significant that the last three letters of the alphabet are prominent here – R Sh T. What's at the start of the Bible is also at the end of the alphabet. This is because the root of the word RShYT is RSh – meaning head, and most important. We will see this theme with the letter R – that what's important is seen at the start and at the end. The ultimate end goal must be stated and understood right from the start. There is the thought that God does things in cycles so that the finish of something has a close relationship to the start – it's come round in a full circle to the same point. Not that events will come back to exactly the same point, but we should be able to see a pattern repeating through history.

R has the numerical value of 200 and is the 20th letter in the alphabet. It's one of the three letters at the end of the alphabet which refer to the tri-nature of Father God – the head. The three elements of His tri-nature are the will, spirit and body (which are physically represented as order, energy and physical manifestation). In the last three letters, the R (head) represents the will of the Father, the aspect which is about direction. The Father is the head of the family.

There are three locations in the Bible where we can often observe a correlation between the last few letters of the alphabet, R Sh and T, and Scripture. Firstly, they are the Psalm whose chapter number relates to the position of the letter in the alphabet. In the case of the letter R, (being the

20th letter in the alphabet), it relates to the 20th Psalm This Psalm talks about trusting the King – the head (R)

Secondly, Psalm 119 has sections relating to each letter. For R, that is verses 153 to 160.

Thirdly, the book of Revelation has the final chapters whose numbers relate to the position of the letter in the alphabet. For R that is Revelation chapter 20.

Let's look at Psalm 119:153-160: Here are the words which start each line:

153: RAH[1] ⨯⨯⨯ [rah] (to look upon).

> **Look** upon my suffering and deliver me, for I have not forgotten your law.

154: RYB[2] ⨯⨯⨯ [riib] (plead, defend).
155: RXWQ[3] ⨯⨯⨯ [rakhowq] (far).
156: RXM[4] ⨯⨯⨯ [rakham] (compassion, mercy, tender love.

> Your compassion is great, O LORD; preserve my life according to your laws.

157: RB[5] ⨯⨯ [rab] (many, numerous)
158 and 159: RAH ⨯⨯⨯ [rah] (to look upon).
160: RASh[6] ⨯⨯⨯ [rash] (beginning, summit, chief, most important).

There does appear to be a theme of the manifest reality of the presence of God – which may agree with the next chapter in Revelation 20.

In Revelation 20, we see the manifest arrival of Jesus to earth to rule as the head (R ⨯) for a thousand years. If people had any doubt about the reality of God, they will come face to face with the full reality. What's most important (R ⨯) will become abundantly clear at this time. After the 1000

---

[1] RAH Strong's 7200
[2] RYB Strong's 7378
[3] RXWQ Strong's 7350
[4] RXM Strong's 7356
[5] RB Strong's 7227
[6] RASh Strong's 7218

years, the Serpent and all deceit will be thrown into the lake of burning sulphur.

ARGMN – Purple

*Exodus 26:31 "Make a curtain of blue, **purple** and scarlet yarn and finely twisted linen, with cherubim worked into it by a skilled craftsman."*

The root of the word ARGMN[1] [argaman] is RG. Notice how RG is made up of the head (R) and foot (G) – the two opposite ends of a person and they represent two concepts at opposite ends of the spectrum. The head is the most honourable part of a person, while the foot is on the dirty ground. The head represents being high up as a ruler, while the foot represents the humility of a servant.

The order of these letters in the alphabet is G and then R. In the root RG, they have been crossed over like weaving. A child word of RG is, ARG[2] [arag], (to weave). Other children of RG include

RG[3] [rag] (thought),
HRG[4] [harag] (kill, slaughter),
YRG[5] [yirag] (sledge – for trampling/ crushing grain).

G and R are in exact reflective symmetry in their positions. G is the third from the start and R is the third from the end.

When we map the alphabet onto the colour spectrum, G relates to red, and R relates to violet/blue. The combination or weaving together of these

---

[1] ARGMN Strong's 713
[2] ARG Strong's 707
[3] RG Strong's 7454. Alternatively written as RƐ
[4] HRG Strong's 2026
[5] YRG Strong's 3407

two colours gives us purple (ARGMN). Purple is not found in the colour spectrum but is technically the combination of red and blue.

But colours are only the physical meaning. The spiritual meaning of G is both red and humanity. The letter G (foot) also talks about humility, which Jesus represents as He came as a baby, washed our feet and died on a cross in humility.

The spiritual meaning of R (head) is both blue and headship, which represents the divine Father.

Jesus was dressed by the soldiers at his crucifixion in a purple robe. It was intended as a mockery of His kingship. Little did they realise that it was prophetic of His nature – that He was both human (red) and divine (blue) woven together. They took the robe off Jesus when they put Him on the cross, but He would have been red with blood, blue and purple all over with bruises from his beatings the night before. Chances are good that no natural skin colour would have been visible at all.

The word spelt RG means, 'thought'. This likely relates to the weaving together of ideas.

RWX – Spirit

*Genesis 1:2 And the earth was without form, and void; and darkness was upon the face of the deep. And the **Spirit** of God moved upon the face of the waters.*

The word translated as 'spirit', is spelt in Hebrew as RWX[1] [ruwakh], which means, 'wind' and 'refresh' – refreshing wind. It also means, 'smell' and 'spacious'. Put these all together and you get a very pleasant picture.

Humanity is alike to God in that we also have a spirit:

---

[1] RWX Strong's 7307

> *Psalm 51:10 Create in me a pure heart, O God, and renew a steadfast **spirit** within me.*

Spirit gives us a unique relationship to God like no other created creature.

RWX is from the root RX whose children include:

RXT[1] ᚆᚒᚆ [rakhat] (shovel – used for winnowing grain in the wind),
ARX[2] ᚆᚒᚆ [arakh] (travel, wander – go with the wind?),
ARXH[3] ᚆᚒᚆ [arekha] (caravan, travelling company),
AWRX[4] ᚆᚒᚆ [awrakh] (path, way of living),
ARWXA[5] ᚆᚒᚆ [aruwkha] (food allowance – while travelling),
RXH[6] ᚆᚒᚆ [rekheh] (millstone – which turns around on the same path),
RWXH[7] ᚆᚒᚆ [ruwakhah] (relief, respite),
RYX[8] ᚆᚒᚆ [riyakh] (aroma),
YRX[9] ᚆᚒᚆ [yerakh] (month, moon – which follows a prescribed path).

A common theme to all these children has to do with travelling a path. Like an aroma, it has a source. Wind has a source and a path.

The letter R (head) brings the idea of a source – like the head of a river.

The letter X (wall) brings the idea of something beyond the wall of our house – a journey. So put together, we get the idea of a path from the head (source or something important) and moving out on a journey/path. The X also brings the idea of something beyond the physically visible which relates to wind and spirit.

The Spirit of God leads us on the path towards our ultimate destination. That destination was also our source because we started out as family

---

[1] RXT Strong's 7371
[2] ARX Strong's 732
[3] ARXH Strong's 736
[4] AWRX Strong's 734
[5] ARWXA Strong's 737
[6] RXH Strong's 7347
[7] RWXH Strong's 7309
[8] RYX Strong's 7381, 7382
[9] YRX Strong's 3391, 3393, 3394

dwelling with God in the garden of Eden. That origin and destination is the most important thing (R ꩟). Spirit is all about relationship, and our destination is family. Relationship is the path to family.

As said before, I don't believe that the Holy Spirit is a separate person. The idea that the Spirit of God is a separate person is not made obvious in either the Hebrew scriptures nor the New Testament. It is clear to me however, that God is two persons – Jesus the Son and God the Father, with each having a tri-nature as explained earlier in the book.

Here's some of the key scriptures Trinitarians use to say that God is three persons – making the Holy Spirit a person. I include my response to those claims:

> *Matthew 28:19 Therefore go and make disciples of all nations, baptising them in the name of the Father and of the Son and of the Holy Spirit.*
>
> *2 Corinthians 13:14 May the grace of the Lord Jesus Christ, and the love of God, and the fellowship of the Holy Spirit be with you all.*
>
> *1 Peter 1:2 who have been chosen according to the foreknowledge of God the Father, through the sanctifying work of the Spirit, for obedience to Jesus Christ and sprinkling by his blood: Grace and peace be yours in abundance.*

My response to all the above verses is that the person of God has three facets, not three persons. A person should have a spirit. If there are three persons, then there should be three spirits. The Bible says there is only one Spirit and one Lord.

But at the end of the day, I'm not making a doctrine out of this – that is, expecting other people to believe my view – because the only doctrine that identifies us as Believers, is Peter's statement that Jesus is the Messiah, the Son of the Living God.

I wrote 30 pages on the nature of the Holy Spirit but Ihave chosen to keep these for a different book.

RʕH – Friend, Shepherd

> *Psalm 23:1 A psalm of David. The* LORD *is my* **shepherd**, *I shall not be in want.*

The word translated as 'shepherd' is spelt RʕH [1][raʕah]. It's from the root Rʕ. Other children of Rʕ include:

Rʕ[2] [reaʕ] (friend),
MRʕYT[3] [mirʕiyt] (pasture),
RʕH[4] [raʕah] (to feed, provide pasture),
RʕWT[5] [reʕuwt] (desire, chase after),
RʕYH[6] [raʕyah] (my love, darling, companion – used as a name, 'my love', mostly in Song of Solomon.) Perhaps RʕYH could just as well have been translated as something like, 'my desire', since the root doesn't relate so much to love.

The letter R (head) brings the idea of a leader or head of the flock.

The letter ʕ (eye) brings the idea of watching. The shepherd is one who leads and watches over his sheep.

> *Isaiah 40:11 He tends his flock like a* **shepherd***: He gathers the lambs in his arms and carries them close to his heart; he gently leads those that have young.*

> *Jeremiah 31:10 Hear the word of the* LORD, *O nations; proclaim it in distant coastlands: 'He who scattered Israel will gather them and will watch over his flock like a* **shepherd***.'*

---

1 RʕH Strong's 7462
2 Rʕ Strong's 7453
3 MRʕYT Strong's 4830
4 RʕH Strong's 7462
5 RʕWT Strong's 7469, 7470
6 RʕYH Strong's 7474

> Ezekiel 34:12 As a **shepherd** looks after his scattered flock when he is with them, so will I look after my sheep. I will rescue them from all the places where they were scattered on a day of clouds and darkness.
>
> Matthew 2:6 "But you, Bethlehem, in the land of Judah, are by no means least among the rulers of Judah; for out of you will come a ruler who will be the **shepherd** of my people Israel."
>
> John 10:11-16 "I am the good **shepherd**. The good **shepherd** lays down his life for the sheep. The hired hand is not the **shepherd** who owns the sheep. So when he sees the wolf coming, he abandons the sheep and runs away. Then the wolf attacks the flock and scatters it. The man runs away because he is a hired hand and cares nothing for the sheep. "I am the good **shepherd**; I know my sheep and my sheep know me – just as the Father knows me and I know the Father – and I lay down my life for the sheep. I have other sheep that are not of this sheep pen. I must bring them also. They too, will listen to my voice, and there shall be one flock and one **shepherd**."

Jesus had also observed that the people of Israel were without a shepherd. The hired hand He spoke about, was likely the religious leaders, who were not concerned for the people as much as their own self-righteousness and reputation. So, it was a significant claim for Jesus to say that He owned the sheep as the Shepherd. He is basically stating that He is God. His other sheep, which are not in that sheep pen, are obviously those who are not Israeli. They also will listen to His voice and join as one flock with one shepherd. An amazing picture.

Note that the root RƷ is also used in the context of a husband and lover. Jesus is also our husband and lover. All aspects of the root are included in His role as shepherd.

> Song of Solomon 5:16 His mouth is sweetness itself; he is altogether lovely. This is my lover, this my **friend** (RƷ), O daughters of Jerusalem.

Jeremiah 3:20 "But like a woman unfaithful to her ***husband*** *(Rʕ), so you have been unfaithful to me, O house of Israel," declares the LORD.*

RXB – Liberty

Psalm 119:45 I will walk about in ***freedom*** *(RXB), for I have sought out your precepts.*

Children of the root RXB include:

RXB[1] 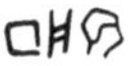 [rakhab] (wide),
RXWB[2]  [rekhowb] (street),
MRXB[3]  [merkhab] (wide, spacious place).

A wide-open space is used as a metaphor for freedom.

Perhaps the letter R (head) may be telling us about something which is of utmost importance. Or is it talking about our start/original state – which is the state we need to return to?

The letter X (wall) signifies being beyond the walls – in a spacious place.

The letter B indicates relationship. It appears that freedom is not necessarily about doing your own thing outside of relationship. On the contrary, it should lead to relationship which gives true meaning and life.

2 Samuel 22:20 He brought me out into a ***spacious place*** *(MRXB); he rescued me because he delighted in me.*

Psalm 118:5 In my anguish I cried to the LORD, and he answered by setting me ***free*** *(MRXB).*

---

[1] RXB Strong's 7342, 7338
[2] RXWB Strong's 7339
[3] MRXB Strong's 4800

What's the most liberating or wide-open space I've experienced? I think it was when I was undergoing a marriage separation. But it wasn't just that which contributed to the liberty. As a result of the separation, I could no longer work for the Christian mission agency I was with. So, I was no longer a 'good, respectable person' in the church because I had initiated a divorce, and I was no longer a missionary hero. I no longer needed to keep my halo polished, in fact, I could use it to play frisbee – yippee! The fact that I had no self-righteousness left was a huge relief – a freedom – a wide open space. This might sound like blasphemy to those who disapproved of my actions – but indeed, I actually experienced a greater closeness to God because it wasn't me anymore, it was all about what He could do for me – trust. The marriage had its ups and downs but I did feel closed in and controlled for most of those 20 years. And I don't blame anyone except myself for the result. There's no doubt about it – I'm a sinner, end of story. We didn't have any children, so that made it easier – though it was the hardest thing I've done in my life. I was very disappointed that things hadn't worked out the way they were supposed to. I thought that God was directing me to be married to that specific person. I had added up the divine signs pointing in that direction and weighed the pros up against the cons and the equation seemed to point in that direction. It wasn't all good to start with, but I thought that with God's help it would work out. Not so…

Now, how could I trust what I thought I was hearing? I've learnt since, that there doesn't have to be logical answers to everything. Trust in God means that I don't have to have every question answered. That's freeing!

I'm married again and have five children, all girls, of whom none are my biological children. One would think that was constraining. It is constraining practically and financially speaking, but spiritually and emotionally, I do feel free in it. Look at Proverbs 14:4:

> *Where there are no oxen, the stall is clean, but from the strength of an ox comes an abundant harvest.*

In my situation, I interpret that as, where there are no children, the house is clean and orderly, and I have money to spend to be free. But children and family bring a great blessing. Good relationships are liberty! Controlling relationships are not.

Regarding wide open spaces, I did enjoy my travels in the deserts of the Middle East. We would drive across the rocky desert for many hours, sometimes at night using the stars to guide our direction. There were no street signs, only tracks in the desert which criss-crossed everywhere, sometimes turning off just to avoid a bumpy patch, sometimes turning off to an entirely different direction. We usually had a local guide with us. Often it was just a matter of heading towards the evening star and following a valley or ridge.

Now, back home in New Zealand, with a full-time job and family, I do look forward to the times when we can get away and go camping in our caravan – to be in wide open spaces.

RXM – Compassion

𐤌𐤇𐤓

*Psalm 103:13 As a father has **compassion** (RXM) on his children, so the LORD has **compassion** on those who fear him.*

Children of the root RXM include:

RXM[1] 𐤌𐤇𐤓 [racham] (compassion, bowels), and

RXMH[2] 𐤄𐤌𐤇𐤓 [rakhamah] (womb, maiden – the H is a feminine marker). This word appears to bring the meaning of a love from deep within.

The R (head) may refer to the source of something. Or it could mean something which is most important or central for us.

The letter X (wall) infers something hidden from view, bringing the idea of something deep within.

---

[1] RXM Strong's 7355
[2] RXMH Strong's 7361

The letter M (ocean) may be referring to something awesome and unfathomable.

*Psalm 18:1 I **love** (RXM) you, O LORD, my strength.*

*Proverbs 28:13 He who conceals his sins does not prosper, but whoever confesses and renounces them finds **mercy** (RXM).*

Sin is very much something we try to conceal. That's where it thrives – in secret and dark places. But if we bring it out in humility, we move beyond the wall of the physical (X) and walk in trust (M). Compassion is very much about choosing to look beyond the visible (X) fault in someone and instead walk the unfathomable (M) path of trust so that relationship can continue through forgiveness.

RShϾ – Wicked

*Genesis 18:23 Then Abraham approached him and said: "Will you sweep away the righteous with the **wicked** (RShϾ)?"*

Meanings of RShϾ[1] [rashaϾ] include (depart, wicked – to depart from the path).

The word starts with the letter R which speaks of our original state in the beginning. But we move on from there to the letter Sh (teeth) which indicates a separation from what we knew at the beginning. From there, it goes to the letter Ͼ (eye) which refers to seeing something. Could this be referring to the command of God in Eden not to eat from the tree of knowledge of Good and Evil whereby people move away from their trust in God and replace it with their own knowledge? This is not to say that they didn't have knowledge before because they certainly did, but the problem came when they put their own limited knowledge ahead of trust in God. By eating of the tree of the Knowledge of Good and Evil, they then discovered

---

[1] RShϾ Strong's 7563

evil and separation as well. It seems that the fruit in itself wasn't as much a problem as the act of disobeying God and moving away from a trust relationship.

Another similar word spelt RƷ[1] [raƷ] also means, 'wicked'. Note the identical spelling except the Sh. Curious, because the word RƷ also means shepherd and friend. This is because apparently in ancient times the word meaning 'wicked' was spelt RGh. The letter and sound 𐤏 [gh] is not used in more recent times in Hebrew but remains in many other Semitic languages. This letter was represented by a black twisted rope and brought the meaning of dark or evil. The letter Gh was later merged into the letter Ein Ʒ but the underlying meaning can still be seen.

> *Genesis 13:13 Now the men of Sodom were **wicked** (RƷ) and were sinning greatly against the LORD.*

---

[1] RƷ Strong's 7541

Sh – Shin – Teeth

The letter and sound Sh were written with the symbol of teeth. This is quite appropriate because the teeth are involved in the making of this sound, where air is pushed through the teeth – though it can still be produced if you haven't got teeth by alveo palatal friction (at the top of the gum behind the teeth).

The name is spelt ShN, and is the root for the following children:
ShN[1] [shen] (teeth),
ShNH[2] [shaneh] (year, sleep),
ShNY[3] [shaniy] (scarlet – the colour of the gums.),
ShNN[4] [shanan] (sharpen, teach incisively),
ShNYNH[5] [sheniynah] (sharp word – with the meaning of a byword or taunt),
ShAN[6] [shaan] (rest),
ShNA[7] [shanaa] (change),
ShNY[8] [sheniy] (second time, again),
YShN[9] [yashen] (previous, sleep).

The general idea which ShiN brings is about cutting or dividing something off. For example, a year (ShNH) is a division of time, the idea of 'again' involves the cutting or marking off time so that something can be repeated – made into two parts.

---

[1] ShN Strong's 8127
[2] ShNH Strong's 8141, 8142, 8139, 8140
[3] ShNY Strong's 8144
[4] ShNN Strong's 8150
[5] ShNYNH Strong's 8148
[6] ShAN Strong's 7599
[7] ShNA Strong's 8132, 8133
[8] ShNY Strong's 8145
[9] YShN Strong's 3463, 3465

The letter N (sprouting seed) has almost the opposite meaning to Sh because N talks about a continuation rather than a discontinuation or cutting off. But curiously, the letter N is last, meaning that continuation has been restored. This is the ultimate story of humanity; our relationship with God was cut off but we have the opportunity to continue the relationship once more.

The opposite spelling of ShN is NSh – which brings an opposite meaning of: debt, deception, interest, loan, forget, despair. The continuation of life has been cut off.

The letter Sh is the second to last letter of the alphabet and I think it's prophetic of end times where everyone will be separated out (Sh) for eternity (N).

It's also the 21st letter of the alphabet, and so, in Psalm 21:8-11 we see a prophetic description of end times separation:

> *⁸ Your hand will lay hold on all your enemies; your right hand will seize your foes. ⁹ At the time of your appearing you will make them like a fiery furnace. In his wrath the LORD will swallow them up, and his fire will consume them. ¹⁰ You will destroy their descendants from the earth, their posterity from mankind. ¹¹ Though they plot evil against you and devise wicked schemes, they cannot succeed;*

We see this separation confirmed again in Revelation chapter 21:7-8:

> *He who overcomes will inherit all this, and I will be his God and he will be my son.*
> *But the cowardly, the unbelieving, the vile, the murderers, the sexually immoral, those who practice magic arts, the idolaters and all liars – their place will be in the fiery lake of burning sulfur. This is the second death.*

ShBYʕY – Oath, Seven

*Genesis 2:2 By the **seventh** day God had finished the work he had been doing; so on the **seventh** day he rested from all his work.*

ShBYʕY[1] [shabiyaʕy] (seventh) is from the root ShBʕ whose children include:

ShBʕ[2] [shabaʕ] (seven, swear),
ShBWʕ[3] [Shabuwaʕ] (week – seven days),
ShBWʕH[4] [shabuwaʕah] (oath, curse),

What does the idea of an oath and curse have in common with the number seven?

Perhaps because seven is about the completion of the physical – in the seven days of creation – the last day being the rest or Sabbath – which is also a requirement of the law. But we can't come to God by physical means to obey the law. So, the oath is a physical attempt to show that a person has the physical means to bring about a result. But they can't – so the breaking of the oath brings a curse.

The letter Sh indicates a dividing, decision and separation. An oath is a decision on a situation.

The letter B talks about a relationship. An oath is a relationship between two persons. There's an element of trust and hope in it.

The letter ʕ is the eye. An oath is something which needs to be witnessed by a second party and is usually an agreement between two parties.

---

1 ShBYʕY Strong's 7637
2 ShBʕ Strong's 7650
3 ShBWʕ Strong's 7620
4 ShBWʕH Strong's 7621

ShBT – Sabbath

*Exodus 16:23 He said to them, "This is what the LORD commanded: 'Tomorrow is to be a day of rest, a holy **Sabbath** to the LORD.'"*

The word spelt ShBT[1] [shabat] (sabbath), means, 'to cease'. It's often used in the context of the seventh day being set aside as a day of rest.

ShBT has a clear connection in spelling and meaning to the word ShBƐ[2] [shabaƐ] meaning, 'seven', and 'oath'. The meaning the two words have in common is the value of seven. And the letters they have in common are the letters Sh and B.

So how do the letters ShB bring the idea of seven? I can't see anything in the numerical value of the numbers which would bring us to seven- Sh has the value of 300 and B has the value of 2. Sh is the 21st letter in the alphabet so there's a noteworthy relationship where $3 \times 7 = 21$. 21 appears to relate to the completion of human life on earth.

There is an interesting symmetry pattern with the two letters – B is the second letter in the alphabet and Sh is the second to last. They also have a symmetry of opposite meaning: B represents relationship and Sh is being separated. It appears that relationship and separation are being brought together.

It could be that the Sh (separation) is talking about something which is set apart as special. The Sabbath day is certainly described as being set apart for a special purpose (holy):

The word, 'holy' is spelt QDSh (see section on 'Holy') and so also uses the Sh to bring the idea of being set apart as special.

---

[1] ShBT Strong's 7676
[2] ShBƐ Strong's 7651

The word, 'rest' is spelt ShBTWN[1] ⟨shabatown⟩ [shabatown] and is also from the root ShBT. The sabbath rest is a time for us to separate ourselves out from the business of life and to find rest in God's presence. There is a sense where we need to do this every day in our lives, but it certainly does help to set aside a day to rest our bodies and minds from the rat race of life.

The letter B represents relationship and family. There is an important concept of resting in our relationship with God – to cease from striving in our own strength.

ShBT then takes us further to the letter T which is the completion of a contract and our final destination. The Sabbath rest helps us to come aside from the physical and enter into relationship with God and one another. In the Old Testament, the Sabbath was a once-a-week event, but the New Testament describes it as being a continual spiritual practice – to cease from spiritual striving and working to be good in our own strength[2].

The letter T also represents our ultimate rest from work and struggle because it's the start of our eternity of dwelling with God.

ShXT – Pit of Destruction

Isaiah 38:17 Surely it was for my benefit that I suffered such anguish. In your love you kept me from the pit (ShXT) of destruction; you have put all my sins behind your back.

The word ShXT[3] [shachat] (pit) is from the root ShX whose other children include:

ShX[4] [shakh] (low, humble),
ShXX[5] [shakhakh] (to sink low, bow),

---

[1] ShBTWN Strong's 7677
[2] Bible, Hebrews 4:1-11
[3] ShXT Strong's 7845
[4] ShX Strong's 7807
[5] ShXX Strong's 7817

ShXH[1] 𐤔𐤇𐤎 [shaxah] (to bow).

The letter Sh brings the idea of separation. The letter X brings the idea of being out of sight or going beyond the physical into the spiritual.

A word with a similar meaning which uses the same letters but in a different order, is XShK 𐤇𐤔𐤊, meaning 'darkness'. This also indicates being separated and out of sight.

A second word also translated as 'pit' is BWR[2] [bowr] also spelt KWR (well for water), possibly the origin of the English word 'bore'. Arabic is pronounced 'biir'.

> Psalm 30:3 O LORD, you brought me up from the grave; you spared me from going down into the **pit BWR** .

A third word translated as 'pit' is ShXH

If people reject the continuation of God's purpose and design through Jesus, then the only logical option is discontinuation – being cut off and out of sight. There is an abyss prophesied at the end of the human story on earth, where all who reject God will be sent. This is the Great Separation and is eternal. Of course, many don't believe in an after-life – or after-death. But I would have thought it's better to be safe than sorry – there's no going back! I have a saying – Don't not do now what you will later regret not doing!

Our youngest daughter, at age 7, had a favourite saying, 'I don't care' - when told about a consequence of antisocial behaviour. I try to communicate to her that she will certainly care about the consequences when she is experiencing them. But it's hard for her to see what's down the track. I suspect she says 'I don't care' as an immediate effort to deflect something she doesn't want to do in the present.

Interestingly, a child of the root ShX, is ShXH, meaning, 'worship' (this will be dealt with in detail in the following section).

This seems to contradict everything I've just said about the pit. Could there be two entirely different ways to interpret the letters? One thing which

---

[1] ShXH Strong's 7812
[2] BWR Strong's 953

is in common between a pit and worship is the idea of being low. In the first, we are cast down low by another. In the second, we ourselves choose to be low in relation to God in reverence of Him.

I hear of many who come to believe in Jesus out of fear of the pit. But is seems to me this isn't a good basis of a love relationship – especially between bride and groom. Fear is more of a self-preservation idea rather than an outward looking relationship. There are many self-gain reasons why people call themselves Christians, but Jesus said:

> *Matthew 7:21-24 "Not everyone who says to me, 'Lord, Lord,' will enter the kingdom of heaven, but only he who does the will of my Father who is in heaven.*
>
> *Many will say to me on that day, 'Lord, Lord, did we not prophesy in your name, and in your name drive out demons and perform many miracles?'*
>
> *Then I will tell them plainly, 'I never knew you. Away from me, you evildoers!'*
>
> *Therefore, everyone who hears these words of mine and puts them into practice is like a wise man who built his house on the rock."*

ShXH – Worship

> *Genesis 22:5 He said to his servants, "Stay here with the donkey while I and the boy go over there. We will **worship** (ShXH) and then we will come back to you."*

One of the first uses of the word ShXH[1] [shachah] translated as 'worship' is when Abraham climbs the mountain to sacrifice his only son Isaac. It was certainly an act of submitting his most precious to the will of God.

His first act of ShXH is when he meets three messengers of God (angels):

---

[1] ShXH Strong's 7812

> *Genesis 18:2 Abraham looked up and saw three men standing nearby. When he saw them, he hurried from the entrance of his tent to meet them and **bowed low** (ShXH) to the ground.*

The word ShXH has the physical meaning of 'to bow'. It's from the root ShX which has the underlying meaning of a low place.

So, worship as defined by the word ShXH is all about putting oneself low. It's especially about putting ourselves low in relation to God and submitting to His will for our lives. The letter Sh (teeth) talks about being separated out as special – related to the word, QDSh (holy). It could also be talking about not trying to be the same and equal but being separate. The Serpent tried to be the same and equal to God but that was the opposite to worship of God. In worship, we need to recognize that God is set apart and we are lower than Him. Humanism believes in putting humanity up high without recognition of God.

The letter X refers to being beyond the physical. Our physical person has a hunger for putting self first, but if we go beyond the physical, we enter into the realm of relationship. By putting ourselves in a relationship to God as the lower, we connect with His greatness.

> *Isaiah 27:13 And in that day a great trumpet will sound. Those who were perishing in Assyria and those who were exiled in Egypt will come and **worship** the LORD on the holy mountain in Jerusalem.*

> *Psalm 29:2 Ascribe to the LORD the glory due his name; **worship** (ShXH) the LORD in the splendour of his holiness.*

Worship of God is about lowering ourselves in humility before God. If we don't, we'll likely find ourselves in a low place by default – without choosing to do so.

In worship, we enter a holy place, separated (Sh) out from the wild world around us. And worship certainly is beyond the physical (X). The letter H talks about a state of awe and wow, which we have as we consider the awesomeness of God and our low place in comparison. Putting ourselves low in humility before God is central to worship. If worship becomes about a sense of euphoria and lacks humility before the awesomeness of God, then I think we're not worshipping. Worship should never be defined as singing a song, though song can be helpful.

ShWH – Equalise, Stilled

Psalm 131:2 But I have stilled (ShWH) and quieted (DMM) my soul; like a weaned child with its mother, like a weaned child is my soul within me.

The word translated in Psalm 131:2 as, 'stilled' is spelt ShWH[1]  [shawah] and is from the root ShH. It has the underlying meaning of equalising something. It can be used to bring the meanings of levelling, agree with, resemble, to be level within oneself, behave, smooth, still.

The letter Sh (teeth) brings the idea of cutting and dividing. It's often used to talk about a decision – weighing up two or more options – which relates to levelling. It can also talk about coming aside from the noise of life in a spiritual sense and, when possible, in a physical sense. The H (existence of a person) is often associated with a breath of life. Perhaps it includes just taking a quiet breath.

ShLM – Completion

*Genesis 37:14 So he said to him, "Go and see if **all is well** (ShLWM) with your brothers and with the flocks and bring word back to me."*

---

[1] ShWH Strong's 7737

ShLWM[1] [shalowm] (completeness) is from the root ShLM whose other children include:

ShLM[2] ᨕᨕ∠ᨖ [shalam] (verb: to complete, be at peace),
ShLMWN[3] ᨕᨕ∠ᨖ [shalmown] (payment).
ShYLM[4] ᨕᨕ∠ᨖ [shiilem] (recompense).

ShLWM is often translated as 'peace', but we need to look at the word in the Biblical context to find the full depth of the meaning. I suppose if we took peace as the main meaning, then we could reasonably conclude, as one dictionary writer did, that the letters meant, 'destroy (Sh) the authority (L) attached to chaos (M)'. But the Hebrew word doesn't necessarily map directly onto the range of meanings which we understand from the English word 'peace' which English speakers understand to relate to the absence of war or chaos. The city of Jerusalem is widely understood by many in Israel to mean, 'City of Peace'. However, in reality, it hasn't lived up to its name! Jerusalem has seen much war and chaos in its history through to the present time. Perhaps there's another meaning.

The root ShLM appears to talk about being in a state of completion. Derivatives of this root meaning talk about the completion of a contract or agreement by means of a payment. So how do the letters Sh-L-M bring that meaning? Here's my take on it, keeping in mind the context of God's ultimate purpose for humanity – to bring us to completion through marriage to His Son.

The letter Sh (teeth) talks about being cut off or separated. It could also talk about being set apart as special. However, Sh is at the start of the word indicating that it could refer to the start of the story about completion of a payment or contract. Payment is required because at the start of the human story we became separated from God. Now God must buy us back. Could part of that buying back be about teaching us to trust in Him? When Jesus allowed Himself to be crucified, that was payment of the bride-price, but we have to accept that gift and trust in Him. I often wondered about who Jesus

---

[1] ShLWM Strong's 7965
[2] ShLM Strong's 7999, 8000
[3] ShLMWN Strong's 8021
[4] ShYLM Strong's 8005

had to pay to purchase us back. God, being the Judge, ruled that the penalty for sin (disobeying or setting oneself against Him) is to be death. Jesus paid the penalty to the High Court of Heaven. A two-fold meaning of Jesus' payment.

The letter L (shepherds' staff) talks about leading or directing. After being separated, God began to lead us, at first through the Torah (law) which taught us that we can't come to Him in our own strength. It led us to recognise our need to trust God. Then Jesus came to earth to pay the bride-price and leave us His Spirit to guide us. Once He paid the bride-price, the courtship period of the law was over, and we are now given the opportunity to accept His offer of marriage and to be betrothed to Him. But even though we accept His offer of marriage, we still need to undergo the test of life to grow in our trust and love of Him. During this time, the groom is away preparing a room for us in His Father's house. Though we are separated physically from Him now, we are one in spirit with Him when we accept His marriage proposal. His Spirit guides us.

He is leading and courting His bride-to-be – which is Jerusalem – spelt in Hebrew as YRWShLM – which is comprised of two words. YRW means to throw and teach – basically to destine, which is certainly about leading. YR is the root of the word translated as Torah. ShLM has the meaning of completion, so together Jeru-salem is talking about destined for completion – which to me, brings the idea of being betrothed, someone who is under contract for the completion of being a bride. The Hebrew word translated as 'bride' is KLLH[1] [kallah] (refer to the section on KL) which is from the root KL which also means completion. The bride is one who has been made complete by joining with her husband. This is the completion of God's purpose for humanity.

The letter M (water, ocean) refers to a great, awesome, unfathomable unknown. It has the numerical value of 40 which talks about a time of testing. But the idea of completion of an agreement should finish on an idea which relates to something more certain.

---

[1] KLLH Strong's 3618

Psalm 23 may offer some clues in the sentence: "He leads me beside still waters."

There we have again the idea of leading. What's the significance of God leading us beside *still* waters? I think we can retain the idea of the waters being awesome and unfathomable. The letter M is used in God's name Elohim where it brings the idea of an immeasurable, unfathomable awesomeness like the ocean. It brings the idea of majesty.

Jesus stilled the waters of the sea of Galilee. This brings the idea that Jesus is in control, and He does bring peace to the storm and chaos. Chaos is not the end of the story. At the end of the story, we have the still, unfathomable nature of God.

So, to me, the story of Sh-L-M seems to tell the story of being separated from God, at first. But then He leads us and courts us to trust in Him. Finally, we can rest beside His still and calm awesomeness. He is unfathomable but we don't need to understand everything – that's what trust is all about.

ShMYM – Sky, Heaven

*Genesis 1:7,8 So God made the expanse and separated the water under the expanse from the water above it. And it was so. God called the expanse "**sky**".*

The word ShMYM[1] [shamayiim] is from the root ShM. Children of the root ShM include:

ShM[2] ᴍᴄ∽ [sham] (breath, sky, there – another place, aroma),
ShMH[3] ⴕᴍᴄ∽ [shamah] (desolate),

---

[1] ShMYM Strong's 8064
[2] ShM Strong's 5561, 8033, 8034, 8036, 8064
[3] Sh MH Strong's 8047

AShM¹ ᄽᄊ𐎀 [aasham] (guilt),
ShWM² ᄽᅟYᄊ [shuwm] (garlic),
YShYMWN³ ᄂYᄽ᚛ᄋᄊᄂ [yeshimown] (desert).

It's not easy seeing what concept these children have in common. There is an idea of being separated (Sh) from water (M). Guilt has the idea of being separated (Sh) and in an unknown place (M). Perhaps an aroma is something which has become separated from its source. I'm not sure of the science of aroma, but perhaps it is activated in the smelling senses by contact with moisture in the nose. For example, the burning of frankincense will produce wafting smoke particles devoid (Sh separated) of moisture, but when they make contact with the moisture (M) in the nose, they will activate the senses.

The letters Sh and M tell a clear story of how sky came into being.

The letter Sh (teeth) talks about separating something out. God separated the water under the expanse from the water above.

The letter M (ocean) talks about the water which is being separated.

Sky is a physical concept, but what does this tell us about the spiritual concept – which is the real truth we're after? I guess heaven is a separated-out place – a holy place (Sh). And it is a great unknown and awesome place (M). It's a place we don't understand but we must trust beyond our limited human understanding.

ShNA – Hate

*Genesis 29:31 When the LORD saw that Leah was **not loved** (ShNA), he opened her womb, but Rachel was barren.*

---

¹ AShM Strong's 816
² ShWM Strong's 7762
³ YShYMWN Strong's 3452

The word ShNA[1] [shanaa] is from the root SN. Here we see again the crossing over or seemingly free variation between the letters Sh and S. Could this be the ancestor of the English word, 'sin'? The root SN means, 'thorn', which is clearly connected to the letter S meaning, thorn. Children of the root SN include:

ASN[2] ⌒ǂỴ [asan] (harm),
SAN[3] ⌒Ỵǂ [saan] (pierce, weapon),
SNA[4] Ỵ⌒ǂ [sanaa] (hate),
SYN[5] ⌒⌣ǂ [siyn] (shield).

It seems that the Hebrew word SN isn't limited to the idea of a deliberate hate as is the English word. The Hebrew word seems to include a neglect of love as shown in Genesis 29:31 regarding Jacob and Leah. I'm sure Jacob didn't deliberately hate Leah.

Regarding Joseph and his brothers:

> *Genesis 37:4 When his brothers saw that their father loved him more than any of them, they **hated** him and could not speak a kind word to him.*

What do the letters S and N bring to the meaning?

In this context, the letter S (thorn) may bring the idea of a painful piercing, which would have been the experience of Leah being neglected.

The letter N (sprouting seed) may bring the idea of a continuation – in this case a continuation of pain.

Let's contrast SN to the root NS with opposite ordering of letters which brings an opposite meaning. The root NS includes the idea of forgiveness. The letter N talks about the continuation of life and the letter S talks about holding onto that continuation.

---

[1] SNA Strong's 8130
[2] ASN Strong's 611
[3] SAN Strong's 5431
[4] SNA Strong's 8130, 8131
[5] SYN Strong's 6793

So, it seems that a neglect of love for someone can often be as painful to them as a deliberate hate. This is especially true for someone who is part of our family who may have a reasonable expectation and need of love.

It seems that Joseph's brothers felt hatred towards Joseph because they felt a neglect from their father in the form of favouritism towards Joseph. Joseph didn't help the matter by telling his brothers about the dreams he had of his family bowing down to him.

> *Genesis 37:8 His brothers said to him, "Do you intend to reign over us? Will you actually rule us?" And they* **hated** *him all the more because of his dream and what he had said.*

Joseph was telling a truth, but it was certainly more than his brothers were able to cope with – especially from their youngest brother. To say that one's parents and older brothers would bow down to you would also go against all their traditional practice. Should Joseph have refrained from telling the dream or should his brothers have had more grace towards him? It's a hard call either way.

ShQTh - Quiet

> *Isaiah 30:15 This is what the Sovereign LORD, the Holy One of Israel, says: "In repentance and rest is your salvation, in* **quietness ShQTh** *and trust is your strength, but you would have none of it.*

I understand that noise is taking us away from our sense of existence. ShQTh[1] (quietness) [shaqath] helps us to sense our existence as a human. We need to put aside the manic business of life in order to hear clearly.

The letter Sh (teeth, separation) talks about coming aside from the noise.

---

[1] ShQTh Strong's 8252

The letter Q (sun on horizon) may talk about a peaceful awe and concentration or focus.

The letter Th (basket) may talk about storing up the precious things in life – putting them aside in a safe place. This letter is used in the word BThX meaning trust.

Here's some more context for the word:

> Joshua 11:23 So Joshua took the entire land, just as the LORD had directed Moses, and he gave it as an inheritance to Israel according to their tribal divisions. Then the land had **rest** from war.

> Ezekiel 16:49 "Now this was the sin of your sister Sodom: She and her daughters were arrogant, overfed and **unconcerned (ShQTh)**; they did not help the poor and needy."

It seems we need to be quiet spiritually to hear, but active in our bodies to outwork what we hear God telling us.

ShQWTs – Abomination

> Daniel 9:27 He will confirm a covenant with many for one 'seven'. In the middle of the 'seven' he will put an end to sacrifice and offering. And on a wing of the temple, he will set up an **abomination** that causes desolation, until the end that is decreed is poured out on him.

ShQWTs[1] [shiqowts] has the meaning of 'filthiness' and is from the root ShQTs who's other child ShQTs[2] [shaqats] means 'detest'.

Could this end-times abomination be a contamination in the temple of the human body? I tend to think it is. Jesus Himself told us that He will tear

---
[1] ShQWTs Strong's 8251
[2] ShQTs Strong's 8262

down the physical temple and rebuild it again in three days. He was talking about raising His own body from the dead.

If we are to presume that we are currently in end times, then we see that there is no physical temple made of stone. The last temple was destroyed in 70 A.D.

And so, neither is there a physical daily sacrifice in the temple. This all leads me to think that the prophesy is referring to the temple of the human body, which is sacred.

The abomination will be a genetic interference with the human gene – in human bodies (our bodies are now the temple of the Holy Spirit)[1]. This will likely be delivered by humanism into the bodies of humanity by means of a medication which alters the human DNA.

This will serve the purpose of the Serpent by sabotaging God's creation of humanity. It will serve the purpose of naive Humanists of reducing the human population through sterilizing (desolating) those it is injected into – and their genetic descendants. Is it mere chance that the word ShQTs visually resembles the word 'shots'? Daniel 9:27 talks about the abomination being set up in a wing of the temple. The word translated as 'wing' also talks about the wing of a bird – which could well reference the arm of a person.

The word ShQTs talks about a filth and contamination. Sure, the human body has been contaminated over many centuries by what we have put into our bodies, but never before has the human gene been contaminated or altered. This is what I believe will happen in the last days. The contamination will bring desolation to the human gene.[2]

> *Daniel 12:11 From the time that the daily sacrifice is abolished and the abomination that causes desolation is set up, there will be 1,290 days (3 and a half years).*

What is the daily sacrifice all about? There hasn't been a daily sacrifice since the temple was destroyed or before. Perhaps the daily sacrifice is about

---

[1] 1 Corinthians 6:19,20
[2] https://www.ncbi.nlm.nih.gov/pmc/articles/PMC6453514/ and do your own research into gene editing and chip implants in humans.

an institutional honouring of God on a regular basis. Was there a date when the world's governments – perhaps an agreement from a humanist international group such as the United Nations or World Council of churches stated that God was not central to human direction and that Humanity alone is the saviour of humanity?

YHWShʕ – Joshua, Jesus

*Deuteronomy 31:23 The LORD gave this command to **Joshua** (YHWShʕ) son of Nun: "Be strong and courageous, for you will bring the Israelites into the land I promised them on oath (ShBʕ), and I myself will be with you."*

The same Hebrew word YHWShʕ[1] [yehuwshaʕ] is used for both the words 'Joshua' and 'Jesus'. The early New Testament translators chose to use the Greek version of 'Jesus' to divorce Christianity from its Hebrew heritage. There was no good reason for the translators of the Bible to translate as 'Joshua' in the Old Testament and 'Jesus' in the New Testament, and so remove a very important link between the two persons.

The word YHWShʕ is two words – YHW and Shʕ. The word YHW is short for YHWH, often Anglicized as Jehovah – God.

The children of the root Shʕ include:
Shʕʕ[2] ⊙⊙ᴡ [shaʕaʕ] (delight),
ShʕH[3] ᴡ⊙ᴡ [shaʕah] (watch),
ShWʕ[4] ⊙Υᴡ [shawaʕ] (cry, rich),
YShʕ[5] ⊙ᴡ⊐ [yashaʕ] (rescue, save, deliver).

---

[1] YHWShʕ Strong's 3091
[2] Shʕʕ Strong's 8173
[3] ShʕH Strong's 8159
[4] ShWʕ Strong's 7768
[5] YShʕ Strong's 3467, 3468

The letter Sh (teeth) brings the idea of cutting – setting apart as special. The root contains the idea of rescuing – which involves separating animals out from danger. The letter ʕ (eye) brings the idea of watching. So combined, the root Shʕ brings the idea of watching over something special and separating (Sh) the flock from danger – such as in a stronghold. It likely applied to the shepherd watching over his sheep – which naturally extended into rescuing them when they were in trouble.

> *2 Samuel 22:3 my God is my rock, in whom I take refuge, my shield and the horn of my **salvation** (YShʕ). He is my stronghold, my refuge and my saviour – from violent men you save me.*
>
> *Psalm 12:5 "Because of the oppression of the weak and the groaning of the needy, I will now arise," says the LORD. "I will **protect** (YShʕ) them from those who malign them."*
>
> *Psalm 18:46 The LORD lives! Praise be to my Rock! Exalted be God my **Saviour** (YShʕ)!*

Back to Jesus' name actually being YHWShʕ – the same as what was translated as Joshua. It's no insignificant chance that God gave YHWShʕ the Son of God the same name as Joshua who led the Israelites across the Jordan River. The life of Joshua is a picture of the ministry of Jesus.

Both grew up and were trained in the Law of Moses. The Law of Moses couldn't bring the people of Israel into the promised land. The people were cursed under the Law. So too, in Jesus' time, the people couldn't come into the Promised Eternal life because of their inability to keep the Law. Law doesn't bring us into relationship with God.

Joshua was the son of Nun. The name Nun is also the name of the letter Nun – which means, 'sprouting seed'. This brings the meaning of the continuation of life and is the spiritual picture of forgiveness – the continuation of relationship. Jesus also is the son of forgiveness – bringing the continuation of relationship with God.

Joshua was one of the 12 spies who were sent into the Promised land to spy on it. Only Joshua and Caleb returned with a report based on faith and trust in God. The others said it was too difficult. With trust, not law, Joshua led the Israelites into the Promised land. So too, Jesus leads us into the Promised Eternal Life through our trust in Him. Just as we followed by trust into the Promised land, so too, we follow Jesus by trust and forgiveness into Eternal Life.

Note how in Deuteronomy 31:23, the word ShBʕ (oath, promise) is used in relation to Joshua leading the people into the promised land. There's a similarity in the root Shʕ and the word ShBʕ. The two are closely and importantly linked. It's the purpose of Joshua and Jesus (Shʕ) to lead God's people into the promised (ShBʕ) land and eternal life.

YShʕ-NAH – Hosanna

*Matthew 21:9 The crowds that went ahead of him and those that followed shouted, "**Hosanna** to the Son of David!" "Blessed is he who comes in the name of the Lord!" "**Hosanna** in the highest!"*

Hosanna is an Anglicized version of the original Hebrew word spelt YShʕ-NAH – which is two words YShʕ meaning, 'rescue' and NAH 'pasture'.

This compound word doesn't appear in the Old Testament and is used only in the context of Jesus being welcomed into Jerusalem.

It's no chance that the name Jesus also comes from the word YShʕ. It's translated as Joshua in the Old Testament. It has the idea of a shepherd.

The combination of shepherd, rescuer and pasture, recalls the beginning of Psalm 23

*The LORD is my **shepherd**, I shall not be in want.*

*2 He makes me lie down in green **pastures** (NAH), he leads me beside quiet waters,*

3 he restores my soul. He guides me in paths of righteousness for his name's sake.

T – Taw – Marker

✝

The name of the letter T is Taw, written as TW .

It was drawn with the symbol of a cross, which was an instrument used in agriculture. When ploughing a field with oxen, a marker was pushed into the ground at the far end of the plough line to act as a target in order to keep a straight plough-line. Towards the top of the stick a horizontal bar was fastened which made it easier to push the stick into the ground with both hands.

The idea of a target fits very well with the position of the letter T as the last letter in the alphabet – representing completion.

The name Taw spelt TW means 'mark'. The letter T represents a plough marker, and the letter W represents a peg – which was often also pushed into the ground to connect a tent to the ground. It was also used to connect curtains together.

There are not many two-consonant roots beginning with T – only 20. Roots with three consonants and that start with a T only have 12 occurrences.

T has the numerical value of 400 but its position as the 22nd letter in the alphabet has significance, too.

The letter T is used as a prefix on verbs to bring the idea of 'she/you/they will'. It talks about an action which is intended but not yet completed. The letter T indicates an intended end result or target. How does the letter T talk about she, you and they? The only connection which comes to mind is that T represents the completion of the marriage covenant by which the woman is joined to the husband (son). We also see T used to make BN (son) into BNT (daughter – which is also used for daughter-in-law).

The letter T is used as a suffix spelt -ot on the end of a noun and it's adjective to mark the noun phrase as feminine plural.

T – TAW – MARKER

In its use to mark 'you will', the T is used to mark second person and the suffix on the end of the verb marks number and gender.

Psalm 119 is divided into sections according to the letters of the alphabet, with sentences beginning with the letter of each section. The section relating to the letter T is naturally at the end in Psalm 119, verses 168-176. The first seven sentences begin with the letter T. In each instance we are given the idea of determining a direction like a target which we aim for. This concept is translated using the English words 'may', 'long for', 'let'. Each goal is a critical element for our relationship with God:

> *Psalm 119:169* **May** *my cry come before you, O LORD; give me understanding according to your word.*
>
> *170* **May** *my supplication come before you; deliver me according to your promise.*
>
> *171* **May** *my lips overflow with praise, for you teach me your decrees.*
>
> *172* **May** *my tongue sing of your word, for all your commands are righteous.*
>
> *173* **May** *your hand be ready to help me, for I have chosen your precepts.*
>
> *174 I* **long for** *your salvation, O LORD, and your law is my delight.*
>
> *175* **Let** *me live that I* **may** *praise you, and* **may** *your laws sustain me.*
>
> *176 I have strayed like a lost sheep. Seek your servant, for I have not forgotten your commands.*

The final verse 176 is a confession that at times we haven't set our eyes on the target and so, have strayed. Despite us taking our eyes off God, David asks God to keep His eyes on us because we still have in mind His commands – despite being distracted at times.

Psalm 22 (remember the letter T is the 22nd letter of the alphabet) was referenced by Jesus when he was on the cross. It was custom, before there were chapter numbers, to refer listeners to a section of scripture by quoting the first line of the section. In the case of Psalm 22, the first line is: "My God, my God, why have you forsaken me?" This Psalm is prophetic of his suffering on the cross, and it then goes onto describe the end result:

Psalm 22:27,28 All the ends of the earth will remember and turn to the LORD, and all the families of the nations will bow down before him, for dominion belongs to the LORD and he rules over the nations.

Revelation 22 is the last book in the Bible, and so describes the end result of everything – the ultimate destination:

14 Blessed are those who wash their robes, that they may have the right to the tree of life and may go through the gates into the city.

17 The Spirit and the bride say, "Come!" And let him who hears say, "Come!" Whoever is thirsty, let him come; and whoever wishes, let him take the free gift of the water of life.

TW – Completion

𐤕𐤅

*John 19:30 When he had received the drink, Jesus said, "It is **finished**.(TW)" With that, he bowed his head and gave up his spirit.*

We don't know exactly what Aramaic word Jesus used on the cross when He said, 'It is finished'. The earliest translation of His words we have, is written in Greek. The Greek word used is 'teleo'. The Aramaic word he most likely used is 'taw' – which is very similar to the Greek word.

Taw (the letter T), as we've seen, depicts a cross – on which Jesus was nailed. Taw also has the meaning of a completion of a contract. I don't get this meaning from a modern Aramaic dictionary, but it's a word I learnt in a southern dialect of Arabic where it has the meaning of good or complete. In the Aramaic language of Jesus' time, people would have known the meaning of Taw as the final letter of the alphabet – where it carried the meaning of completion. In the context of Jesus saying, 'It is finished', I believe He was talking about the completion of the marriage contract, which was completed with the payment of the bride-price – His death on the cross.

The Hebrew word TW[1] is used in the Old Testament to bring the idea of an intention or goal:

> *Job 31:35 Oh that one would hear me! behold, my **desire** is, that the Almighty would answer me, and that mine adversary had written a book.*

It's also used with the idea of a mark:

> *Ezekiel 9:4 and said to him, "Go throughout the city of Jerusalem and put a **mark** (TW) on the foreheads of those who grieve and lament over all the detestable things that are done in it."*

That mark on the head determined a destination for the person. In this case, the person who had the mark would live. What form did that mark take? It would be natural to assume that the mark was the letter T (cross) which has the meaning of a mark and carries the idea of being destined for a purpose.

The word Taw, as we've seen, is the name for the 22nd and completing letter of the alphabet. Jesus pointed us to Psalm 22 on the cross when He quoted the first line of it "My God, my God, why have you forsaken me?" The last line of that Psalm is,

> *Psalm 22:31 They will proclaim his righteousness to a people yet unborn – for he has **done** it.*

---

[1] TW Strong's 8420

The word translated as 'done' is ʕShH[1] [ʕashah] which means 'to do' and to accomplish. Jesus accomplished the task which would bring righteousness and eternal life to all future generations.

TMM – Perfect, finish

𐤕𐤌𐤌

*Daniel 9:24 "Seventy 'sevens' are decreed for your people and your holy city to finish transgression, to put an **end** (TMM) to sin, to atone for wickedness, to bring in everlasting righteousness, to seal up vision and prophecy and to anoint the most holy.*

This prophesy from Daniel is talking about the end times – a time when evil will have reached its maximum and fullness. At this point God will bring it to an end.

The word TMM[2] [tamam] (whole, finished) is from the root TM. Children of this root include:

TM[3] 𐤕𐤌 [tam] (whole),
TAM[4] 𐤕𐤀𐤌 [taam] (double),
TMH[5] 𐤕𐤌𐤄 [tamah] (marvel, wonder),
TMHWN[6] 𐤕𐤌𐤄𐤅𐤍 [timahown] (confused – overwhelmed – the proverbial bucket filled up),
TWMH[7] 𐤕𐤅𐤌𐤄 [tuwmah] (mature, integrity),
YTWM[8] 𐤉𐤕𐤅𐤌 [yatowm] (orphan).

---

[1] ʕShH Strong's 6213
[2] TMM Strong's 8552
[3] TM Strong's 8535
[4] TAM Strong's 8382
[5] TMH Strong's 8539
[6] TMHWN Strong's 8541
[7] TWMH Strong's 8538
[8] YTWM Strong's 3490

The Arabic word spelt TMAM [tamaam] brings the idea of good and satisfied. The Arabic word 'tam' means to wait – presumably with the idea of looking forward to completion.

TϽH – To Wander Away

*Psalm 119:110 The wicked have set a snare for me, but I have not **strayed** (TϽH) from your precepts.*

The word TϽH[1] [taϽah] comes from the root TϽ whose children include:
TϽTWϽ[2] ⵙⵢ+ⵙ+ [taϽtuwaϽ] (error),
TϽϽ[3] ⵙⵙ+ [taϽaϽ] (deceive),
TϽH[4] ⵯⵙ+ [taϽah] (wander).
All these meanings have in common the idea of veering away from or losing sight of the destination.

The word starts with the destination (T), but then our own knowledge (Ͻ - eye) lead us astray. In the same way, Adam and Eve *saw* that the fruit of the tree of Knowledge was attractive and good to eat, so they ate of it and put aside relationship and family with God, which was the central destination.

Deception will be the central theme in the last days. Its rapid increase will be a key marker for the times.

> *Matthew 24:3-5 As **Jesus** was sitting on the Mount of Olives, the disciples came to him privately. "Tell us," they said, "when will this happen, and what will be the sign of your coming and of the end of the age?"*

---

[1] TϽH Strong's 8582
[2] TϽTWϽ Strong's 8595
[3] TϽϽ Strong's 8591
[4] TϽH Strong's 8582

> ***Jesus*** *answered: "Watch out that no one **deceives** you. For many will come in my name, claiming, 'I am the Christ,' and will deceive many."*

The reply of Jesus indicates that the primary sign of the last days will be deception. Deception is the primary tool of the Serpent, so it makes sense that he will pull out all the stops when his time is near.

One of the important signs of deception will be the increased importance given to human knowledge (ע) – which will become the golden calf to worship.

We will think it makes perfect sense and many Believers will fall for it. There will be just enough sugar in it for us to receive it. A cheap and poorly designed deception is a blatant lie, but a well-crafted deception is one which makes us think that we're in for a good thing - that we're saving lives and the planet and giving freedom to people.

How do we know we're being deceived? One important thing to do, is to keep our eye on our ultimate target – to be family with God. If anything steers away from that, then it's deception. Listening with our heart to God's Word is a good way to know the best path. Our physical family on earth is also a good model God has set in place as a picture of His Eternal Family. If anything cuts across that physical family model which He created, that's a sign that we're heading in the wrong direction.

The Completion

This book has shown us the completion which YHWH has in mind for humanity – to dwell with Him as His family for eternity. And what leads up to that is a lifetime of learning to trust in Him through a wilderness of unknowns, tests and not being able to see Him face to face.

Two questions which require a response in this book are:

Is each letter of the ancient Hebrew alphabet truly a communication (AWT) from God (YHWH) to humanity (ADM) or is this all just made up? Bearing in mind that the letters of the alphabet are only one level of God's communication to us.

If the alphabet, Bible and patterns within it are a divine communication to humanity about God's ultimate purpose for humanity and how to get there, then what is our response to that communication?

For myself, making the discoveries communicated in this book, inspires me to greater trust and understanding of what YHWH has in mind for my life and humanity. It gives me clarity of direction. It gives purpose and hope for every day and the whole of my life. The meaning and purpose of my life is found in relationship to God and to those around me who have opportunity to become part of God's Eternal Family. Every person I meet may be my eternal brother or sister.

This all seems other-worldly in our current life, but it does speak to the way we need to relate to each person around us and what gives us worth as a person in the here and now. It is also a matter of trusting beyond what we can perceive with our physical senses and mind – which is all temporal. We need to cross over beyond the immediately visible and enter into the spiritual realm which is the eternal reality. Don't wait till you leave this physical body to do that – because that will be too late. We need to cross over and enter into His family lifestyle in the here and now. This means living as a family, not as individuals struggling to survive in our own bubbles. Our identity, meaning and worth is found in family, not in our own achievements or physical bodies.

I hope the divine truths embedded into the Semitic language will reach not only the Semitic peoples, but also the whole of humanity, because, after all, the language was given originally to Adam, the father of all humanity.

If this book has impacted your life, or you have discovered new insight based on Paul's discoveries, please join the discussions regarding the content of this book which can be found on Facebook on a page called, The Eternal Family in the Alphabet.

URL: https://www.facebook.com/profile.php?id=61553474849709

About Paul Devereux

Paul Devereux obtained diplomas in ministry, teaching, horticulture, field linguistics and translation as preparation for working on language analysis and a dictionary for a Semitic language, which included living and travelling in various regions of the Middle East for 10 years. This involved learning four dialects of Arabic and two dialects of Southern Semitic languages.

During this time, he also worked with agricultural aid projects in the region which included a yearlong survey of water resources in a large Bedouin region.

In 2010, he returned to his family property in New Zealand where he aims to live off the land to feed his wife and family of 5 foster and step children.

If you found this book of use to you, do please leave a review on Goodreads, or email Paul at paulrdevereux@outlook.com.

www.ingramcontent.com/pod-product-compliance
Lightning Source LLC
Chambersburg PA
CBHW062031290426
44109CB00026B/2591